A Century of Faith

O·YE·ICE·AND·SNOW·
BLESS·YE·THE·LORD·
PRAISE·HIM·AND·
MAGNIFY·HIM·FOREVER

Since 1922 this illustration by Eustace Paul Ziegler has been the iconic representation of the Episcopal Church of Alaska, instantly recognizable to readers of The Alaskan Churchman *and* Alaskan Epiphany. *It translates to an Alaska setting the Nativity of Our Lord and the Feast of The Epiphany. The Christ Child is held by His mother, the blessed Virgin, who is an Indian maiden. The Magi are a trapper, a miner, and a fisherman, bringing their gifts and adoration from afar. A fishnet, a screen of stately spruce trees, and towering, snow-clad mountains form a lovely reredos. On either side stand members of the "glorious company of the Apostles" to guard the Holy Child. A related story about the artist appears on page 21.*

A Century of Faith

1895 • CENTENNIAL COMMEMORATIVE • 1995
EPISCOPAL DIOCESE OF ALASKA

CENTENNIAL PRESS
FAIRBANKS, ALASKA

A Century of Faith

© Copyright 1995, Centennial Press
All rights reserved
First Edition

Library of Congress Catalog Card Number: 95-67397

A CENTURY OF FAITH/Carol A. Phillips, Editor

1 - Episcopal Church   2 - Diocese of Alaska   3 - Clergy
4 - Biography   5 - History   6 - Bibliography

ISBN #0-9645828-0-5 Hardbound
ISBN #0-9645828-1-3 Softbound

Excerpts from *Cry in the Wilderness* are reprinted with permission of the author, Tay Thomas.

ACS Hosannah cartoons are reprinted with permission of the artist, the Rev. Scott Fisher.

Excerpts from Bishop Rowe's obituary are reprinted with permission of *The Living Church*.

Unless otherwise noted, photographs are from the files and archives of the Episcopal Diocese of Alaska and St. Matthew's Church, Fairbanks.

Published by Centennial Press
        Episcopal Diocese of Alaska
        1205 Denali Way
        Fairbanks, Alaska 99701

Printed in Alaska by Northern Printing, Anchorage

A Century of Faith

is dedicated
to the Mission of the
Diocese of Alaska:

~ to proclaim the GOOD NEWS
of God in Christ

~ to seek and serve Christ in all persons,
loving our neighbors as ourselves

~ to strive for justice and peace among all people,
respecting the dignity of every human being

Bishop Gordon follows the procession of choir, acolytes, and clergy into St. Timothy's Mission, Tanacross, May 30, 1957, for the ordination of David Paul to the Diaconate. (Photo by Dick Kezlan)

Contents

Young archers, David, Peter, Julius, Luke, and Charlie, practice their marksmanship at St. Mark's Mission, Nenana, 1910.

FOREWORD

What you hold in your hand is a book of dreams. Not the kind that slip by in the night, half-remembered and half-forgotten, but the kind that are real, solid, and lasting. They are all of these things because they are the tangible evidence of the people who created them. Generation after generation, for many years, men and women in Alaska dreamed of the Gospel of Jesus Christ carried to every corner of the Great Land. They dreamed of a community which would embrace all cultures and languages. And they dreamed of a Church that would honor God just as it cared for God's people.

The reality of these dreams is contained here in the images and stories of the people who shared them. Here you will see and hear the vision of Episcopalians from many different times, experiences, and walks of life. The book of dreams is rich and varied.

You will see how the Gospel did move through Alaska, how it did bring a new community to life, and how the Church has always sought to honor God and care for the people in God's family. The book of dreams is faithful and constant.

Most of all, you will see the mystery of how God works in everyday human life. Look at the faces, read between the lines, listen to the honesty and the humor, and feel the quiet presence of the Spirit as it has shaped the Episcopal Church through events both great and small. The books of dreams is a message for those who seek to learn.

Finally, this book is a testimony to every person who at any time has helped to make the Episcopal Church in Alaska what it is today, and what it is becoming for tomorrow. It honors the memory of those good people throughout this diocese in every decade who made their gift to the life of the Church. It celebrates the strength, beauty, wisdom, compassion, and abiding faith of the Episcopal Church for all generations to come. The good news is that people make dreams come true when they make Christ the center of what they are dreaming. The Good News for Alaska is: that dream never ends.

~ Steven Charleston
Bishop of Alaska

INTRODUCTION

Here is a most unusual saga: the courageous and colorful history of our Episcopal Diocese in a vast land of extreme climate and great isolation. It includes the stories of indomitable leaders, men and women who have labored for God with a vision strong enough to endure the many obstacles in a place remote from the mainstream of the Episcopal Church. It includes the stories of lay people who have maintained strong Christian lives by relying on their own faith and personal resources, often with little support from clergy or community for lengthy periods of time.

Our first tribute rightly goes to the earliest Anglican missionaries who crossed the border from Canada into what was then Russian Alaska. The Reverend William Kirkby was the first to arrive at the Fort Yukon trading post in 1861. He taught hymns and held services which he translated into the local Athabascan language. He was followed by Archdeacon Robert McDonald, who not only translated the entire Bible, Hymnal and Prayer Book into the Takudh dialect, but also trained laymen to assume leadership.

Other early milestones were the establishment of the first Episcopal mission in 1889 at Anvik, where the work was led by the Chapman family for 61 years, and the arrival at Point Hope on the Arctic Coast of Dr. John Driggs. As a layman and doctor, John Driggs spent 18 years teaching school, running a medical clinic and introducing the region to Christianity. He remained forever isolated from the outside world, preferring to stay among his Eskimo people, and he, too, raised up a number of lay leaders.

In 1895 the National Church appointed the first Bishop of Alaska, Peter Trimble Rowe. He was followed by other strong leaders, but behind these individuals and the milestones in our Church's history in the north stand many unsung heroes, dynamic Native lay leaders as well as the women who ran missions and schools for years. Their stories illuminate many of these pages.

This book is also a saga of change in the Great Land: wrenching change from a centuries-old nomadic and subsistence lifestyle to settled life based on a cash economy. It is the story of the growth of towns and cities from a simplistic rural life to the complex modern society of the "Lower 48." The boom times of the gold rush and the discovery of vast reserves of oil, the arrival and development of air travel, instant communications and television have transformed even this Arctic land and have left many challenges in their wake.

It is good to look back occasionally, especially on a landmark 100th anniversary. We can be justly proud of our heritage — of the courage, hard work and unwavering faith of those who preceded us. We, like them, must continue to find ways to deal with the often harsh demands of our northern latitudes. We must continue to honor the strong lay leadership so essential to the Alaska Church, while maintaining the tradition of trained, dedicated clergy. We must continue to work together — lay and ordained, men and women of all races — in steadfast faith as we walk together into the future with our Lord Jesus Christ at our side.

- Tay Thomas
St. Mary's Church, Anchorage

"Anvik was our first mission station in Alaska...and Christ Church was a little log church at that mission, the first building of our church to be erected...I have always been proud that I was ordained a deacon in that little church."

- Bishop John B. Bentley
Second Bishop of Alaska

We have heard with our ears, O God, our fathers have told us,
what work thou didst in their day, in the times of old.

Psalm 44:1

I

THOSE WHO BROKE THE TRAIL

In his book, *The Alaskan Missions of the Episcopal Church*, published in 1920, the Venerable Hudson Stuck, Archdeacon of the Yukon, wrote: "...before we pass on to the story of our own missionaries in Alaska, it is well to pause for a moment and think of the debt we owe to the pioneers of our Mother Church who broke the trail for those who were to come after them." The pioneer missionaries of whom the Archdeacon wrote were the Reverends William Kirkby, Robert McDonald, Thomas H. Canham, Vincent C. Sim, a Mr. Hawksley, and Bishop William C. Bompas of the Diocese of Selkirk.

The Rev. William Kirkby, the first missionary of the Church of England and later Archdeacon, crossed the Rockies from the Mackenzie country of Canada in 1861 to minister to the "servants" (as they were called) of the Hudson's Bay Company at the fort they had established on the Yukon near its conjunction with the Porcupine River and mistakenly believed to be in Canada. The fort, named Fort Yukon, was not built as protection from the Native people with whom the company had trade and friendly relations, but as a defense against a possible attack by Russian traders who had established posts on the lower Yukon River.

In a report to the Smithsonian Institution, Kirkby wrote of the ready acceptance of the Gospel by the Native people, but there is no record of a church being built during his visit.

Kirkby was followed in 1862 by the Rev. Robert McDonald, of whom Stuck wrote, "The name of this man, afterwards made Archdeacon of the Yukon, is as notably associated with the middle part of that great river as is the name Veniaminov with the Aleutian Islands. He travelled far and wide upon the Yukon and its tributaries, evangelizing the Indians; he translated the whole Bible, the Book of Common Prayer and the Hymnal, into the Indian tongue and he is still (in 1920) remembered with reverence and affection by the Indians of many thousands of square miles." To Stuck's comments must be added that McDonald first developed a syllabarium and composed *A Grammar of the Takudh Language*, published in London in 1911 by the Society for Promoting Christian Knowledge. He then proceeded to teach the Native people to read and write their own language.

Credit has been given to McDonald for the discovery of gold in the vicinity of Circle City, Alaska and the rush for gold which at that time established the largest

tent city in the territory and became the location for Jack London's novel *Burning Daylight*. When asked why he did not look for gold on his travels, McDonald is said to have replied, "If I want to, I can scoop up gold in a teaspoon in those hills." A creek named Preacher's Creek is a memorial of that remark and its subsequent gold rush.

The Church of England. under the superintendence of Bishop William Bompas, continued to establish missions along the Yukon and its tributaries, with clergy of the English Church Missionary Society. The Rev. Thomas Canham was sent by the bishop in 1888 to Nuclacayette (a corruption of the name Nuchalawaya "the land between the rivers"), the site of Fort Adams and Tanana, and established St. James' Mission. Like McDonald, Canham had learned the Native language and had translated much of the prayer book and had baptized three hundred people by 1891 when the Rev. Jules Prevost of the Episcopal Church arrived to take charge of the mission (see sidebar). Canham remained there until the following year, continuing his translation work.

The Rev. Vincent Sim travelled the Porcupine River as both priest and teacher and died there (see sidebar). Later, after the first visit of Bishop Rowe to the Interior, the Church of England continued to provide
Continued on page 4

Canadian Clergy

Upper left: Bishop William Carpenter Bompas of the Diocese of Selkirk, Canada, sent clergy into Alaska but repeatedly appealed to the Episcopal Church to take over the work and to the House of Bishops to elect a bishop for Alaska. Bishop Bompas retired in 1905 and died at Carcross the following year.

Upper right: The Rev. William West Kirkby was the first Church of England missionary to minister in the territory of Alaska, traveling from the Mackenzie country in 1861 to Fort Yukon. Enthusiastic about the work in Alaska, he wrote, "On the whole continent of North America it would be difficult to find a more important and interesting field for Missionary operation."

Lower left: Archdeacon Robert McDonald, shown (far left) with Bishop Isaac O. Stringer circa 1906, settled at Fort Yukon in the 1860s, learned the Native language and developed its written form, preparing translations of the Bible, Prayer Book, and Hymnal which are still in use today.

Lower right: The Rev. Thomas H. Canham, shown here with his wife, established St. James' Mission at Fort Adams and Tanana, "the land between the rivers," became fluent in the Native language, and translated the Prayer Book, staying on for a year to complete his work after the arrival in 1891 of the first Episcopal missionary, Fr. Jules Prevost.

(All photos on this page courtesy of Yukon Archives/Anglican Church of Canada)

VINCENT C. SIM...ONE OF THE FIRST

It was springtime now...and the young priest was dying. Weakened to the point of exhaustion by his travels and caring for the sick around him, he now would share in their way of dying as he had shared in their way of living. Through the early stages of the sickness he had kept up with his teaching, for there was much to teach and the people were eager to learn, but now, in this last month, even that had become impossible....

They had taught him too, of course, how to survive and how to live in this land. They had accompanied him on his travels and now, for this last journey, they would care for him too. Perhaps one of those caring for him, there in the little cluster of cabins in the high canyons of the Porcupine River, was a tall young man, noted among his people for his wrestling ability. He would remember him.

Within the cabin there was only the sound of the labored breathing, now slower... and the words the dying priest repeated, now slower, over and over again, softer and softer, he repeated the words of the 46th Psalm: "...The God of Jacob is our refuge."

As the ice on the river broke, and water began to run once more on the Porcupine...he died. It was May 11, 1885. His friend and fellow priest, Thomas H. Canham, reported back to Bishop Bompas: "...his spirit passed to the presence of his Saviour, whom he had so faithfully served. He was laid to rest in the Indian graveyard — a quiet, secluded spot on the top of a high hill. A neat rail and headboard were made and placed by an Indian around the grave."

The name carved on the headboard read: "The Reverend Vincent C. Sim." He was barely 30 years old. He was one of the first.

...The young man noted among his people for his wrestling ability...would tell his son about the priest, always referring to him as Mister Sim. His son would become the first Athabascan ordained to the priesthood... the Reverend David Salmon of Chalkyitsik.

~ Excerpts from "Vincent C. Sim... One of the First" by the Rev. Scott Fisher, *Alaskan Epiphany*, Vol. VI, No. 2, Summer 1985

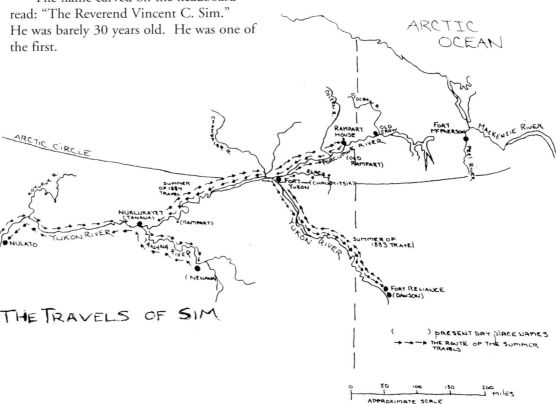

THE TRAVELS OF SIM

DR. JOHN DRIGGS

A physician and devout Episcopal layman, Dr. John Driggs arrived at Point Hope in 1890 to begin a mission and school. The village council, reacting to the ravages of the whaling era, had passed a resolution prohibiting white men from landing on their beaches, but after hours of negotiation they relented and allowed Driggs to come ashore. While his belongings were being unloaded from the

Dr. John Driggs -- selfless devotion to the Arctic Coast people for 18 years (Photo courtesy of Andrew Tooyak Sr.)

Revenue Cutter *Bear*, waves swept away most of his coal supply and nearly all his clothing. Despite this inauspicious beginning, he settled into a two-room house (school and living quarters) and began his 18-year tenure on the arctic coast. At first the people left him strictly alone, but a breakthrough came in the form of a curious young boy, Kinneeveeuk, who wanted to see the inside of Driggs's small hut. The doctor showed him around and cooked him some pancakes. Kinneeveeuk returned next day with a friend, then another, then another. With kindness, and pancakes, Driggs won trust, and eventually a school room full of pupils.

He postponed classes and religious services until he had won the confidence of the people and could communicate with them in their own language. He maintained his modest home, hunted driftwood for fuel, cut ice for his water supply, and traveled many miles to outlying camps to give medical aid.

Tragedy was part of everyday life along the coast. Supplies ran out if winter came early and the annual supply ship couldn't get through. During his first year three of his pupils were lost to drowning or bears, another was killed by dogs. Many people succumbed to white man's diseases: one year a measles epidemic killed every baby in the village.

After four years at his solitary station, the Church sent Driggs an assistant, the Rev. E.H. Edson, who took over teaching duties, leaving Driggs free to undertake prolonged journeys to minister to the sick.

Ordained a Deacon in 1903, Driggs continued his life of service, but by 1908, at only 54 years of age, his health had failed. He retired to Cape Lisburne, 50 miles north of Point Hope, where he spent the last years of his life, trapping and hunting for his food and supplies. When he was stricken ill in 1914 his Eskimo friends attempted to get him to the Point Hope mission by dog team, but he died en route and was buried near the cliffs of Cape Lisburne.

Despite the trials and hardships, Dr. Driggs saw many positive results of his efforts to improve the lives of the Point Hope people. Education, literacy, improved treatment of women, and a genuine sense of community growth were the tangible rewards of his exemplary life.

- Excerpts from *Cry in the Wilderness* by Tay Thomas

✝

Continued from page 1

clergy. In 1886, Bishop Rowe begged Bishop Bompas for the loan of one of his men to serve Circle City, and Bompas sent the Rev. Mr. Bowen. The Rev. Mr. Hawksley continued the work at Fort Yukon.

Of Anvik, the first mission established in Alaska by the Episcopal Church, Archdeacon Stuck wrote, "...the Domestic and Foreign Missionary Society (of the Episcopal Church) entered into a contract with the United States Bureau of Education to provide a teacher for a school in the Yukon valley, and the Rev. Octavius Parker, a missionary of Oregon, volunteering, was sent out to St. Michael at the mouth of the Yukon." A mission was established at Anvik with the arrival of the Rev. John Chapman and at the invitation of the Native people. The Rev. Dr. Chapman built a home, a school and a sawmill, and, in 1894, Christ Church. Dr. Mary Glenton, a physician, and Deaconess Bertha Sabine were sent out to Anvik that same year (see Mrs. Chapman's story, page 5) The Rev. Dr. Chapman traveled to the nearby villages of Shageluk and Holikachuk and ministered to the people of the area for forty-three years. He was followed by his son, Henry.

Point Hope, the second mission of the Episcopal Church, was established after a Lt. Commander Stockton, U.S.A., sent a request in 1889 to Dr. Sheldon Jackson, the General Agent for Education in Alaska. Jackson negotiated with the Episcopal Church to send a teacher, and Dr. John B. Driggs, M.D., of Maryland was selected. Driggs arrived at Point Hope in 1890 and remained there for eighteen years.

Continued on page 7

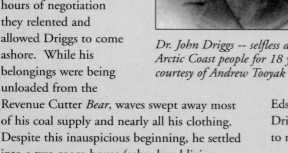

It was in the afternoon of the 8th day of August, 1894, that the four of us — Mr. Chapman returning from his first furlough in the States, Sister Bertha W. Sabine, come out to teach, Dr. Mary Glenton, physician, and myself, landed in Anvik. We had left the port of St. Michael on the coast in the last week in July, in a small, flat-bottom, stern-wheel steamer, about 60 feet long. This was the approved type of boat for the Yukon River, and she was named *The Yukon*. The captain was Russian-Eskimo, the engineer a Swede, the crew and the cook, Eskimo boys. Ourselves and our belongings, and provisions for the trip, were the only passengers and cargo. The journey up the swift waters of the Yukon was slow and tedious, but we were well fed and cared for, and when the engi-

Dr. John Wight Chapman "at home on the Yukon" for 43 years.

neer was off duty he entertained us with tales of his adventures, Alaskan and otherwise. The strange and almost uninhabited country and the beauty of the great river fascinated us.

This eventful day had been misty in a fine rain and we had been housed in the small dining room, kept at our lessons in the Ingilik dialect and folklore by our indefatigable teacher, for we were coming to live among people who could speak or understand very little English, and if we were going to be able to understand them, we must learn something of their language and their conceptions of the universe. We were at work upon the legends, handed down by word of mouth by their forefathers, trying to make the sounds of which the strange words were composed, when the call came that we were nearing Anvik and that landmarks were already in sight.

We rushed out to see, regardless of lessons. We were still on the broad Yukon, but the fishing point, where the Anvik joins the Yukon, was a pretty sight, idyllic, with the white tents and the little brown huts set in the green grass, smoke rising from the fires, the scarlet salmon hanging to dry upon the racks, against the silvery green of the willows and the dark spruces in the background, low blue hills in the distance.

At our left rose the high rocky bluffs of the Yukon, crowned with thickets of spruce and feathery birch and alder. Slowly our little steamer rounded the last rocky point and came into the clear quiet waters of the Anvik. Young natives had come out in their canoes and paddled swiftly all about the boat in welcome.

The mission premises came into sight, the new little log church with its white bel-

fry and surmounting cross. Within hung the bell, the gift of a devoted churchwoman of New York, probably the first church bell to send its sound across those rivers. There were the storehouse and the sawmill, more useful than a gold mine to the mission and the natives, and the gambrel-roofed log building where school was held. Our own log cabin home sat high upon the hill.

Just then, as the boat came to the landing, the clouds parted, the sun shone out, and a rainbow, a rare sight in that latitude, stood above our new home.

The boy Hazyan, who had been left in charge of the mission, stood at the steps of the landing to welcome us at the end of our 6,000-mile journey. We went up the paths, through the groups of waiting people, into the cabin, and knelt to give thanks and to ask a blessing upon the new life upon which we were entering.

We went into the church. The logs had been cut and the foundation tiers laid before Mr. Chapman had left in the summer previous. The native men had given one day at cutting logs without pay, as their gift, and when the foundation was completed, the Doxology had been sung. The walls were raised by the native men voluntarily. The building was completed by Maurice Johnson, a Swede, and he had done careful and substantial work.

The room was 25-feet square, and there was no furniture excepting the handsome stone font, given by our faithful friends of the Woman's Auxiliary in Newark, and the small Estey organ from Vermont.

This was on a Saturday afternoon. Sister Bertha found an empty packing box, covered it with turkey-red calico and draped it in white, and it was set between the two eastern windows to serve as altar. Its only furniture was the small wooden cross given by Miss Julia C. Emery to Mr. Chapman when he first set out upon his mission. We found glasses and filled them with the brilliant red spires of the deerweed and feathery tipped grasses gathered from God's own garden along the river bank in front of the mission, and set them on each side of the cross upon the altar.

A large sheet was hung across one corner of the room to serve as a limited "vestry." Benches were brought in from the school room, and the church was as nearly ready for the service next day as we could make it.

The people came to church, 85 persons crowding into the room. The men sat upon the benches, the women crouched on the floor, abject figures with their hair falling over the downcast faces. The babies were snug in the parki hoods on the backs of the mothers, and we were hardly aware of them until we saw their very bright black eyes looking out at us. Probably we were the first white women they ever had seen.

The toddlers, comical replicas of their elders, ran about in the open spaces, even up to the feet of the minister, for as yet there were no chancel or steps. Some of the little ones, released from the parki hoods of their mothers, in which they had been brought, were fine in bright calico shirts, vests like those of their fathers, and blue denim trousers.

Little boys played quietly in the corners. Some had deerskin parkas, others wore coats of striped ticking, very gay, belted in with strips of hide with sets of caribou teeth sewn on in perpendicular rows, or strips of cloth ornamented with large white agate buttons,

a much-admired decoration, or fringes of empty cartridge shells which made a pleasant tinkling. A wolverine tail, proud trophy of their father's hunt, was attached to the back of the belt of some of the little boys.

The little girls had earrings and bracelets of the large blue-and-white Russian beads or pendants of delicate shells, rare in that region. The boots or moccasins were of reindeer or fish skin.

Familiar hymns were sung, with the accompaniment of the organ. The men looked up, listening to the service and the words of the interpreter, one of the school boys, as he stood at the side of the preacher.

All the congregation had come from their work at fishing just as they were, in old smeared clothes, unwashed, uncombed, excepting one woman whose hair was neat and her calico dress clean. She was the wife of the chief man of the village, and the first communicant. She reverently recited the Creed, as she stood at that period of the service.

The church door stood open to the summer air and sunshine, but to keep the swarms of mosquitoes from coming in, smudges of decayed wood and grass had to be kept going in the vestibule.

When the service was ended, the people still sitting quietly in their places, the minister came from the vestry and said, "Come, children," and while we newcomers doubted whether they would understand or come, one by one those boys and girls of that first school came and stood in a semicircle to be catechized before him, a collection of dirty little rag dolls, just as they had come in from their play. No one had told them to make themselves neat for church, and perhaps they had no clean clothes anyway.

They stood with their uncombed hair, dirty little hands and faces, damp boots and moccasins making muddy spots upon the floor.

The children knew what was expected of them, for as the minister began, in English, the familiar questions of the Catechism, they looked up with attention, each pronouncing their own name, for they all had been baptized, then they went on with the answers, and though they had not recited during the whole year past, they remembered. Whenever there was hesitation, some could say what others had forgotten, and so the lesson was said by those little children of another race, in that first church built in the wilderness of the Yukon country.

We have lived to see many of those children, and their children, grow to manhood and womanhood, with households and families of their own.

~ May Seely Chapman

JULES PREVOST

Fr. Jules L. Prevost, highly principled missionary, educator and editor, described by Archdeacon Stuck as a member of the "muscular school of Christianity"

When the American Episcopal Church was asked to take over work begun by the Anglicans, Father Jules Prevost went to the mission of Our Savior at old Fort Adams, downriver from the present townsite of Tanana. He worked with Anglican priest Thomas H. Canham, who was completing the translation of the Book of Common Prayer into the Native tongue. Fr. Prevost traveled extensively by dog team and boat throughout the area, among 37 Athabascan villages, and set up a school at Tanana under contract with the Bureau of Education.

An uncompromising opponent of the bootleggers who preyed upon the Native population, the priest often dealt personally and harshly with the offenders, leading Archdeacon Stuck to label him a member of "the muscular school of Christianity." Mrs. Prevost's strength of character and gentle disposition made her a perfect helpmate to her husband in his work: she was, according to Archdeacon Stuck, "the perfect missionary wife." (Read excerpts from Prevost's letters to his wife, "Letters to Louise," page 129)

To meet social and communication needs of the widely scattered settlements, Fr. Prevost brought in a small printing press, a gift from Episcopalians in the Lower 48, and began publishing the first newspaper in the Interior, *The Yukon Press.* He helped establish numerous missions, including Epiphany mission at Valdez and St. Mary's in Nome. He was the first Episcopal missionary to cover the vast territory of the Fortymile country.

Every leader earns at least one story that is "told on him," and this is Fr. Prevost's: At Bishop Rowe's request, Prevost traveled by dog team from Tanana to Nome, an arduous trek lasting 43 days. With him he had a horse, which died en route. When a group of prospectors later came across the carcass of the horse, they butchered it and, upon catching up with the priest on the trail, sold him some "moosemeat."

It was a significant loss to Bishop Rowe and the missionary district when the Prevosts left Alaska in 1906 after 15 years of service.

✝

Continued from page 4

At the time of the election of the first Bishop of Alaska there were three missions of the Episcopal Church in the territory: Christ Church, Anvik; St. Thomas', Point Hope, and St. James', Fort Adams (Tanana). In spite of this and the urgings of Bishop Bompas, the House of Bishops was reluctant to elect a bishop for a vast territory which they, along with most Americans, believed to be mostly uninhabitable and a wilderness of ice and snow. The Rt. Rev. Thomas Jenkins in his book *The Man of Alaska* records that the Rev. Dr. John Chapman was elected Bishop of Alaska in 1892 but does not explain why the clergyman from Anvik did not accept. When asked about this later, Chapman's son Henry said, "I do not know why my father did not become the first Bishop of Alaska. It may be that the very long time it took for a letter from the House of Bishops to Anvik and for a return letter to have been received by the bishops that they assumed he was not interested. My father never mentioned it." Certainly, the House of Bishops never pursued the matter.

Finally, at the General Convention of 1895 meeting in Minneapolis, after several attempts to elect a bishop for Alaska had failed and a motion had been adopted to add Alaska to the Missionary District of Olympia (Washington), calling the bishop by a double title, the matter was reconsidered through the urging of a prominent layman, J. Pierpont Morgan, and the Episcopal Church Women. A motion to elect a Bishop for Alaska was carried. The House of Bishops nominated the Rev. Peter Trimble Rowe and, the House of Deputies concurring, he was elected and consecrated the first Bishop of Alaska on St. Andrew's Day 1895.

~ The Ven. Norman H.V. Elliott

✝

PETER TRIMBLE ROWE
First Bishop of Alaska

Born in Meadowville, Ontario, Canada, Nov. 20, 1856, son of Peter Rowe and Mary Elizabeth (Trimble). B.A., Trinity College, Toronto, 1878; M.A., 1880; D.D. 1895. Ordained to the diaconate, 1878, and to the priesthood, 1880, by Bishop Fauquier. Missionary, Garden River, Algoma, Canada, 1878-82. Married Dora H. Carry, June 1, 1882; she and the Bishop had two sons. Missionary, Sault Ste. Marie, Michigan, 1882-95. Consecrated Bishop, Nov. 30, 1895, by Bishops Doane, Whitaker, Starkey, H.C. Potter, Talbot, A. Leonard, Davies, and Brooke. Appointed Missionary Bishop of Alaska, 1895. Dora Rowe died May 22, 1914. He married Rose H. Fullerton, Oct. 21, 1915; they had three sons. Bishop Rowe died June 1, 1942 in Victoria, British Columbia. His ashes were interred in the churchyard of St. Peter's by-the-Sea, in Sitka, Alaska.

P. T. Rowe

...to be in all things a faithful pastor and wholesome example for the entire flock of Christ.
- Examination of Candidate for the Office of Bishop
Book of Common Prayer

II

THE BISHOP ROWE YEARS
1895 - 1942

"A single man with a loaded sled pulled by two dogs, passed us on the trail....When he drew opposite, I saw it was Bishop Rowe, of the Episcopal Church....We rested on his sled while we visited together. He then went on north, pushing..."

- From the Diary of
Judge James Wickersham
March 21, 1901

The living memories are few now. It has been a long time. There are fading photographs on church walls that show an elderly, white-haired man in church robes. There is an imposing portrait that once hung in a place of honor in the Washington National Cathedral; now it hangs in a two-story office building in the older part of Fairbanks. It shows a stern, older Episcopal bishop. The living memories are few.

Anyone alive now who remembers the day Bishop Rowe died is over the age of fifty. The Rev. Patrick Attungana is gone now, but he was there at Point Hope in 1927 when Bishop Rowe landed in the first airplane, and he remembered: "Archdeacon Goodman told us the Bishop was coming, but in a new way, and we needed to clear the rocks off the beach and make it smooth.

All us boys worked at it...and then we heard this noise, far off, high up. We could see this black thing in the sky, coming over the cliffs, over Cape Thompson, coming towards us. We stood and watched it fly around and around and around over us. And then it landed. AND THERE WAS THE BISHOP! He got out of the plane and reached in his pocket and got his pipe and tobacco. Finally, somebody said, 'Gee, Bishop, Point Hope boys are pretty low on tobacco' — because we were. He smiled and handed his tobacco pouch over and said, 'Here, boys, help yourselves.' It was always good to see Bishop." Joe John of Tanana is gone now, but he used to speak with pride of how he sometimes interpreted for the Bishop when he came through. A few aging grandparents recall: "Bishop Rowe? I remember him. He confirmed me. He was big. He was old. And he had strong hands."

There was a time when he wasn't old, when he wasn't an elderly figure in fading photographs on church walls. There was a time when he was that solitary figure Judge Wickersham passed on the trail, and they sat together on the sled while the dogs rested, and they smoked their pipes in the brightness of the springtime sun. He was 44 years old that day, with dark, curly hair. He had

been Bishop and in the country for over five years. He would be Bishop for another 41 years.

Peter Trimble Rowe was not the first Episcopal Bishop to enter the Alaska Territory. Bishop Paddock of Washington visited Southeast Alaska briefly, sometime before 1886, exploring possible Church outreach; nothing came of this. Nor was he the first Bishop of the Anglican Communion to enter the Territory. The Rev. William Bompas of Canada came north in 1866, was made Bishop in 1874, and had been covering both Northwestern Canada and Alaska since. Nor was he the first one chosen to be the Episcopal Bishop of Alaska. Minutes of the 1890 General Convention mysteriously record that the Rev. John W. Chapman of Anvik was elected Bishop of Alaska, but through "some technicality" his election was not confirmed.

But Peter Trimble Rowe was the one, that St. Andrew's Day (November 30th) in 1895, who journeyed from the woods and snow and lakes of his scattered missions in Northern Michigan to St. George's Church in New York City and had the hands of eight bishops laid on him and was consecrated the first Episcopal Bishop of Alaska. "Believe me," he later wrote, "as I walked up that aisle to the altar I felt like a lamb going

9

to the slaughter. Everyone believed it to be an impossible job and that it would be bitter for whoever accepted it." He was the one who then went home to Sault Ste. Marie, collected his wife and two sons, headed west to San Francisco and Seattle, settled his family in Tacoma, and caught the ship north. He never left.

Bishop Peter Trimble Rowe, early in his episcopacy (Photo courtesy of St. George's Church, Cordova)

For the next 47 years, he was THE Bishop. The story and record of the Church in this country is HIS story, HIS record. He laid the foundations and set the style. His achievements are those on which the Church still strives to build.

When Rowe sailed north in the spring of 1896 to Juneau (hardrock gold had been discovered in Southeast in 1880 and, from that discovery, Juneau had sprung), this was the populated area of the Territory, estimated by Rowe at "about 1800 whites with some hundreds of Natives." There were four missions in the entire 600,000 square miles of his episcopal jurisdiction, three along the Yukon River, all separated by hundreds of miles of complete wilderness. Dr. John Driggs, the Rev. John Chapman, and the Rev. Jules Prevost were already laboring at mission outposts.

At Fort Yukon, the true historical beginning of the Anglican Church in Alaska, the Canadian missionaries had been at work for years, with the Rev. William Kirkby holding the first services there in July 1861. (Over 130 years later, The Ven. David Salmon of Chalkyitsik, can still recount oral stories passed on about that first service.) Archdeacon Robert McDonald had arrived the following year, beginning his historic translations of the Bible, Hymnal and Book of Common Prayer into Takudh. "McDonald is the most unappreciated and unknown figure in the history of this State," a University scholar once remarked to me. "The work he did was incredible, and hardly anyone really recognizes or knows about it." (The Gwich'in people know. His translations are used to this day.) The heroic work of McDonald, Bishop Bompas, and others,

traveling down the Porcupine River to Fort Yukon, and up and down the length of the Yukon, laid for the Americans a foundation of such dimension that even such figures as Archdeacon Hudson Stuck were humbled by their achievements.

Canadian William Ogilvie, Dominion Land Surveyor, passed through Rampart House on the Upper Porcupine in 1887 and reported the results of the Canadians' labors: "They hold every Sunday a service among themselves, reading from their books their prayers and lessons of the day, and singing in their own language to some old tune a simple hymn. They never go on a journey of any length without these books, and always read a portion before they go to sleep."

This was the Church to which Rowe arrived as Bishop. Four widely separated and scattered missions. "The prospects of country or work did not look good," he would later write.

Forty-six years later, when he came to the end of the trail in the early morning hours of June 1, 1942, there would be 24 staffed Episcopal congregations or churches in 21 communities across the land: one on the Arctic coast, ten in the Interior, five in the Southcentral/Anchorage area, and five in Southeast. From Ketchikan in the south to Point Hope in the high Arctic, the Gospel was being proclaimed and Episcopal services regularly held, in a variety of language. Additionally, there was the thriving mission school in Nenana and the Hudson Stuck Memorial Hospital — the sole continuing survivor of hospitals Rowe had erected in every camp and community he came to — *Continued on page 17*

HUDSON STUCK

Archdeacon Hudson Stuck, 1907, three years after his arrival in Alaska

It is a formidable job to try to do justice to a character as complex as Hudson Stuck, Bishop Rowe's indispensable "Archdeacon of the Yukon and Tanana Valleys and of the Arctic to the north of the same." In historian David M. Dean's biography, *Breaking Trail* (see Suggested Readings), we are provided with a provocative study of Hudson Stuck's impact on the Alaska Church. From the moment of his arrival in Alaska until his untimely death at Fort Yukon in 1920, Stuck justly earned a reputation for effective, forthright leadership second to none.

An Englishman by birth, Stuck came to Alaska via Dallas, Texas in 1904 at the age of 40, bringing his considerable talents as a writer and speaker, along with fervent commitment to the Church. He often expressed admiration for the earlier missionaries who had labored under conditions "unlike our more comfortable times." His "more comfortable times" included thousands of miles and months'-long trips by dog team or river boat, camping under rough and often hazardous conditions, and frequent ventures into unfamiliar territory.

Living first in Fairbanks and later in Fort Yukon, Stuck traveled throughout the Interior on journeys that covered from fifteen hundred to two thousand miles a year, supervising or serving Allakaket, Anvik, Chena, Circle City, Eagle, Fairbanks, Fort Yukon, Nenana, Rampart and Tanana as well as almost 24 smaller missions along the route. Between trips he wrote five books which today are collectors' items (see Suggested Readings).

While Bishop Rowe developed a special kinship with Alaska newcomers, Archdeacon Stuck grew to know and love the Athabascan people in a way almost unmatched by any other missionary. He knew the problems they faced, and he insisted on preserving their customs, skills, and way of life. He condemned the exploitation of the Native people and never hesitated to champion their causes. Their welfare was always dear to him, and because of his candor and contentious nature he became a highly controversial figure to incoming Caucasians.

Not least among his numerous accomplishments, Stuck made the first successful ascent of Denali in 1913, leading a group comprising his favorite traveling companion, Walter Harper; seminary student Robert Tatum; and guide/mountaineer Harry Karstens. (See color section for additional information)

Bishop Rowe could not have had a more valuable assistant nor the Church a more dedicated leader than this transplanted Texan who left a legacy of colorful legend among his indelible marks on the Church and on the country, from its smallest settlements to its highest summit.

Hudson Stuck

Assisted by two young Native interpreters--one Athabascan, one Eskimo--Archdeacon Stuck conducts Christmas services at Allakaket, 1909. (Photo courtesy Archives of the Episcopal Church)

Archdeacon Stuck with one of his dogs

The Archdeacon capitalized on his name. His personal motto: "HAEREO" -- I Stick." The incident illustrated here by Scott Fisher's cartoon, when Stuck's boat was hung up on a sandbar as another boat came by, may be apocryphal but is still widely circulated in the Interior.

THE ARCHDEACON TRAVELED 1500 TO 2000 MILES A YEAR BY DOGSLED OR BOAT AND PASSED INTO PEOPLE'S HEARTS. ONE SUMMER, TRAPPED ON A SANDBAR, HE ENTERED POPULAR FOLKLORE...

John Fredson of Fort Yukon returns from a hunting trip. An essential member of the conquest of Denali by the Stuck party, Fredson was educated at St. Mark's, Nenana, Mount Hermon School in Massachusetts, and the University of the South, Sewanee, Tennessee, then returned to serve as a leader in his home state and community.

The mission staff at Fort Yukon, about 1910: Left to right: Archdeacon Stuck, Miss Annie Cragg Farthing, the Rev. Charles Betticher, Miss Clara Heintz (later Mrs. Grafton Burke), and Dr. Grafton Burke. Miss Farthing died at Nenana in November 1910.

In his spare time the scholarly Archdeacon wrote five books which provide an unparalleled history of the Alaska Church during the early part of the century, as well as a record of his successful ascent of Denali in 1913. His biographer, David Dean, notes: "As perceptive and accurate records of conditions in Alaska, they have a value which the passage of time has only enhanced."

Bishop Isaac O. Stringer of the Yukon officiates at a service of dedication of the cross marking the grave of Archdeacon Hudson Stuck, 1922. Stuck died in November 1920 at Fort Yukon.

13

WALTER HARPER

W alter Harper's death at age 25 was so shattering to Archdeacon Stuck that he recorded in his diary when he received the news: "I will not believe it at present." Harper had been his pride and joy, his protege, his companion on journeys covering hundreds of miles, when Harper's knowledge and skills in wilderness survival often "saved the day" in hazardous situations. Stuck said of him: "In all the arts of travel, in all the wilderness arts, he was past master. With a rifle, an axe, a dog team, a boat of any kind from a birch-bark canoe to a power launch, he had few superiors. ...I had rather he were by my side in times of stress or danger than any other I ever knew." Later, Stuck wrote: "Have I climbed a mountain? — I climbed it largely by his legs. Have I made memorable journeys? — I made them largely by his powers. He has given me his eyes and ears, his hands and feet, his quick intelligence, his coolness and splendid self-reliance in times of stress or danger, his resourcefulness in emergency."

This promising young life was cut off prematurely in the October 1918 sinking of the *Princess Sophia* in Lynn Canal. Walter and his wife, nurse Frances Wells Harper, who had been married at Fort Yukon by the Archdeacon only six weeks earlier, were

The Archdeacon and Walter Harper prepare to leave Allakaket, 1917

The ascent of Denali, June 1913. Stuck wrote: "This photograph was taken on the upper glacier, at about 17,500 feet....The lowest rock in the picture is about 1,000 feet above the man bowed down with his burden. Appearances are very deceptive at great heights."
(Photo by Hudson Stuck)

Left: Back row, left to right: Walter Harper, Dr. Grafton Burke, two unidentified men, and the Rev. Robert Tatum (Harper and Tatum accompanied Stuck to the summit of Denali). Front row: Archdeacon Stuck and explorer Vilhjalmur Stefansson, at Fort Yukon, 1918. Stefansson had been seriously ill and spent several months recovering at Fort Yukon, during which time he and Stuck indulged in lively dialogues heated by their sharply polarized views about religion and the life and people of the north, dialogues which Clara Burke later recalled as "a liberal education in the extremes of scientific opinion." (Photo courtesy Archives of the Episcopal Church)

Below: Walter Harper on the trail with Stuck's dog team. Stuck's unique, beaded sled bag hangs from the sled handlebars. (Photo courtesy Archives of the Episcopal Church)

en route to Seattle when the steamer ran aground in a heavy snowstorm only 45 miles from Juneau and, although rescue was virtually assured, the captain's misplaced confidence in his ship's ability to stay afloat resulted in the unnecessary loss of more than 350 human lives.

At age 19 a member of the 1913 conquest of Denali by the Hudson Stuck party, Harper had been the first person to stand on the summit of North America's highest peak. It is appropriate that an Alaska Native, in whose language the mountain was named, was the first to achieve this honor.

✝

DR. GRAFTON BURKE

One—among many— of Archdeacon Stuck's positive contributions to the well-being of the Church was when he persuaded his friend Grafton Burke to come to Fort Yukon in 1908 as a medical missionary. Burke stayed for 31 years; his wife, Clara, worked alongside him as a nurse for 29 of those years. Personally devoted to Stuck as well as to the medical and spiritual needs of the area, Grafton and Clara Burke had an impact evident even today in the upper Yukon region, where the name "Grafton" is still often favored as a name for newborn male children.

Stuck's affection for the Burkes, and theirs for him, was an influential force for good in their mutual ministries. Although well aware of Stuck's cantankerous qualities (Clara Burke spoke of him as the man "under the porcupine quills"), but tolerant as only the closest of friends can be, the Burkes were staunch supporters of the Archdeacon to the end of his days, tending him with tireless though futile nursing care during his terminal illness in 1920. Burke's wrenching account of Stuck's death plumbs the depths of the respect and devotion that existed between the two. When Dr. Burke died in Sept. 1939, he was buried beside Stuck's grave in the Native cemetery, close to the burial site of William Loola, the first Athabascan deacon at Fort Yukon.

✝

Above: Clara and Dr. Grafton Burke at Fort Yukon with their sons, Grafton and Hudson (Drane collection, University of Alaska Fairbanks Archives, acc. #91-046-53N)

Left: Dr. Burke in the old Hudson's Bay cemetery in Fort Yukon, 1934. The Hudson's Bay Company left Fort Yukon in 1869, two years after the U.S. purchased Alaska from Russia.

The Bishop with the mission staff at Nenana, May 1929. At his left is Deaconess Thompson, the vivaciuos little Irish woman who was a major influence at St. Mark's Mission for many years. The woman next to her is believed to be Bessie Blacknall; the other two women have not been identified. (Photo courtesy Anchorage Museum of History and Art)

Continued from page 10

in Fort Yukon. (Two years earlier, the National Church had proposed closing the Fort Yukon hospital for budgetary reasons. In stunned irritation, Rowe had written back that he "would recommend the closing of every Mission in Alaska rather than that of Fort Yukon." It stayed open.)

But in the spring of 1896, all of this, and more, was still to come. Rowe's first task, he felt, was visiting these scattered missions and seeing their needs for himself. That meant heading north and entering the great Interior; from Juneau it meant crossing the forbidding Coastal mountains into the lakes and headwaters of the Yukon. He left from Juneau in April 1896 by tugboat to the beginning of a yet little known trail across the mountains. The summit was only some four miles away, but a long way up — 3,500 feet. Near the top the trail rose to a grade of more than 35 degrees before it crossed the summit into Canada and the lakes.

Rowe joined a parade of hundreds of men crossing the Chilkoot Pass that spring, bound for Fortymile and Circle. Gold had been discovered in the area in 1893, and within a year the town of Circle had sprung up and was producing $400,000 in gold. By the following year Circle would be almost a ghost town, but the whole world would know the name of Chilkoot Pass, and the hundreds who tried to cross it in '96 would have turned into the tens of thousands who tried in '97 and '98. Rowe, on the edge of seeing what his Church looked like, was also on the edge of literally world-changing events.

Across the Pass, hauling his own sled of 450 pounds across the still-frozen lakes, holding services along the way, he reached the timber and whipsawed boats for the trip down the Yukon. Hauling his boat across the rotting spring ice, he finally reached the trail's end and began descending the Yukon. By June, after two months of constant travel for over a thousand miles, he reached Circle.

Bishop Rowe's own account of the action of General Convention in the matter of the election of a bishop for Alaska: "...this wisdom has been justified."

"The first Bishop of Alaska elected. It was at the General Convention, held in Minneapolis, Minn., October 1895. The Church was anticipating that this should be done. The delegates of the Woman's Auxiliary came to the Convention, instructed and inspired, to give its United Offering towards the support of a Bishop for Alaska. This was an indication of the general desire of the Church.

"When the motion came up in the House of Bishops it was intensely debated. The debate continued for two days. I know for I was present and listened to it. The older Bishops opposed the motion. They quoted the criticisms made against Seward's purchase of Alaska—that Alaska was a hopeless territory, an 'Ice Chest.' The vote against the motion prevailed. But Mr. J. Pierpont Morgan, the lay delegate from New York Diocese, who had his 'ear to the ground,' told the Bishop of New York, Henry C. Potter, that he thought the bishops had made a mistake and advised reconsideration. This was done. The motion then prevailed. A Bishop was elected. And this wisdom has been justified."

In the summer of 1896, this was the "Paris of Alaska." A music hall, two theaters, eight dance halls, and twenty-eight saloons served a population of 1,200. Town lots were selling for $2,000 apiece, and gold production was now over a million dollars. Here Rowe also discovered the results of the Canadian work, noting "to my surprise, the Indians had Bibles, Prayer Books, Hymnals which they could use." He held services for both Indians and whites in a vacated saloon for five weeks, before departing for downriver. After one service, he overheard one of the miners remark: "Had a poor opinion of preachers, but if that is Christianity, then I'm for it!" Before leaving Circle, Rowe had purchased the saloon for a church and was making plans for a hospital and library.

That summer he continued down the river, stopping in Fort Yukon (where he appointed William Loola as lay catechist), Fort Adams (where Martha Mayo became his first confirmand), and finally, on the first of August, Anvik, where he remained for several weeks.

Back upriver in Canada that August, the stampede for gold had begun with a landmark discovery on a creek flowing out of a tributary of the Yukon known locally as "Thron-diuck." That tributary would give the name for all of what happened next, as "Thron-diuck" became corrupted into "Klondike." As Rowe continued down to the mouth of the Yukon, word of the Klondike discovery spread to the miners in the Interior. The Rush was on.

It would actually last for only about 18 months, but it would change the North utterly and completely and would shape the work of the Church for the future. The four isolated missions were about to get swamped. The proud Alaska Native cultures were about to be inundated. The harsh Alaska wilderness, with mosquitoes in the summer and 70 below temperatures in the winter, would soon be covered with gold-seekers on the Trail of '98, many of them ill prepared for the conditions that lay ahead of them. Historians estimate that at least 100,000 men left home and family to head north in the winter of '97-'98; less than half actually reached Dawson. The rest would scatter from the Aleutians to the Canadian prairies.

In the spring of 1898, Rowe was once more on the trail to Chilkoot Pass. He estimated there were 40,000 on the trail with him this time. His diary records why he was again ascending the steep mountains:

The Bishop dressed for the trail.

It gave me an opportunity of getting close to these men, as I could get in no other way, and I think I fairly succeeded. It was a surprise to them that I should be sharing their life, and for no other object than to tell men the story of God's love. I find in my experience that the only way to reaching men and preparing them to receive God's message is to reach, with a brother's heart of interest and sympathy, the individual man. Many of these men would find their way into our territory, where this Church of ours is almost exclusively ministering the Word and God and Blessed Sacraments, and to meet them and know them was an important preparatory step.

Again climbing the summit, again whipsawing the timbers into a boat, again crossing the rotting spring ice, again descending the canyon, rapids, and lakes to the Yukon, Rowe formed bonds on that trip and established a reputation that lasted the rest of his life. Years later, at a formal dinner in Washington, D.C., a waiter serving the Bishop whispered in his ear, "Wouldn't you rather have some beans?" Startled, the Bishop turned and saw a man he had met on that trail years earlier. They spent the rest of the night swapping gold rush stories.

To recount Bishop Rowe's life, even in summary, and record his achievements and the growth of the Church over a fifty-year span, is impossible to do in a few pages, but even in these first two journeys to the Interior, the style and direction of the future Church in Alaska can be seen.

Before Rowe left Circle on that first

The Frances Wells Harper Memorial Solarium at Fort Yukon, part of the Hudson Stuck Memorial Hospital, was named for the young nurse who perished with her husband, Walter Harper, in the tragic sinking of the Princess Sophia *in 1918. This facility assisted in the treatment and recovery of tubercular patients in the Interior for many years.*

trip, he was already making plans for a hospital, a library, had purchased a building for church services, and saw the need for more workers. He continued this in every community he came to, and he came to every camp just about as fast as it sprang up. In many places he was the first minister to arrive. Episcopal hospitals would stretch from Ketchikan to Point Hope, opening when the need arose and continuing as long as the need remained. The hospitals, in Skagway, Fairbanks, and other communities, as in Circle, always came first, frequently before the church buildings. There still are people living today who owe their lives to the medical care received in these hospitals.

When he left Anvik on the first trip, Rowe was encouraging John Chapman to continue the school he had started and was envisioning larger schools to meet the education needs of the people. Episcopal mission boarding schools would continue in Anvik, Nenana, Tanana and other communities, run by dedicated workers and staff.

When he left Fort Yukon on that first trip, Rowe had already met and appointed
Continued on page 27

The Bishop visits with patients in the Wells solarium at Fort Yukon

With more pretentious people we might term it a "dynasty," but the 61 years of service of the Chapman family at Anvik was marked by such selfless devotion that any word implying power or privilege would be totally inappropriate. Rather, the elemental simplicity of their way of life among the people of the lower Yukon qualifies them as true "Alaska Gothic," if such a category indeed exists.

John Wight Chapman arrived in 1887 at Anvik, where he spent the next 43 years, succeeded after his retirement by his son Henry, who carried on the work until he was transferred to Sitka in 1948. The son's role might be termed "foreordained," considering an incident during Bishop Rowe's first visit to Anvik in 1896, when the young Henry was just learning to talk. The Bishop, sitting at the table opposite Henry, said to him, "Well, baby..." to which the tiny boy instantly responded, "Amen!"

John Chapman later wrote, "To the Bishop's declaration to the congregation at that first confirmation service that, 'This is a great day for this place,' we also said, 'Amen!'"

May Seely Chapman and Susan Chapman, working alongside their husbands as teacher, nurse, caregiver, each played an essential role in the life of the Anvik mission. (See story by Henry and Susan's daughter, Laura Chapman Rico, page 125.)

Dr. John W. Chapman - a man with a mission.

The Rev. Henry H. Chapman -- He followed closely in his father's footsteps

People of the Anvik mission with the fruits of the harvest: hundreds of pounds of potatoes, turnips, rutabagas, and cabbages ensured that the mission would be well fed during the following year.

Eustace P. Ziegler, the "little minister" of Cordova and gifted artist

To many who benefitted from his unique role, Eustace Ziegler was "the little minister." Arriving in Cordova in 1909 as a lay volunteer, he became supervisor of the Red Dragon, a clubhouse built by the Church a year earlier in accordance with a suggestion from the priest at Valdez, the Rev. Edward P. Newton. A recreation hall and free reading room for railroad workers, and an alternative to the 25 or more bars flourishing in the town, the Red Dragon was transformed into a church on Sundays, with an altar lowered from the rafters and a cover draped over the pool table. Ziegler became known as "one of the outstanding characters" of the Copper River valley district. Providing meals, advice, and friendship, he was like a brother to many homeless, penniless men, some of them men of education and former refinement who were in the North seeking adventure and employment, indulging their wanderlust, or sometimes sunk low in the social scale from dissipation. They came with the boom days of Cordova, when the "Iron Trail" of which Rex Beach wrote was under construction, then later drifted away to other frontiers. These wanderers and outcasts found a sincere welcome at the Red Dragon.

There was no hint of institutionalism about the clubhouse or its supervisor, undoubtedly one secret of their success. Although Ziegler studied at Berkeley Theological Seminary and was ordained to the diaconate and, in 1916, to the priesthood, he had "such a true catholicity of religion, such freedom from bias, such a receptive friendliness to all beliefs" that he drew to his services men of all creeds "and men of no creed." In the clubhouse/church he talked to his motley congregation about the simple virtues of life and the beauty and truth of the teachings of Christ. This ministry became the foundation of St. George's Church in Cordova.

Ziegler spent a year at Yale Art School, then returned to Alaska in 1920 and became editor of *The Alaskan Churchman*. His distinctive cover design has identified that publication and *Alaskan Epiphany* ever since. He is recognized today in the secular world as one of Alaska's foremost artists.

A woodcut by Ziegler, "Alaskan Boanerges"

FREDERICK B. DRANE

For ten years, starting about 1915, Archdeacon Frederick B. Drane made his headquarters in Nenana, traveling from that home base throughout the vast expanse of the Tanana and upper Yukon valleys of central Alaska. Fortunately for us, he kept journals of his incredible wilderness treks, journals now housed in the diocesan archives in Fairbanks. They are a fascinating reading experience. Drane also carried out the duties of census-taker over a huge area of the Interior; those figures provide insights into the lay of the land and its far-flung settlements.

Drane's extensive photo collection, presented to the archives of the University of Alaska Fairbanks, records the diverse work of the missionary district. The University also possesses Drane's unpublished manuscript, *Circuit Rider on the Yukon*. Preservation of such records is a gift beyond measure to historians, and we have Drane's daughters to thank for these treasures. It would behoove a serious scholar to investigate and publicize these resources.

Archdeacon Drane was about to return to Alaska after a stateside furlough in the mid-1920s when he was stricken ill, developing tuberculosis which may well have had its roots in his sacrificial ministry to the Native people during the pandemic influenza of 1919-20, described in his journal. He did not return to Alaska; however, his health recovered, he lived out an active ministry in North Carolina to the age of 91.

These are some entries from his journals:

<u>November 19, 1917</u> - Left for Tetlin with dogs and the long sled. Camped at the 17-mile cabin. The next day as I was crossing over the range of hills between the Tokio River and the Tetlin country, an immense herd of caribou passed all around me, moving south toward the Mentasta Pass to the Copper River country. Only by turning over the sled and sitting on it could I check the dogs' mad flight after them. Finally got the dogs tied up around some bushes and tried to keep them quiet. The caribou paid little attention to the wild barking, but placidly strolled past us on both sides. Finally one of the bulls came at us with lowered head but turned aside before I felt it necessary to shoot him. The country was full of meat and I did not care to kill needlessly, but finally I shot one bull. Took part on my sled to be used as dog feed at Tetlin, and the rest I cached on an old pole cache that had been built for that purpose in times past.

The next fall an Indian named Moses walked up to me and shook my hand. He held it tightly and, looking me in the eye, said, "Mr. Drane, you saved my life. The caribou you cached on the Tetlin hill was used by me during the cold spell last December when I was out of food for my family and dogs, and carried me until I could kill some meat." And with that he gave me a beaded money poke much used in the country.

Archdeacon Frederick B. Drane – He left a rich legacy of journals and photographs. (Photo courtesy of Frances Drane Inglis)

November 1917 — On this visit to Tanana Crossing, Ketchumstock, Chicken and the Tetlins, I baptized 17 children and adults and married in all six couples.

March 12, 1919 — Ala Kellum and I leave Tanana for Rampart and Stephens Village. Have a head wind and a hard pull. Next day wind blowing hard downstream and minus 24 degrees. It is a cruel fight against a wind that cuts like steel. Here and there a bend in the Yukon gives us protection. When we reach the Rapids we get the full force of a frightful wind pouring through this canyon. The ice is swept clean of snow for long stretches. This robbed both men and dogs of any foothold. Often the dogs would be swept off their feet and blown around like sacks of leaves. Often the sled would be caught by a gust of wind and swung in a large circle until it banged against the crouching dogs and knocked them along. Sometimes Ala would be blown off his feet and rolled over and over like a log on the glare ice. Often the only way we could advance was on hands and knees. We finally snapped a dog chain to the harness of the leader and led him on, walking when we could stand up and crawling when the gusts of wind were too fierce. Our faces were frozen in several places. Ala with his dark skin and the white frosted areas looked rather ghastly. This was not the worst. The cold wind made tears come into our eyes which froze to the eyelashes, causing the eyes to shut tight. Sometimes we could break the ice that held the lashes together by rubbing our gloved fist over them. Sometimes it could only be done by baring the hand, which was a very painful

thing, as the fingers would immediately start to freeze. Finally after four hours of this struggle, we reach Anderson's place three miles above the Rapids. Here we found a cabin, made lunch and rested.

March 28, 1919 — Back at Rampart — I arrange with mail carrier Al Woods to take my suitcase to Hot Springs and I start out walking. It is about 52 miles there. Stop at the mining camp of Eureka the first night and arrive at Hot Springs at 2:20 the next day.

April 2, 1919 — Back at Nenana. On this trip I covered 810 miles; held 34 services; baptized 13 children; buried 1 (adult).

May 3, 1919 — On the way to Tanana Crossing — Cannot find the trail. Make for a hill through a haze of falling snow, but the compass is playing tricks and I again come out to the Tanana River. Camp for the night at the foot of a range of hills. Off at 6:45 a.m.; follow the trail up the hill and over the ridge. Along the ridge it offers a wonderful view of the Tanana and the Alaska Range and the Roberson River country. Find a blazed tree with charcoal drawings. There are 11 caribou and 1 moose in the picture. Somebody made a fine kill and wanted to tell the other hunters. Ration out the last ounce of dry meat and rice between me and Sam the dog. I write up my notes while the supper cooks. Mine scorches and I cannot enjoy it. I give it to Sam, and I eat his with relish. Not the first nor last time I have enjoyed dog food.

May 1919 — Tetlin — Just after the death of the benevolent and much loved Chief David, the men and women of the village started up their songs of lamentation. Their wails are heartrending. I had a service. The people have asked for "lots of church." They have accepted the coming of the missionary at this time as a token that Chief David in departing had summoned me to come.

May 19, 1919 — Tetlin — Ole Esbloom the trader leaves loaded with muskrat skins....Bishop Rowe stopped with him from Chitina the spring of 1915. Ole told him of trying to drive a moose to his cabin before shooting it to save hauling the meat. The moose became mad and suddenly charged him. Before he could shoot he got tangled on his snowshoes and the moose caught him in his horns and pitched him over its shoulders. "Did it hurt you?" asked bishop. "No," replied Ole, "but I lost my hat."

I gave a "cook" for the Indians and two white men who are here and ate with them while the other whites ate in the mission dining room. Old Charlie rose to make a speech and thank me for the feed. He spoke in the high-pitched tone used by the Indians when they are eloquent in praise. The two white men, not knowing Indian ways, thought Old Charlie was "giving me hell." However, he was saying, "In the days that are gone we used to have a great Chief named Isaac. He ruled us wisely and well and he looked after the poor and needy. He was like a father to us all. Then he died. Later you arrived. Now we acclaim you our father in Isaac's place." All this was in many words and an excited tone. Had I not known their way of oratory and been able to catch some of his words, I too would have thought I was "catching hell."

At Nebesna — For our benefit Frank Sam and Walter Northway go off to a cache and come back with 50 lbs. of flour, some sugar, rice and dried fruit. They give us a supper that seemed like a banquet after the straight meat diet.

March 1920 — En route home from trip to Toklat and Eureka — I reached an Indian camp and spent the next day (Sunday) with the people in their camp. Was given a feast Sunday afternoon, with beaver and moose meat. The beaver is sweet and fat — very good. My sermon for this trip is "Man doth not live by bread alone." Reached the railroad the next day at noon and boarded train for Nenana by 7:30. Was receiving $4.00 per day plus traveling expenses. The distance traveled was 259 miles.

November 1920 — At Tanana Crossing Chief Sam of Ketchumstock came over and announced that at Chicken Creek he had been told that Archdeacon Stuck was dead. The news had come from Fort Yukon by last boat....On my arrival at Nenana I got more details. The Archdeacon died at Fort Yukon of bronchial pneumonia Oct. 10 (actually Oct. 11). I found a letter to me dictated on his death bed, saying he had a return of his old trouble, neuritis, and possibly complications and would take the last boat out. That he wanted me to make the visitations in his place. At the same time he sent me a pair of mooseskin trousers he had had made for me. Bishop Rowe wired his approval of my making the trip and authorized funds for the purchase of a dog team. I secured Moses

The Nenana staff in 1921: Myrtle Rose, Archdeacon Drane, Bessie Blacknall, and Fern Rose (Drane collection, University of Alaska Fairbanks Archives; acc.# 91-046-775N)

Cruikshank, a youth of Fort Yukon who had spent nine years at St. Mark's Mission and who was now working on the railroad. He was big, strong and reliable and knew dogs and sledding, and he agreed to go with me. I gave him $50.00 per month and some extras.

Moses Cruikshank, Archdeacon Drane's trusted assistant and trail companion, also traveled and studied with Archdeacon Stuck and Walter Harper during summer trips to missions along the rivers. (Drane collection, University of Alaska Fairbanks Archives; acc.# 91-046-23N)

"JE-SUS CHRIST!" *Bishop Rowe shouted loudly from the pulpit of St. Philip's in Wrangell as he started his sermon. The congregation sat up, startled.*

"JE-SUS CHRIST!" the Bishop repeated, looking fiercely around at the packed pews. "These are the words I heard a bit ago as I walked through town on my way to the church. Right in front of me a man stumbled out of a saloon. When he fell, he shouted out, 'JE-SUS CHRIST!' I thought I could use these same words to begin my sermon today."

When Bishop Rowe came to Wrangell in the early 1900s, it was a big event. He would stay for several days — a week or more if necessary to catch a steamship back to the north — and had plenty of time to visit with families in the St. Philip's congregation.

One of these families was that of young Bill Taylor, whose mother, Ada, was one of several people who would translate parts of the services from English to Tlingit. Bill remained a lifelong member of St. Philip's until his death in 1984. He vividly recalled that sermon and the preceding incident as he and his family had walked with Bishop Rowe from their house to the church that afternoon.

This was one of Bill's favorite stories, told to Alice Hunt Rooney.

~ Madelyn Stella

A clergy meeting at St. Matthew's, Fairbanks, about 1930. Left to right: Bishop Rowe; the Reverends M.L. Wanner, Fairbanks; William MacPherson, Anchorage; M.J. Kippenbrock, Cordova; M.F. Williams, Fort Yukon; E.A. McIntosh, Nenana; and C.E. Rice, Juneau. (Photo courtesy Anchorage Museum of History and Art)

The age of flight -- and Bishop Rowe -- arrive at Point Hope, August 3, 1927. Ordinarily the 700-mile trip from Nome to Point Hope would have taken nearly a month. The Bishop is shown standing near the tail of the plane; his guest, Major Simpson, is at his right. During this visit the Bishop confirmed a class of thirty prepared by Archdeacon Goodman. The excitement of Point Hope residents at the first sight of an airplane is recounted at the beginning of this chapter. (Photo courtesy Anchorage Museum of History and Art)

25

HYMNS
465
285
507

Bishop Rowe in the sanctuary of St. Mathew's Church, Fairbanks (Drane collection, University of Alaska Fairbanks Archives; acc. #90-173-453N)

Continued from page 19

the lay catechist, William Loola, who had been trained by Bishop Bompas and Archdeacon McDonald. Rowe ordained Loola a deacon in 1903 and would follow with the ordinations to the diaconate of Arthur Wright in Tanacross and Albert Tritt in Arctic Village, and Paul Mather of Ketchikan to the priesthood. His commitment to the development of Alaska Native leadership, and respect for their cultures, was evidenced early on, and perhaps had its roots in his early years of ministry with the Ojibway of the north shore of Lake Huron. His struggles to preserve Native hunting, fishing, and land rights — as when canneries closed off fishing in the Yukon or railroads crossed burial grounds — sometimes drew criticism (Judge Wickersham once privately referred to him as a "dear fool"), but he never backed down. When Archdeacon Stuck fought to preserve the teaching of the Native language in the school in Fort Yukon, and stopped to allow Walter Harper, an Alaska Native, to be the first on the summit of Denali, he was only continuing a commitment his Bishop and Church had made earlier.

When Rowe arrived in the booming Circle, he was the first; and the notice he put up announcing services was quickly taken down to be preserved for the historical archives. Though some other churches (chiefly, Russian Orthodox, Roman Catholic, Moravian, and Presbyterian) were also ministering to and with Alaska Natives, Rowe was frequently the first to arrive in the white mining camps, his visits usually soon followed by the construction of hospitals, libraries, and churches. His multicultural work led to the multicultural Church that continues to this day.

Canadian Bishop Bompas had set a precedent of simplicity and adaptation in his travels, occasionally being mistaken for a ragged trapper and often serving people who were astounded to discover he was their bishop. Rowe continued in that pattern, ascending the Chilkoot like everyone else, building his own boats, cutting his own wood, mushing his own dogs, and asking no special favors. He reached out to all he encountered with "a brother's heart" and won the love of the North.

He was absolutely fearless. He was the first to successfully descend the rapids along the Chilkoot trail. He thought nothing of striding into a saloon and announcing he was borrowing it for a service. It was no surprise he was in the first airplane to land at Point Hope in 1927.

For almost half a century he set a trail of sacrifice and commitment that has molded the shape of the ministry of our Church. He set that trail by his deep faith in God and his deep love for Alaska, the land and the people. He was later called to be Bishop in Colorado, South Dakota, and Southern Ohio, but he always refused to leave Alaska. Even though he was in his eighties and a world war was raging, he was making plans for a tour of the Aleutians when his final illness overtook him.

Among the worries he carried into his final days was the church at Point Hope. He was searching for a replacement for the aging Archdeacon Goodman and could not seem to find a suitable priest. "I am beginning to lose faith in the present generation of younger clergy," he sighed. He need not have worried. The year after his death, the replacement for Archdeacon Goodman would arrive at Point Hope — the young William J. Gordon Jr.

– The Rev. Scott Fisher

✝

Once, so the story goes, Rowe met a lone prospector to whom he was unknown, floundering along over lumpy ice with weary dogs. The Bishop, too, had his difficulties, and asked the stranger about the trail ahead. "It's hell," the prospector replied, and proceeded to relieve his frustrations with a vehemently profane account of just how bad the trail was, to which the Bishop listened quietly. "And how's it been your way?" the stranger asked. With sincere conviction the Bishop responded, "Just the same."

(From Bishop Rowe's obituary in *The Living Church*, June 7, 1942)

"The Bishop is dead." These four short words, in several Indian dialects, in Eskimo, and in English are bringing to the residents of Alaska the news that the Rt. Rev. Peter Trimble Rowe, D.D., will no longer be seen on the apostolic visitations that marked the year's high point in many an Alaskan town.

In the United States, Bishop Rowe, who died June 1st, in Victoria, B.C., was given many affectionate nicknames, one of the best known being "Bishop of All Outdoors." To Alaskans, however, he was simply "The Bishop."

...Stefansson and other Arctic explorers have known him, loved him and written about him. Bishop Rowe and Jack London mushed many a weary mile together through the wilds behind huskies, while the famous author was gathering material for his short stories and novels....Rex Beach made Bishop Rowe one of the lovable characters in a novel based on his experience with the missionary in the Far North. River men, prospectors, trappers, storekeepers, lumber-jacks, whalers, natives were all sworn friends of the Bishop who, gentle, soft-spoken, devout, went sturdily on his way through 47 years, preaching the Gospel of Christianity with earnestness and fervor, but always with human, practical sympathy for his fellows in whatever conditions he encountered them.

...The Bishop was always alert for the welfare of the Indian people. He baptized them and confirmed them and tried to minister in every way to their physical welfare. When White men sought to commercialize the salmon fishing at the mouth of the Yukon by spreading nets and establishing a cannery, with consequent starvation for the Indians in the interior, Bishop Rowe, with Archdeacon Stuck, fought to prevent them, in 1919 and 1920, and finally won. Approximately one-half of the Indian population of Alaska today are baptized members of the Episcopal Church.

...As Depression financing made deeper and deeper inroads into missionary work in the 1930s, Bishop Rowe was deeply hurt by the cruel necessity of closing work that had been flourishing for many years. At one time he offered to relinquish his entire salary to avert the catastrophe of further cutting of items that he believed to be essential. Among the hardest blows were the closing of the Indian mission school at Anvik and the elimination of the $2,000 fuel fund for the hospital at Fort Yukon. Any possibility of retirement and rest was dismissed, and the Bishop resolved to carry on with the aid of his able young suffragan, the Rt. Rev. John Boyd Bentley, who was consecrated in 1931. At that time, he wrote:

"To sacrifice this work in Alaska built up from nothing, the work of devoted men and women and the sacrifices and offerings of thousands of children of the Church as well as by the gifts of saintly men and women and the self-sacrificing work of knightly souls such as Hudson Stuck and A. R. Hoare, is just unthinkable. Before I yield to any such thing, I will live and fight. I may die, but I will die fighting to the end."

BISHOP BENTLEY RECALLS ROWE'S DEATH

(When Bishop Rowe died in Victoria): It was during the war (1942)...and I couldn't get transportation from Fairbanks to Seattle. Everything was military. The Bishop was to be buried from his parish church and then interred at Sitka, where he had first lived in the early days, interred next to the first Mrs. Rowe. Finally I did get down there in about two weeks. After the burial office had been read at Victoria, I went over and saw Mrs. Rowe and the boys. Mrs. Rowe had the Bishop's body cremated. From the undertaker I got the Bishop's ashes and urn, a little box, and on my way back home to Nenana I stopped at all the missions and churches around the coast. And all along the way, until I got to Sitka, when I'd go to a hotel or wherever I stayed, I'd smile to myself and think, "Oh, Bishop, bless his heart, he'd smile too to think that I put him on a shelf in the clothes closet until we made the next move."

We got to Sitka, and we planned to have the Bishop's ashes buried Sunday afternoon in the cemetery next to the church. But I was told the City Council had passed an ordinance that there could be no more burials in that cemetery, so I went to see the commissioner, who was the highest civil officer in town. He had known Bishop Rowe, and I think he was a member of that parish. He was very patient in explaining to me that it was the law, that he just couldn't do it. But I said, "I make a real effort to keep the law. But you knew Bishop Rowe and what he meant to Alaska and what Alaska meant to him. His dear wife is buried here, and I'm sure he wanted to be buried here. And at four o'clock tomorrow afternoon I am going to inter his ashes here. If you want to call on the civil authority to arrest me or stop me, that's up to you, but that's what I plan to do." The next day the commissioner was there with a considerable company of people to attend Bishop Rowe's funeral. I never heard anymore about that.

(Portrait by Neale Ordayne)

I wrote to Mrs. Rowe and asked if the missionary staff in Alaska might have the privilege of putting a stone at the Bishop's grave and she said yes. It was still wartime, and transportation was difficult. I didn't know any stonemason in Seattle or Portland, but I knew one in Hampton, Virginia. So I wrote and told him what I wanted, a granite stone about as wide as this table and five feet long, and gave him the inscription we wanted: "Peter Trimble Rowe" with the dates of his birth and death, and "Bishop of Alaska" with the dates he'd been Bishop. And he cut the stone and put the inscription on it and crated it very carefully and shipped it through the Panama Canal up to Seattle, and from there it was sent to Sitka. I went down to Sitka and had a service when the stone was put in place.

There'll never be another Bishop Rowe. He was just the man for the time.

✝

"The Man of Alaska," Bishop Peter Trimble Rowe and his suffragan, later successor, Bishop John B. Bentley. (Photo courtesy University of Alaska Fairbanks Archives)

JOHN BOYD BENTLEY
SECOND BISHOP OF ALASKA

Born in Hampton, Virginia, February 9, 1896, son of Charles Headley Bentley and Susan Elizabeth (Cake). Graduated from College of William and Mary, 1919; Doctor of Divinity, Virginia Theological Seminary, 1932; Doctor of Sacred Theology, General Theological Seminary, 1948; Doctor of Humane Letters, St. Paul University, Japan; Doctor of Divinity, College of William and Mary, 1985. Ordained to diaconate in Anvik, July 1922, by Bishop Rowe; to the priesthood, June 1929, by Bishop Tucker. Married May 29, 1921 to Elvira Wentworth Carr. Assistant, Christ Church, Anvik, 1921-25. Master, Charlotte Hall School, Maryland, 1925-26. Assistant, Bruton Parish, Williamsburg, Virginia, 1926-30. Archdeacon of the Yukon, 1930-31. Consecrated Suffragan Bishop of Alaska, September 29, 1931; served as Suffragan, 1931-42; Bishop-in-Charge, 1942-43; Bishop of Alaska, 1943-47. Director, Overseas Department; Vice President, Episcopal Church Executive Council, 1948-64. Phi Beta Kappa. Died in Hampton Virginia, June 12, 1989.

(Photo courtesy of St. Mark's Mission, Nenana)

III

THE BISHOP BENTLEY YEARS
1943 - 1948

A story written by Mark Twain was entitled *A Connecticut Yankee in King Arthur's Court*. A fitting title for an article about the Rt. Rev. John B. Bentley could be, *A Southern Gentleman in King Winter's Court*, for such a gentleman and soft-speaking Phi Beta Kappa scholar was the second bishop of Alaska, who signed his name Jno. B. Bentley. Born in Hampton, Virginia, educated at the College of William and Mary, served in a horse-drawn field artillery regiment of the Virginia National Guard in Texas and overseas in World War I, worked in the shipyard at Newport News as a ship's carpenter helper, studied at The Theological Seminary in Alexandria, Virginia, and married in May 1921 in Alexandria, John B. Bentley came to Alaska as a lay volunteer with his wife, Elvira, at the invitation of Bishop Rowe and was assigned to assist the Rev. John Chapman at Christ Church, Anvik.

He described his duties in Anvik as being "the handy man at the mission." He said, "We had a small boarding school there for Indian boys and girls, about forty children and three wonderful women on the staff. My job was to see that they had wood and water,...assist at the service by reading the lessons, doing odd jobs. I rang the bell and built a fire in the church....Mrs. Bentley

Bishop Bentley in the early 1940s, when he, too, was in his early 40s.

became the Postmaster." Although he told Bishop Rowe he was not prepared to be a deacon, he was ordained in Christ Church in 1922 and later said, "I have always been proud that I was ordered a Deacon in that little church. I have been very sentimental about it." Evidence of his love for Christ Church is to be found in a brick inserted in the altar which he obtained from the church in Jamestown, Virginia. It is fitting that a brick from the first church established in the colonies in 1607 should be placed in the first church established in Alaska.

In 1925, due to Elvira's illness, it was necessary for the Bentleys to leave Alaska. Five years later, having served as Master of Charlotte Hall School in Maryland, Chaplain of Students at the College of William and Mary, and assistant at Bruton Parish, Williamsburg, Virginia, he returned with Elvira to Alaska and was appointed Archdeacon of the Yukon. Because Nenana gave the best access to travel to the villages on the Tanana and Yukon rivers and their tributaries, he settled there and later, as Bishop, built a log home and furnished it with furniture which he made. The skills he had learned as a ship's carpenter served him well.

As Archdeacon he visited all of the missions in the interior of Alaska, traveling alone by dog team in the winter and accompanied by Elvira on a boat in the summer. Of these journeys he said, "I had a little sled and five dogs. And I had a small boat. Bishop Rowe had a splendid boat built for us in the summer of 1931 and shipped up. It was named *Pelican* IV. *Pelican* I and II had been used by Archdeacon Stuck and a third *Pelican* by later archdeacons. The name came from Psalm 102:6: 'I became like a pelican in the wilderness.'" During the depression years, when it became too costly to operate the *Pelican*, he had a small boat built by the maintenance man at St. Mark's Mission; it was 28 feet long, very narrow, and powered by an outboard motor. He named it *Discovery*. Furnished with a tent and camping gear, he would leave Nenana on the first Monday in June and return in mid-August.

Traveling along the Yukon and its tributaries, he would stop at every fish camp, holding services, baptizing the children, celebrating the Holy Communion, and, as he said, "Having a wonderful time." He believed that he had been appointed as Archdeacon because Bishop Rowe knew he was, in his words, "Perfectly at home in a small boat. I grew up on Hampton Creek in a small boat. Sailed and fished, camped out on the beaches of Chesapeake Bay."

He reported the extent of his travels by boat in an article in the November 1938 issue of *The Alaskan Churchman*: "The log of the *Discovery* shows that during the past four summers that little vessel traveled over 10,000 miles on the Yukon River and its tributary streams under her own power. Three times she made the long run upstream from the mouth of the Koyukuk to St. John's-in-the-Wilderness at Allakaket, fighting the current all the way for 450 miles. Once she went the whole length of the Tanana...a distance of about 800 miles,

Continued on page 36

Marguerite Bartberger, a devoted worker in the missionary district for 25 years, is shown here (left) with John and Elvira Bentley at the Anvik mission in 1922.

The Rev. and Mrs. Wilfred (Shorty) Files, stationed at Tanana, were expecting a visit from Bishop Bentley, who was coming downriver from Nenana in the mission boat. Like any clergy wife, Ann Files was organizing her time around the estimated date of arrival, making preparations for meals and hospitality, and seeing to other details to ensure the Bishop's warm welcome. One day early, however, on a rainy, mosquitoey evening, a young boy sighted the Bishop heading downriver toward the mission. He ran to Mrs. Files at the mission house and reported, "The Bishop is coming...well, it's either the Bishop or a log." Mrs. Files replied grimly, "Well, I hope it's a log!"

In all my writing and talks to various organizations, I have strongly emphasized the hard and dedicated work performed by the Episcopal mission and their personnel.

Archdeacon Stuck was the first minister I remember meeting. In 1920 he baptized me and my brother Jim and others during the winter, going through on the Koyukuk River dog team trips that they took sometime. I do know that Archdeacon Stuck during 1906 got the people of Arctic City to move to Allakaket with the promise to build a mission there, which they did. They continued to make their winter overland route to the upper Koyukuk River till about 1928. I don't know who made the last trip. From my findings 1920 was the last dog team trip on the Lower Koyukuk by the mission.

I met Bishop Rowe in June 1920. He gave burial service for my mother at Hog River where we lived at that time. He came on a scow-type houseboat; I would say probably 10' x 40' long. How many trips were made before 1920 I do not know.

Our dad was unable to care for us properly, so asked Bishop Rowe if they could take us kids to the Anvik mission boarding home and school. It was agreeable to Bishop Rowe, so they loaded us five on his boat to Anvik: Elsie 10; Ada, 7 1/2; myself, 5; Jim, 3 1/2; and Marion 6 months old.

The *Pelican* I used to make a yearly trip from Nenana mission down the Yukon to

The Pelican *IV out of Nenana: Bishop John B. Bentley, captain, pilot, deckhand, engineer. Mrs. Bentley was cook and general helpmate during summers spent visiting camps and villages along the rivers of the Interior.*

the mouth of the Koyukuk River where the Koyukuk enters the Yukon. They traveled as far as Allakaket and Alatna, 470 miles up the Koyukuk. They performed confirmations and baptisms at Allakaket; also stopped at all camps and towns along the river giving church services or baptisms when needed. These trips were quite an event for people along the Koyukuk. The boat generally had a nurse to help care for the sick. Prayers were said also special to the sick. The Mission was always helping people when in need in many respects.

The *Pelican* I got old. Bishop Rowe turned over his post to Bishop Bentley. I saw Hudson Stuck with a dog team at Allakaket making the winter tour. He may have come later too, but I did not see him any more (Ed. Note: Stuck died in 1920). Bishop Rowe I met in 1920. I seen him last in 1925. Bishop Bentley I met about 1920

when we went to Anvik mission. He was a lay leader, just getting out of the U.S. Army service after serving over in France in World War I.

I really appreciated and loved the man in every respect. The late Edwin Simon's definition of him was so true: a real gentlemen and a scholar — to everyone.

I myself had problems after losing my mother. My distrust for other people was hard to overcome. John Bentley at that time seemed to understand my problem. I was only five or six years old. I developed a trust in him. For me he was my guardian angel. When he used to take the boat and dog team trips to Shageluk, a day's travel from Anvik, he took me with him. When he left Anvik to go somewhere before becoming a bishop I cried because to me he was the only person who seemed to care. I am sure I was wrong because I never saw any mission personnel neglect anyone at Anvik mission.

After I came back from Eklutna school in 1927 (leaving Anvik in July 1925-1927) was the last trip of *Pelican* 1, hauling supplies and a crew to rebuild mission quarters for Miss Hill who spent years at Allakaket.

In 1928 we were fishing four miles below Nulato for dog food. One evening a brand-new boat landed, the *Godspeed*. Pushed into the beach. Who steps out to heave me the painter — our new bishop, John Bentley. For me it was a joy to see him.

Above: Services at a fish camp along the Yukon, during the 1930s, when John Bentley was Suffragan Bishop

Right: The Bishop "walks the plank" at a stop along the river

He said he wanted to spend the night with us. We had prayer and service. Before he left he commented on how pleased he and Mrs. Bentley were with the way we supported ourselves. Only the two, Jim and I, at the camp, working hard.

I ran into him quite often throughout the years. The *Godspeed* was a nice boat but needed about two and a half feet of water to make it over the riffles on the Koyukuk. Bishop Bentley didn't let that stop him. He got himself a 24-foot river boat with a 10-hp outboard motor to make his yearly trips down the Tanana and Yukon rivers and up the Koyukuk. After a number of years Bishop Bentley faded from the Alaska picture. The program was taken over by the new bishop, William Gordon. I believe he made one or more boat trips before becoming our Flying Bishop. I have to say all the past bishops and others leaders and mission personnel who dedicated their time to serve the people of the interior of Alaska are part of Alaska history. In meeting the challenges in helping prepare the Natives to meet the change, to adapt themselves to a fast-moving world that has invaded their land and culture.

Because of the Church we are all living a much healthier life, cleaner in every respect. Some practices that the missions turned around are hard to believe, only if you lived it by tradition and culture.

~ Sidney Huntington

Once when I was staying in a cabin with a large Indian family, there was a little boy, an attractive little fellow seven or eight years old who spoke very good English. He watched me dress in the morning and was fascinated by the whole operation. When I put on what we call oversocks or insocks, he was intrigued. It's a sock that is simply the foot of a sock, like a slipper with no upper on it, made of caribou or mountain sheep. You can wear it with the fur on the inside or put it on over your woolen socks. Or you can turn it inside out and wear the fur on the outside. I wore caribou insocks because I could get them anywhere in the Interior, and I always wore the fur on the inside. This little boy watched me and he said, "You wear your sock with hair inside?" And I said, "Yes." "Why you do that?" he asked. "Well, I have a feeling it may be a bit warmer, better to wear it with the hair on the inside than on the outside." He looked closely for a moment, then smiled and said, "Caribou think more better wear hair on outside."

~ From Bishop Bentley's Tapes

David Wallis, layreader and interpreter at Fort Yukon, with Bishop Bentley and chief Esais Loola, late 1930s

Continued from page 33
and then down again. Four times she has made the run of 675 miles from Allakaket down to Anvik."

Although he urged the Bishop to reconsider, he was nominated in 1937 by Bishop Rowe and elected by the House of Bishops as the Suffragan Bishop of Alaska. In addition to his episcopal duties he became editor of *The Alaskan Churchman.*

Highly respected by riverboat captains for his skill in navigating the rivers of Alaska, he was equally admired by the printers of *The Alaskan Churchman* for his ability to write and prepare for printing the Church's quarterly periodical. Robert B. Atwood, publisher and editor of *The Anchorage Times,* which printed the booklet, said, "He had the ability to write and space the words and articles so that no changes had to be made by the typesetters, much to their amazement. Whenever he visited us I would introduce him to the printers and he would explain his methods. Later, when I wrote editorials, I used his methods. He was a charming and gracious gentleman and we looked forward to his visits."

Upon the death of Bishop Rowe in 1942, Bishop Bentley was appointed Bishop in Charge of the Missionary District of Alaska and in 1943 was elected Bishop of Alaska by the House of Bishops.

During World War II, at the invitation of the Commanding General of the Alaskan Department and the Commandant of the Seventeenth Naval District. he visited the posts and stations in the Aleutian Islands. He wrote, "The trip gave me the opportunity and privilege of meeting the officers and men who were stationed there. It was my

BISHOP BENTLEY REMINISCES

I remember at the rapids on the Yukon one day I was having service and there were close to a hundred people present. They put up a big canvas as a shelter against the sun and put a big box under it and from some mysterious place a woman brought a white piece of sheeting and covered it. I carried in my little boat all the things I needed for the altar: the candlesticks, the cross, communion vessels, a little baptismal bowl. And in the midst of the service I saw two young men on the edge of the congregation get up from where they were kneeling and go into a tent and come out, each with his rifle, and walk up the beach, maybe a hundred yards or more. Out of the corner of my eye, I saw two caribou swimming the Yukon. When those caribou came ashore on the other side of the river, the boys shot them and dragged the carcasses up on the beach, came back and put the rifles in the tents and came back to the service, not disturbing the congregation in the least. They had known exactly what had to be done; they had done it, and that was it.

I remember being at Allakaket for Christmas in about 1930. I went over the trail with Moses Cruikshank, my traveling companion from Tanana. It's about a five-day journey from Tanana to Allakaket. The church was jammed, of course, and outside it was far below zero. I had on my Bishop's robes, and as I walked up the aisle the hair on the caribou parkas worn by all the congregation was attracted by the static electricity of something in my robes, and all these hairs just jumped. By the time I got up to the altar I was literally covered by caribou hair, which I wore all during the service. Afterward I hung the robes up in a warm place in the mission house and all the hairs fell off. It was a peculiar experience.

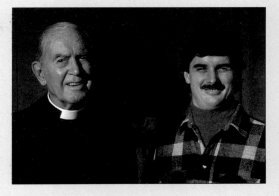

The Rev. Wilson Valentine (now of St. Brendan's, Juneau) visited with Bishop Bentley in Virginia, December 1987. The Bishop died in June 1989. (Photo by Bishop George C. Harris)

Bishop Bentley and the children of St. Mark's Mission, Nenana, participate in a ceremony before the foundation is laid for an extension to the schoolhouse, 1940s.

In all the years I traveled in the Interior and left gas at points along the river, every person on the rivers knew I did it, but I never lost one gallon of gas or oil. They knew it was there, but they knew what it was there for, and they left it alone.

Once I was flying with a bush pilot in a small, one-engine plane, and we got caught in some bad weather. I didn't know where we were but hoped the pilot did. We circled around and climbed up and went down, looking for a hole and something he could recognize. I was sitting two seats behind the pilot. Next to me sat an oldtimer, old prospector going to the north coast. And when we got out of the plane, the oldtimer said to me, "Parson, was you scared up yonder?" I said, "You bet I was scared." He said, "I was too. Did you pray?" I said, "You can bet your bottom dollar I prayed." He said, "I was hoping you would." I said, "My friend, next time you do your part too."

~ From Bishop Bentley's Tapes

good fortune to be in the far Aleutians, on Attu and Shemya, at the time of the Japanese surrender and to be able to have a part in the V-J services there. I think that it served the Church in that it was a means of letting our Church boys know that their Church had not forgotten them and that it was ready to visit them in far outposts."

In 1947 the Rt. Rev. Henry Knox Sherrill, Presiding Bishop, called John Bentley to become the Director of the Overseas Department of the Episcopal Church and Vice-President of the Executive Council. Just as he had resisted being ordained a Deacon and consecrated a Bishop, Bentley went to New York to ask Bishop Sherrill to reconsider. Of that meeting he wrote, "I tried to beg off. I said that perhaps I was the happiest man in the Church where I was and might be left, I hoped. He said, 'I'm not so much interested in your happiness as I am in seeing that you do what the church has called you to do.' To which I could only say, 'I will go, sir.'"

The Bentleys left Alaska in 1948, and the Rt. Rev. John Boyd Bentley, Second Bishop of Alaska, became, perhaps, the most loved Director of the Overseas Department of the Episcopal Church by all of us, both lay and clergy, who were appointed missionaries under his care.

~ The Ven. Norman H.V. Elliott

✟

WILLIAM JONES GORDON JR.
THIRD BISHOP OF ALASKA

Born in Spray, North Carolina, May 6, 1918, son of the Rev. William Jones Gordon and Anna Barrow (Clark). Bachelor of Arts, University of North Carolina, 1940; Bachelor of Divinity, Virginia Theological Seminary, 1943; Doctor of Divinity, Virginia Theological Seminary, 1953. Ordained to the diaconate, January 1943, by Bishop Penick; to the priesthood, July 1943, by Bishop Bentley. Married Shirley Lewis, July 16, 1943; he and Shirley had four children. Deacon-in-Charge, St. Peter's, Seward, 1943; Priest-in-Charge, St. Thomas' Mission, Point Hope, 1943-48. Consecrated Bishop of Alaska, May 18, 1948; served as Bishop until his retirement in 1974. Junior Chamber of Commerce Outstanding Young Men in U.S.A., 1953. Director, Project TEAM (Teach Each a Ministry), 1974-76. Assistant Bishop of Michigan, 1976-86. Died at Midland, Michigan, January 4, 1994. Interred at Point Hope, Alaska.

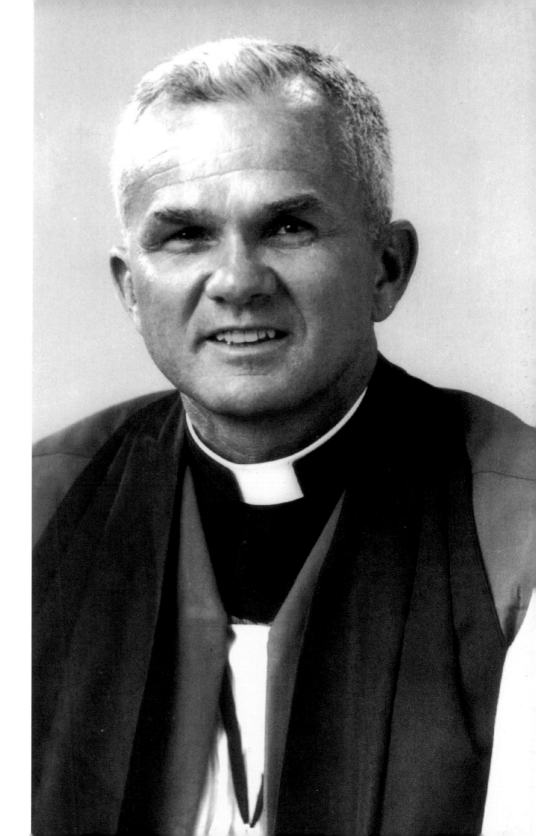

But they that wait upon the Lord...
shall mount up with wings as eagles...
Isaiah 40:31

IV

THE BISHOP GORDON YEARS
1948 - 1974

When Bill Gordon became the third bishop of Alaska on May 18, 1948, twelve days after his thirtieth birthday, he may have been young for the job, but he was no stranger to Alaska and her people. Coming to St. Peter's Church, Seward as a deacon in March of 1943, he served four months there. He and Shirley Lewis, who had met aboard the SS *Yukon* sailing out of Seattle, were married in Seward July 16, 1943. Prior to moving to St. Thomas' Church, Point Hope, in response to Bishop Bentley's request that he succeed Archdeacon Frederick Goodman, Bill was ordained a priest on July 25 at St. Mark's Church, Nenana, and Shirley was confirmed. By the end of the month the Gordons had arrived in Point Hope, which became "home" for nearly five years. It was during a trip from Point Hope to Kivalina by dog team in November of 1947 that Williams Jones Gordon Jr. learned he had been elected by the House of Bishops to succeed John Boyd Bentley as bishop of the then Missionary District of Alaska, which became a diocese in 1971.

Few in Alaska, other than Shirley, called him "Bill" during the 26 years of his episcopate: he was clearly "Bishop," and addressed as such. Later, when they moved to Michigan, calling him "Bill" became easier,

and later still it was an important part of expressing care for him during the years he courageously wrestled with cancer. It was the life and ministry of Bill Gordon, our brother in Christ, which the Church in Alaska celebrated one last time as his ashes were interred at Point Hope in June of 1994.

Bill Gordon had been bishop less than a year when he took his first flying lesson. Although he had enjoyed the summer visitations to the missions along the rivers of Alaska's interior in 1948 and 1949, the length of time involved and the costs of operating and maintaining a riverboat, the *Godspeed*, made the attraction of flying appealing to this young bishop. The size of his jurisdiction and tight budgets necessitated flexible and affordable transportation if the bishop were to be among his people, so this one learned to fly. While commercial flights to the churches in Southeast Alaska remained the norm, as early as April of 1949 the Bishop's trips to the Arctic Coast and interior villages were usually made in a succession of diocesan-owned planes. Two of them, the "Blue Box" and the "Blue Box II", were so named because offerings made in "blue boxes" in homes around the country resulted in grants from the United Thank Offering toward the cost of the planes.

Blue Box offerings and other contributions were important to the development of the Church in Alaska and the Bishop's plans for its future. During his episcopate, funds from the National Church for missionary programs began to be reduced. When the Bishop journeyed "outside" to the Lower States, his many contacts, as well as his own personal charm and charisma, helped win friends for the Diocese. Three movies were made and widely used to tell the story of the Episcopal Church in Alaska. In two of these, *Light of the North* and *The Great Land*, the "Flying Bishop" is the focus. The third film, *One in the Spirit*, recounts the diversity of the Church's mission in Alaska and the growth during the sixties and early seventies of ecumenical work, ministry of the laity, and the calling forth of local church leaders to be ordained and provide the sacraments.

The Alaskan Churchman was published primarily for readers "outside" of Alaska, though it had avid readers "inside" as well. The Bishop was the editor, and the Log of his travels throughout the Diocese included reports on his flying trips and some of the advantages, frustrations and occasional mishaps they involved. Pictures and stories of people in the churches, and visitors from "outside" and as far away as Africa were fea-

The Bishop visits with Rowland and Mary Cox (left) of Point Hope and Al and Joanne Reiners of Kotzebue, 1955.

Shirley Lewis Gordon and baby Paneen, born in 1944 (Kennell-Ellis Photo)

This was the altar of St. Peter's Church, Seward, on July 16, 1943, the day Shirley Lewis and Bill Gordon Jr. were married. (Photo courtesy of Mary Elizabeth Lee)

Tom Osgood assists the Bishop as he prepares for takeoff from Kotzebue. Bush clergy became familiar with the rituals involved in getting the Bishop off the ground.

The Bishop at All Saints, Anchorage, during a reception honoring the 10th anniversary of his consecration, 1958 (Photo courtesy Anchorage Museum of History and Art)

tured. Laity and clergy of Diocese were asked to write of their work and ministry. *The Alaskan Churchman* gave its readers a sense of having a place and partnership in the Diocese of Alaska, and occasion to send support.

Bishop Gordon's experience among the people of the Arctic Coast, and his early visits to the Athabascan Indian villages of the vast Interior, led him to see the need for increasing the teams of nurses, deaconesses, teachers and clergy serving in remote villages. The fifties and sixties witnessed many changes in Alaska: population growth in the

Anchorage and Fairbanks areas; statehood; larger military bases in response to the "Cold War;" mining and exploration for oil which led ultimately to construction of the TransAlaska Pipeline in the seventies; challenges to the traditional life style of Eskimo and Indian people brought about by more people, more education, more money, more development, as well as the Native Claims Settlement Act and the birth of Native corporations. In the midst of these changes, many church workers from "outside," who were placed by the Bishop in remote villages as "missionaries," found themselves chal-

lenged to do things for which they'd had little formal education. They all had some experience and training to teach, preach and conduct church services; what was new was the Bishop's directive to work themselves out of a job. "Don't do anything the people can do for themselves" carried the implication of helping lay people acquire the skills to be the Church in their villages, servants and ministers to one another. Few of us to whom the directive was given would admit to having done an exemplary job! Whatever success we may have had came primarily *Continued on page 47*

BISHOP BENTLEY REMEMBERS

Archdeacon Goodman was ready to retire from Point Hope because of age and disability. I didn't know who I could send up there. I thought I'd go down to Seward and meet Mr. Gordon and see what he looked like. So, I went. He was a tall, fine and handsome, vigorous young man. Pleasant to meet, friendly, and I said to him, 'I don't want to keep you here; I can get somebody else here. This is an easy post. I am going to send you, if I may, to the most difficult, isolated mission we have in Alaska.' He said, 'My goodness, where are you going to send me?' I said, 'I am going to ask you to go to St. Thomas' Mission at Point Hope on the north coast. Will you go?' He said, 'I will go anywhere my Bishop asks me to go.' I said, 'God bless you.' That was my introduction to Bill Gordon.

When I got back home to Nenana, the mail brought a letter from Bill Gordon asking if Shirley might go to Point Hope with him (they had met on the steamer coming from Seattle to Seward). So I got him on the phone — we had communication along the line of the Alaska Railroad. I said, 'What did Shirley say about it?' 'She said she'd go if she's permitted.' And I said, 'Tell her to get packed.' And I went back to Seward and officiated at their marriage. That evening Bill and Shirley and I took a train up to Curry, an overnight trip on the railroad between Seward and Fairbanks. Bill has always charged me with having accompanied him on his honeymoon. Anyway, we went up to Nenana, and Bill and Shirley stayed with us in the Bishop's Lodge for several days. While we were there I ordained Bill to the priesthood, and he presented Shirley for confirmation. Then we went to Fairbanks and engaged a bush pilot to take us to Point Hope.

He (Gordon) had not only a normal conscience, but he had been reared with a keen sense of duty and obligation. He was active, alert, and faithful in his duties. Any man can be faithful. Any man can be hard working. Any man can behave himself. But not every man, indeed very few men, can have a culmination of all these virtues and be a good bishop as a pioneer on a frontier field. But Bill Gordon did all those things, and I have great respect for him and am devoted to him. He and Shirley have been just like a son and daughter to me.

The Holy Spirit surely guided the House of Bishops when it elected Bill Gordon to be Bishop of Alaska. Physically, mentally and spiritually he was prepared in every way to hold that post and meet those responsibilities. And for 25 years he did and became almost a hero bishop in the Church. And I'm proud to have had any association with him and any part in his election.

Confirmation at Grayling

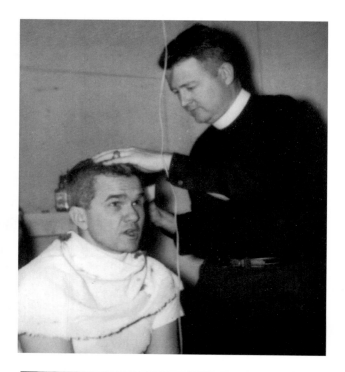

Upper Left: The Bishop gets a haircut from Curtis Edwards in Tanana, 1960.   Upper right: Shirley Gordon unloads groceries from the Blue Box The Gordons never arrived empty-handed at bush missions. How good that fresh produce tasted after weeks without it!   Lower left: Bishop Gordon enjoys visiting with Joe and Gladys John during a potlatch at Tanana, 1972.   Lower right: Clowning around with Shirley   Above: The Gordon family at Kanuga Episcopal Camp and Conference Center in Hendersonville, North Carolina in 1986. Shirley is seated at center near the Bishop. The Gordon children are Rebecca (Becky), standing third from left; Anna Clark, sitting just below Becky and beside Shirley; Paneen, standing behind her mother; and William III at far right beside his wife, Bonnie. Since this photograph was taken, the number of grandchildren has increased by three. (Photo courtesy of Bonnie Gordon)

PEEL TOOYAK, INTERPRETER

Before my dad, Peel Tooyak, began working at St. Thomas' Mission, he was a hunter and a reindeer herder. He got involved working for the late Rev. Archdeacon Frederick W. Goodman at St. Thomas' Episcopal Church and at the mission six days a week, as an interpreter, layreader and organist. He walked to and from the mission each day, and sometimes pulled Archdeacon Goodman around the village on a sled for pastoral visits.

My dad and mother, Beatrice, had ten children, with five now surviving. They sent my brother Enoch to the mission school at Nenana with the goal that when he finished there he would become a priest. (Note: Enoch Tooyak, along with Father Robert Reid and Teddy Mueller of St. Mark's Mission, drowned in September 1949 in the Tanana River near Kantishna, during a hunting trip.)

When Archdeacon Goodman's health became weak, a young man, the Rev. William Gordon Jr., and his wife Shirley, took over the work of ministry in Point Hope, and my dad Peel Tooyak started working with them. Until he became ill, he continued working with them as interpreter and organist. In 1944, the year he was to be ordained a deacon, my dad died on June 28th. He was sorely missed by all of us, and sometimes I have wished my dad and mom were alive to see all of their grandchildren.

When my wife Irene and I became

Peel Toyak, interpreter at Point Hope, with his wife Beatrice (Photo courtesy of Andrew Tooyak Sr.)

elders in Point Hope, we always thought of our parents, who are now resting in peace until the last day. We both learned from our parents, the late Peel Tooyak and Beatrice, and Bob and Helen Tuzroyluke, and we dedicate this story of my late dad to all the readers of this book. May God bless you all.

~ Andrew Tooyak Sr.

After Peel Tooyak's death, William J. Gordon Jr., then priest-in-charge at Point Hope, wrote: "I have never seen anyone face death more calmly. He said to me, 'God knows best,' and his whole life was based on that assumption....I had a communion service for him in his little tent, and Peel insisted on making all the responses. One of the most touching moments of my life came when he read, in Eskimo, the Epistle in the communion for the sick. I was constantly humbled in the presence of this man....He was interpreter here for 13 years. His whole life during that time was devoted to the furthering of the cause of Christ in this village....The whole village has suffered a great loss in his passing....Surely he was one of God's own faithful servants." Archdeacon William Goodman, who during his later years at Point Hope had also benefitted greatly from Peel Tooyak's faithful ministrations, wrote: "Peel was God's good gift to the Church. And now he rests in joy and happiness with Jesus in Paradise. O fairest victory!"

~ From *The Alaskan Churchman* November 1944

Continued from page 42
from learning that to survive amid the harsh realities of the "bush," we ourselves needed to be taught by the people living there. We found ourselves literally sitting side by side at the feet of the elders and youngsters of the villages, learning from them. Their gifts of leadership and witness in the churches distinguished them, and today many are the lay and ordained ministers of their congregations.

Bishop Gordon frequently spoke of the opportunity the Church in Alaska had to take some risks and try things out. If some of these experiments didn't work out and we lost a skirmish, the Church at large wouldn't have been harmed. But if we tested out something that succeeded, the whole Church would benefit. Financial reductions in National Church support for Alaska provided an additional incentive for what has become perhaps the most notable of the successful experiments: ordination of locally trained women and men for celebration of the sacraments in churches which are geographically remote and isolated. Through diocesan training programs for the villages and towns, and parish programs in cities such as Anchorage, Fairbanks, and throughout the Southeast Panhandle, local congregations "raised up" leaders of character and strong faith to exercise priestly functions. Many of these persons were unpaid, and still are; their gift in ministry being matched by the gifts of catechists, lay preachers, lay readers, wardens and vestry (or church committee) members.

Alaska was a leader in the United States with the sacramentalist program. When Bill Gordon completed his work among us, one

Continued on page 56

I once heard Bishop Gordon preach a sermon at All Saints' Church, Anchorage, in which he told of flying north of the Brooks Range and trying without success to locate himself on a map. He finally realized, after poring over the map for the umpteenth time, that he had actually flown off the map. He used this as an analogy for the experience of the Episcopal Church in Alaska. To be sure, the Church in Alaska might, at any given time, be behind in some way and needful of information and help to "catch up." On the other hand, there are other ways where, in faithfulness to its Lord, the Church in Alaska has forged some real break-throughs; has, in a manner of speaking, "flown right off the map," with the result that the map needs to be updated or expanded.

One of those areas is the emphasis the Alaska Church, under Bishop Gordon's leadership, placed on the ministry of the whole people of God. Long before this concern was reflected in the National Church canons, the Commission on Ministry in Alaska had as its first charge: to assist the Bishop in challenging and equipping the laity for ministry. An outgrowth of that was TEAM (Teach Each a Ministry) -- code name for an effort of which Bishop Gordon was an ardent exponent. This has now come to be referred to more generally as "total ministry." Within this context was the emergence, fostered by the Church in Alaska, of ordination of especially qualified persons in remote and ethnically distinct situations for unique but appropriate ministries. The enabling legislation for this was Title III Canon 8. This gave rise to no little controversy in the Church, but, as a result of it, the Church, in my opinion, is incalculably richer. This is only one illustration of how the Church in Alaska, with Bishop Gordon in the cockpit, has at times flown clean off the map.

– Mark Boesser

You have to understand that Bishop Gordon and Walter Hannum did not always agree on everything. They have been known to be at "loggerheads" with one another. But of course that made intermittent periods of peace and tranquillity between them all the sweeter. Such was the context of a feast in the Mission house at Fort Yukon. Walter and Louise were at their genial best, hosting a group of folks at their dinner table, dancing about, serving, would you believe, grapefruit -- GRAPEFRUIT yet, in Fort Yukon, Alaska. Moreover, all the tiny segments had been cut free in advance, the very epitome of gracious hospitality. When all had been served and prayer had been offered, Walter sat down on the far opposite end of the table from Bishop Gordon. Walter dug in for his first bite, and the unthinkable happened. A spurt of grapefruit juice sprang from Walter's spoon, went clean across the table lengthwise -- a guided missile, to be sure -- and landed with unerring accuracy in the Bishop's eye. Bishop howled -- and who could not? -- for no one could doubt that Walter had done it on purpose.

~ Mark Boesser

A REMEMBRANCE

I remember when Bishop Gordon did some miraculous things. He was gifted with many talents, not all of which were widely known. His memory for crucial facts often bordered on the miraculous, and his ability to concentrate was similarly astounding.

I witnessed an example of this once while traveling with him. We had visited two small villages, where he seemed to know everyone, usually by first name. I thought this was interesting, but not too unusual, considering the limited numbers involved.

We finished our trip by attending the annual parish meeting at St. Mary's in Anchorage, which had experienced a rapid growth in its then few years of life. There were the usual dignitaries and visitors at the head table, so before one of his always brief after-dinner addresses, the Bishop stood at the dais and introduced those at the head table to the assembled parishioners. He then began to recognize and introduce those in attendance, young and old. In order from left to right, he introduced well over a hundred people, skipping no one, using their full names, and apparently without a single hesitation or slip. I was convinced he could probably walk on water, if necessary, and, needless to say, his address was personally welcomed and received by everyone.

I remember when Bishop Gordon crashed the "Blue Box" with an "815" representative aboard ("815" is the designation for the National Church headquarters at 815 Second Avenue in New York City). Bishop Gordon must have been one of the greatest bush pilots ever to fly the treacherous and unpredictable skies of Alaska. In his thousands of hours of flight time, he

admitted to only three "misadventures." He was reportedly cautious, ingenious, and wily. None of his flying mishaps was serious, a testimony to his natural skills, but the last crash was amusing, as he told the story, and illustrates the truly human side of a great man of God.

The Bishop didn't cotton much to empty ceremony, hypocrisy, or blustering busybodies. He also didn't care much for pontifications from anyone who didn't know, from experience, what life in a relatively isolated missionary district was like. Ordinarily, this created no problem with visitors from the "south 48," who were awed by the size and complexity of the diocese and the man who was the apostle and chief shepherd in that place. But on this occasion, a representative from "815" was an exception.

This particular individual was an east coast layman who felt the Bishop's attire was only a notch or two above "grunge," lodgings at the Diocesan House quaintly primitive, and the diocesan staff inadequate, at least in quantity if not otherwise. After a hastily curtailed flight to the arctic coast and back up the Yukon, the "815" legate was still critical of almost everything the church had done, was doing, and undoubtedly would do in the future. According to the Bishop, however, he himself was long-suffering and unusually patient, which was quite out of character. At the last of the villages, a landing on skis in spring snow resulted in a minor accident. The plane nosed over in the soft melting snow, throwing the Bishop and his passenger into the windshield and dashboard, despite their seat belts. The Bishop was not injured, but the unpleasant

visitor sustained a cut above one eyebrow. No other damage was done; the plane was quickly uprighted by the waiting villagers, and the flight continued successfully to Fairbanks to return the "815" visitor to New York and "civilization." And none too soon either for him or the Bishop, I suspect.

As the Bishop told this story he broke into a large smile tinged somewhat with mischief, it appeared. Could it be? But I must be mistaken; surely that engaging smile was an expression of his joyful thanksgiving for God's protection and a saintly acceptance of God's all-pervasive will and divine justice.

~ The Rev. Tillman M. Moore, M.D.

A elder of Shageluk presents the Bishop with a woven basket.

Left: A confirmation in Shageluk

Bishop Gordon moved from almost single-handedly deciding many issues bearing upon the life of the Missionary District of Alaska to embracing a participatory decision-making power of lay and clergy representatives from all over the Diocese. That was no small feat! Still, when he was chairing a business meeting, there was little question about who was in charge. Once, however, I saw him a bit off balance. And he was not alone. It was in the early seventies, and the scene was the Convention at which we were moving from Missionary District status to that of Diocese. Considerable work had gone into preparing for this change. New structures had been well researched. The wheels were well oiled, and we were charging along -- that is, until the mid-morning coffee break. Eskimo members caucused. Athabascan members caucused. There was communication between the two groups. When Bishop Gordon called the meeting back to order, Lennie Lane from Point Hope gained recognition to "make a motion," which he proceeded to do in the

The Bishop's Log

June 30, 1959: Made my final trip from Fairbanks to Arctic Village taking the last two passengers (for a work camp program), plus some potatoes, sugar and forty dozen eggs. At 7:30 p.m. at Bishop Rowe Chapel, celebrated the Holy Communion and preached at this most impressive opening of this experience of real family sharing in the Church. Really felt the power of the world-wide Church as the Rev. Isaac Tritt administered the Chalice to his brothers in the Faith from faraway places like Connecticut and Alabama and Ireland.

June 18-19, 1960: This was a busy day in Allakaket with the arrival of the river barge with a whole year's freight for the village. Visited with village people along the bank of the river. In the afternoon we all went up the Alatna River for a picnic with the two DVBS girls along. The girls decided to go swimming up the bar and I warned them to watch out for wolves — and what do you

know —the first wolf I've seen in seventeen years in Alaska appeared on the bar above them!

January 3, 1962: I ordained David Keller to the Priesthood in the lovely and simple setting of St. Luke's Church, Shageluk. Fr. Simmonds preached the sermon and the other clergy joined in the ancient rite of the laying on of hands. Later I thought how my own hands have been used in these ordinations: firepotting the airplane, pushing the tail around, flying the plane — then transmitting the authority of the Apostolic Church by the imposition of my hands as Bishop; then serving as the sacramental representative of the Holy Catholic Church in administering the bread and the wine in Holy Communion. There was a wonderful contrast between the sacramental and the practical as I used the same hands to gas up the "Blue Box" from a drum in Anvik with the temperature at 50 below!

January 21, 1962: Took off (from Cordova) for Fairbanks. Weather OK across the Chugach Range; however, it lowered near the Alaska Range, and with reports of winds from 70-100 knots through Isabel Pass I decided to remain overnight at Paxson Lake. Landed on the field in 3 1/2 feet of snow, and except for a kind man with a Weasel I might be there yet. He pulled me to the highway and out of the deep snow.

January 24, 1962: Tetlin — Temperature dropped here this morning to minus 70 degrees. This is the coldest temperature I have ever seen in Alaska (or in North Carolina either!)

March 29, 1963: Point Hope — Attended the funeral of an elderly Eskimo woman I had known for twenty years. Was impressed anew with the stark reality and simplicity of the Eskimo funeral — the dignified service of the Church, followed by a procession of parka-clad congregation following the simple wooden casket pulled on a sled and the procession of priests in vestments and parkas walking ahead of the sled following the crucifer to the graveyard enclosed by a fence of over eight hundred whalebones. At this time of the year, with the beach gravel frozen rock hard, there can be no interment, so the bodies are buried in a grave in the snow-covered by a canvas and

snow blocks until the early summer when there will be a permanent burial service. How truly Christian is this way of saying a temporary farewell.

June 1, 1964: Flew to Sitka for a visit at St. Peter's-by-the-Sea. Visited in the community with Fr. Stratman and in the afternoon attended a very interesting panel discussion at the Mt. Edgecumbe School on Native Culture. Members of the panel were Indian, Eskimo and Aleut teachers employed by the Bureau of Indian Affairs. What better source of culture than those who live it!

Dec. 26, 1970: Another early start and out to the field and loaded 21 Victor and took off 425 miles to Anvik for my annual visita-

Bishop Tom Greenwood of the Yukon (left) and Presiding Bishop Arthur Lichtenberger join Bishop Gordon for the centennial celebration at Fort Yukon in 1961. Canadian clergy established the Fort Yukon mission in 1861.

Inupiat language. Titus Peter from Fort Yukon seconded the motion and said he'd like to interpret for his people, which he did in Athabascan-Gwich'in dialect. Bishop Gordon, somewhat taken aback, said, "What is the motion?" Both Native groups simply let the question hang in the air. The silence screamed. Gradually it dawned upon us Caucasians that, because the Native people plainly had the votes, someone could "move the question," a vote could be taken, and the motion could even pass, and we non-Natives be none the wiser. The point having been made, Lennie stood and read the motion, which said, essentially: "Considering the importance of the subject matter at hand, and its effect upon the lives of folks for years to come, we should slow down, take time for translation, and put it in simpler language, understandable by all the people."

What effective confrontation, and what a graceful use of power! I can tell you, it fairly turned that Convention around.

~ Mark Boesser

Bishop Gordon arrived at the Juneau airport. Immediately, we headed out the Mendenhall Loop Road. As we neared where the road swung left toward the Mendenhall River we stopped, parked, and set out to walk the bounds of a neat piece of property. The question was: would it be a sound investment for the Church, with an eye to the future, to purchase a five-acre plot of land available for $1,000 an acre? The proposal under consideration: $1,000 from Holy Trinity, $1,000 from the Diocese, and $3,000 to be raised "outside" for this lovely location near the glacier. Up and down we hiked, under beautiful trees, over picturesque knolls, down the valleys, imagining just where a church building might be placed to provide accessibility, visibility, adequate parking. Bishop Gordon moved along like an antelope, exploring in first one direction, then another. As we completed our circuit, the Bishop said without hesitation, "It looks like a winner. Let's go for it!" And so we did. What seemed good to the Holy Spirit and to us then is now the beautiful setting of St. Brendan's, a very much alive and growing church in the Mendenhall Valley. Thanks be to God!

~ Mark Boesser

Greeting parishioners after services, Good Shepherd, Venetie

tion there, with a plane full of food supplies for Jean and Jimmy Dementi and materials for a party plus some goodies for the Anvik community. Encountered a terrific headwind and very cold conditions in the air and it took me four and a half hours before I finally sighted the little village on the Yukon at the mouth of the Anvik River and landed on the snow-covered sandbar in front of the village. Found the temperature an even 40 below zero. It is good to put the plane to bed but this involves pouring 40 gallons of gas out of five gallon cans into the wing tanks, and sitting on an aluminum wing with gloves (and the seat of my pants!) wet with gas. I sure wish sometimes I wasn't a bishop!

December 27, 1970: Celebrated the Holy Communion, preached, and confirmed in

Christ Church Mission, and there was a reception in the Mission house before I went down to the ice of the Anvik River to fire-pot the plane to return to Fairbanks. This is another aspect of winter flying that I would rather do without, particularly since it is down to 40 below again today. I finally got the plane warm and the snow tramped down and started to take off, but just as I was down about 150 feet on the runway the warmth of my breath against the cold windshield completely fogged the cabin and I couldn't see a thing along the snow covered river (or the tree covered bank on the other side), so I had to stop the plane and ended up in deep snow. The pleasure of pushing the tail around in the cold prop wash of the plane in deep snow at 40 below zero is always a memorable experience! Was finally able to get into the air and off for Fairbanks and arrived home just as darkness really settled in. Found the temperature 30 below zero and getting colder. In spite of it all, it was worth any inconvenience to be able to go to Anvik for this visitation.

Dec. 29, 1970: Took my wife to the gala University ball — an odd combination of delicate female finery along with boots and parkys and mittens as the ladies came in from the 35 below zero cold.

Jan. 10, 1971: Anchorage — Had the privilege of celebrating the Holy Communion for an old dear Point Hope friend, Allen Rock, who is dying in the Public Health Service hospital. It is at times like these that I would not trade my priesthood for any job on earth.

Aug. 14, 1971: Flew to Anchorage with Titus Peter, David Salmon, David Keller and Margie John. The weather was fine across the Alaska Range but 40 miles out of Anchorage the ceiling went down to zero and we had to land at the little landing strip at the vacation spot of Big Lake and hold for an hour and a half until the ceiling lifted a little and we were able to tree-top it into Anchorage.

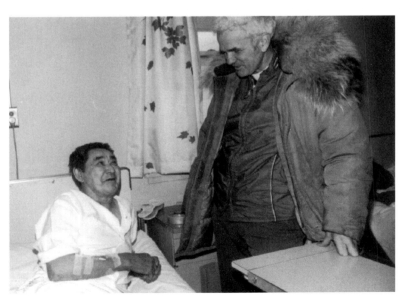

Encouragement and prayers for a patient at the Tanana Hospital, 1972

Aug. 14-16, 1971: Spent these days in a lovely wooded setting at Birchwood Camp outside of Anchorage meeting with nearly 30 members of the family of the Church in Alaska....We discussed in depth the ministry, considering first the needs in Alaska, how God's missionary task may be executed, what hands we need to execute the task and just how these may be provided....The group felt that the one compelling need in Alaska is to provide for some sacramentarians to enable devoted and godly persons to be ordained to the priesthood for primarily a sacramental ministry so that the Holy Communion may be made available to the congregations of the Church throughout Alaska....The chief key to the success of this step will be increased responsibility throughout the congregation by responsible people for the total life of the church with many, many people...seeking further training...so that the Mission of our Lord may be truly carried out by His people.

Aug. 16, 1971: Flew directly from Anchorage to Tanana across the Alaska Range, quite near to the glories of Mt. McKinley. We had been seeing God in His people the past few days and now we are seeing Him in all His glory in His creation.

✝

I remember a "testy time" in 1952 when, as a green deacon at a North Carolina conference center where Bishop Gordon was present, I participated in a debate about Pastoral Clinical Training, a three-month summer program for seminarians encouraged by some seminaries and viewed with considerable suspicion by some others. As it happened, no one at that conference center had been involved in such training, but I had. PCT, as it was then called, was a structured training experience, under the direction of a qualified chaplain-supervisor, at an institution such as a hospital, prison or mental facility; it was designed to give seminarians exposure to people in real-life situations. Upon being asked my opinion of the program, I responded positively about its benefits. I found Bishop Gordon to be the most outspoken opponent, so much so that after some three hours of debate I returned home and told Mildred, "Wherever we may be led to serve, I'm afraid we can scratch Alaska. I've just had a three-hour argument with Bishop Gordon, and I figure I've pretty well done myself in." Some seven years later, when I was serving in Texas, I couldn't have been more surprised to receive a long distance call from Bishop Gordon asking if we would consider coming to the Church of the Holy Trinity, Juneau. I concluded that unless he had suffered a considerable loss of memory (which was highly unlikely, he 1) didn't feel the need for a "yes" man, and 2) respected a person's convictions. Moreover, as later encounters were to bear out, although he was wonderfully persuasive and could be a real "bulldog" in an argument, there was not a rut that could hold him. He was always learning and he had the capacity to change his mind. I really came to appreciate that in him.

~ Mark Boesser

The Bishop talks things over with Dick Clarke at Convocation in Juneau, 1970. Bishop Gordon was noted among his clergy for "putting himself at their disposal" when he visited their parishes or missions, accompanying them on home and hospital visitations, and sharing their pastoral concerns.

Shirley Gordon visits with Archdeacon Frederick Drane and his wife Rebecca (left) and Bishop John Bentley and his wife Elvira at Nags Head, North Carolina, July 1970. When Drane died in January 1982, Bishop Bentley wrote to a friend: "He was always one of my heroes." (Photo by Bishop Gordon)

Worship services at Minto, March 1974

Bishop Bentley, Bishop Gordon and Shirley crack up during Norman Elliott's reminiscences at the Gordons' farewell banquet, Hotel Captain Cook, Anchorage, April 1974.

Anna Clark Gordon surveys high tide in what had been her yard at the Bishop's residence on Kellum Street, Fairbanks, during the 1967 flood in the Interior. Seventeen people waited out the high water here for almost a week while Shirley provided meals and comfort for all.

Continued from page 47

Continued from page 47

of his priorities was to travel and share with the Church in this country and in other parts of the world the methods by which small churches in particular can provide for their own strong lay and ordained ministers. The Bishop's Project TEAM (Teach Each a Ministry), as well as other programs developed subsequently, have provided a vision of what the total ministry of the baptized people of God can be.

Bill Gordon had a big vision of what the Church of Jesus Christ in Alaska could be, and his strong will was a driving force for bringing much of it about. Patience was not first among his virtues, and all who worked with him understood who was "Boss." But he was open to listening to new ideas and would change his mind if he felt the evidence was convincing. His daughter, Paneen, sums it up: "He was a very positive, sometimes scary guy, but if you hung in there long enough he'd listen and learn." He cared deeply about the needs of all the churches and the people of Alaska. At those times when he was aware of really messing something up, or had seriously hurt someone's feelings, his apology came from the heart.

Shirley and the children sometimes had less of Bill's time than they would have desired, and so did some of his lay leaders and clergy. Yet in the work of being a bishop he was a pastor; and it was clear to him, as he'd say to us from time to time, "If y'all aren't something, I'm nothing." It was in that spirit that he knew and remembered so many people on a first-name basis and gave them unfailing encouragement and support.

The work of ministry in the name of Christ was, for Bill Gordon, a partnership. He strove to see such partnership built among the regions of the Diocese; between "Whites" and Natives; in supporting women's ordination to the priesthood; by calling for ecumenical cooperation; through providing means of alternative service for conscientious objectors in the days of the Vietnam War; in promoting wise and environmentally sound resource management; and in supporting dialogue between the Diocese and the wider Church.

Nineteen years after leaving this Diocese, when the Bishop and Shirley visited the state to celebrate their fiftieth wedding anniversary in 1993, friends of many years and newcomers alike were impressed by his hopeful view of the Church. Controversies and thorny issues notwithstanding, he asserted that the Church is in the healthiest condition he'd seen it in years. Problems and difficulties which once could hardly be admitted are now on the table, and the Church is facing them.

While Bishop of Alaska, Bill customarily ended times of discussion and celebration of our partnerships in ministry with prayers. Whether it was with a clergy family when, after one of his visitations in a small village, he was about to fly back to Fairbanks; at a large diocesan gathering; following a visit to a village elder who was seriously ill in an Anchorage hospital; and in thousands of other circumstances, he seized the opportunity to pray, to be silent, to let God have the floor. The life and ministry of Bill Gordon and Christ's flock in the Diocese of Alaska were changed and blessed in that way, and it was good.

~ Dale G. Sarles

✟

The Gordons celebrated their 50th anniversary surrounded by Alaska friends on board the riverboat Discovery *in Fairbanks, July 1993. The Binkley family has operated the Chena and Tanana river tours for many years. Shown here with the Gordons are Captain Jim Jr. (left) and Mary and Captain Jim at right.*

The Blue Box *planes enabled Bishop Gordon to give "wings to the Word" throughout his vast missionary jurisdiction.*

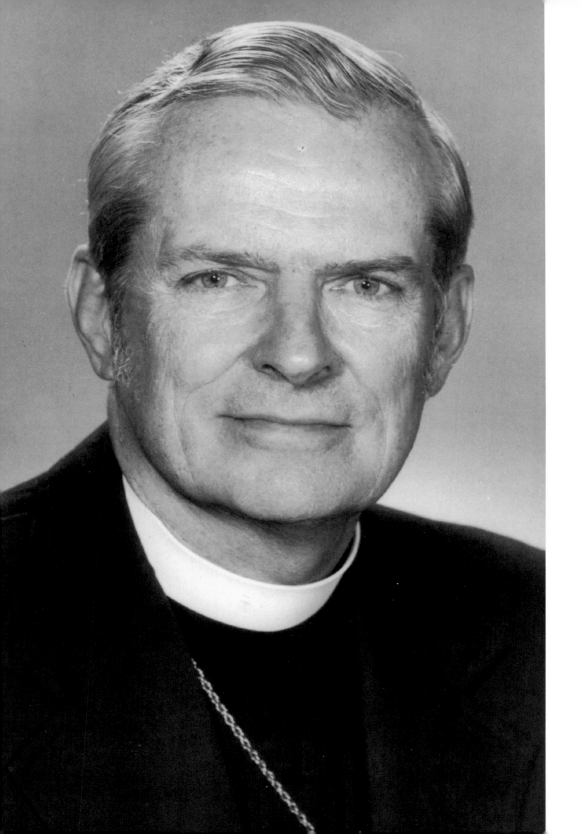

DAVID REA COCHRAN
FOURTH BISHOP OF ALASKA

Born in Buffalo, New York, April 9, 1915, son of Clement Hale Cochran and Agnes (Haynes). B.A., 1936; D.D., 1975, Hamilton College; B.D., 1939, Episcopal Theological School; S.T.D., 1982, Church Divinity School of the Pacific. Ordained to the diaconate, 1940, by Bishop Hobson; to the priesthood, September 1940, by Bishop Whittemore. Married Mary Elizabeth Zabriskie, February 7, 1942; they have three children. Curate, St. Mark's, Grand Rapids, Michigan, 1940-42. Rector, St. Paul's, Dowagiac, Michigan, 1942-44. Chaplain (Captain), US Army, 1944-46. Chaplain, University of Washington, 1946-52. Rector, St. John's, Northampton, Massachusetts, 1952-56. National Commission on College Work, 1956-58. Board of Windham House, 1957-59. Visiting Lecturer, Smith College, 1961. Vicar, Standing Rock Mission, Ft. Yates, North Dakota, 1966-69. Consultant, Board for Clergy Deployment, 1970. Director, Dakota Leadership Program, 1970-74. Board of Theological Education, 1971-76. Bishop of Alaska, 1974-81. Vicar, Holy Family of Jesus Cambodian Church, 1985-88; Director, Cambodian Ordination Program, 1985-present, Tacoma, Washington. He and Mary now reside in Tacoma.

Let the elders who rule well be considered worthy of double honor,
especially those who labor in preaching and teaching . . .
— Timothy 5:17

V

THE BISHOP COCHRAN YEARS
1974 - 1981

Bishop Cochran's story in Alaska began several years before his consecration, when he was living in North Dakota as founder and director of the Dakota Leadership Program. A man whose thinking was firmly rooted in the philosophy of Roland Allen, a turn-of-the-century British missionary in China who advocated giving people charge over their own ministry, Cochran was invited to be the primary presenter at a leadership conference in Fort Yukon in 1967. At this pivotal meeting the stage was set for development of the innovative Canon 8 ministry in Alaska. Under this canon indigenous clergy could be "raised up" from local congregations and trained within the diocese to serve as non-stipendiary ordained or lay leaders in their home communities. Bishop Gordon called these persons "sacramentalists." Cochran later stated that much of what he did as Bishop of Alaska was related to things that began at that meeting.

When David Cochran was consecrated Alaska's fourth bishop in August 1974, he entered a scene marked by rapid and far-reaching change, both in the church and in the state as a whole. Pipeline construction was at its peak, bringing with it opportunities for jobs, big money, inflation and social disruption, particularly in small communities. The Alaska church had just emerged from the status of Missionary District to that of Diocese. Other issues waiting in the wings were women's ordination and the experimental use of a new prayer book.

Bishop Cochran's episcopate got off to an unusual start when, two weeks after assuming office, he attended a meeting of the Synod of the Province of British Columbia to discuss possibilities for a cooperative relationship between the Episcopal Diocese of Alaska and the Canadian Anglicans. Bishop Cochran wrote:

An overenthusiastic Canadian journalist sent out a story on Associated Press which hit a number of papers in the lower 48: "A plan to withdraw the Anglican Diocese of Alaska from the Episcopal Church in the U.S. has been presented at a meeting here." The Living Church picked it up and reported: "Just two weeks after his consecration Bishop Cochran is leading his diocese out of the Episcopal Church." I shortly received a telegram from Presiding Bishop John Allin: "What is going on up there?"

A great deal was going on. Cochran regarded himself as an interim or transition bishop with a two-fold mission: 1) to guide the Diocese through the aftershock of Bishop Gordon's departure and to manage the administrative transition from Missionary District to Diocese, and 2) to follow up on and reinforce the decisions made at the Fort Yukon conference.

As part of a plan to accomplish these goals, a program called NETWORK was

Paperwork — an ongoing element of the Bishop's duties, and always more where that came from

Above: A group from Minto and Beaver poses with Bishop Cochran and the Cessna 180 at the Beaver airstrip: Left to right: Elsie Pitka, Beaver; Kenny Charlie, Minto; the Rev. Luke Titus, Minto; Elman Pitka, Beaver; Arlene Pitka, Beaver; Alice Jordan, Beaver; Bishop Cochran; and Ruth Cruikshank, Beaver; December 1975.

Right: The Bishop presents Bessie Titus with a certificate as a NETWORK Field Associate.

brought into being. This was a vessel for communication, education and training. NETWORK staff published the diocesan magazine, *The Alaskan Churchman*, later renamed *Alaskan Epiphany*. Staff wrote curricula for the training of indigenous "sacramentalist" clergy and lay leaders, conducted training sessions and implemented a correspondence study program. A media library was established for general use throughout the diocese.

Fiscal realities, in the form of diminishing funds from New York headquarters and gifts from Outside, had to be faced. Under Cochran's direction, the first total budget, including gifts and grants from New York, was presented at the 1976 diocesan convention in Sitka.

Through his work in North Dakota Bishop Cochran had been involved in Coalition 14, a group of former missionary districts which came together to negotiate their financial needs with the National Church, as well as to discuss new ideas for ministries and to touch base with others who worked among Native Americans. Cochran brought the Diocese of Alaska into that helpful relationship. It was after a Coalition 14 meeting in 1980 that the Rev. Steven Charleston, new Executive Director of the National Committee on Indian Work, made his first visit to Alaska at Cochran's invitation.

Cochran was instrumental in gathering support for the establishment of the two diocesan conference centers, Meier Lake in Southcentral and Emmaus Center in Southeast. He had a part in introducing the Cursillo movement and Marriage Encounter to the Diocese, and continued to build on the ecumenical relationships begun by Bishop Gordon.

Regarding the second part of his mission "to develop fully indigenous and self-supporting churches in the 'bush,'" he wrote:

A great start had been made in the selecting and ordaining of Native "Sacramentalists," some...replacing seminary-trained white clergy. But because of the diminishing funds this replacing took place more rapidly than anticipated, and we were left without the trained back-up clergy the plan had called for. Many of the Sacramentalists were left without adequate supervision and support. Our attempts to supply this support with diocesan staff or archdeacons did not fully meet this need....So, with this second mission, I felt I achieved far less than I had hoped.

About a year before his retirement, Bishop Cochran happened to be seated at the window of the schoolhouse in Beaver, looking at chunks of ice "sailing majestically and silently down the (Yukon) river." He reflected:

As I sit here...I am very conscious of the fact that less than a year from now I will be retired, and Mary and I will be just beginning to settle down in our new home in Seattle. I have no idea as to who the new bishop will be....But I have some special wishes and hopes for him (or her?)

May he appreciate and enjoy as fully as I have the fantastic opportunity given the Bishop of Alaska to travel the length of this vast land, and to experience the rich diversity of its people and places, its

Left: The new church at Chalkyitsik is dedicated, 1977. Pictured, left to right: David Salmon, Titus Peter, Bishop Cochran, Andy Fairfield, Isaac Tritt and John Williams

Below: Bishop Cochran with a young parishioner at St. Augustine's, Homer, 1976

cultures and climates. Very few persons, including those who have lived in Alaska their whole life, are ever given this privilege.

May a way be found so that the visiting, pastoring, teaching part of his ministry may not always be fighting with the demands for administering with the result that neither is satisfied....

May he be blessed with as creative and supportive a group of co-workers, lay and ordained, as I have been. They make all the difference!

May he have the chance, if only once a year, just to sit for a while and watch the ice move out!

Continued on page 65

61

BISHOP COCHRAN REMEMBERS

With a winter chill in the air, I began sorting out the heavy old wooden storm windows at the Fairbanks rectory, and I noticed that some had different hardware for attaching them. Donning my purple snowsuit (a gift from the Diocese of North Dakota), I went out to the sidewalk in front of the house and with a pair of binoculars scanned the second-floor windows, trying to see in the dusk which storm windows fitted which. I sensed a car had stopped behind me, and when I turned there was a cop. "Aha! A peeping Tom caught in the act!"

Our dogs had some pups, and we gave them away. One was returned after several weeks, the lady saying she had to move and couldn't take the dog with her. While Mary stood holding the rejected creature, she called after the lady, "What is his name?" "His name is Bishop, but we sometimes call him Puddles." The dog had a tendency to wander off, and neighbors sometimes saw Mary going down the street, whistling and calling, "Here, Bishop! Come on home, Bishop!"

Speaking of dogs — one time when I spent a night at Norman and Stella Elliott's in Anchorage, they had to leave in the morning before I'd finished breakfast. Their dog came and sat beside me, uttering low growls. When I tried to get up she bared her teeth and snarled with real menace. There I stayed until Stella came home and rescued me.

On our first trip to Point Hope Mary and I visited Fr. Patrick Attungana in his little house, with sleds and other equipment piled against the outside walls and snow drifted up to the sod roof. We sat under a gasoline lantern, sipping tea. "You know," he said, with his wonderful smile, "this is paradise. God gives us everything we could ask for — whale, walrus, seals, fish, caribou, for food and clothing. And plenty of berries in summer. And good friends and neighbors." We looked out the window at the bleak gray scene and nodded. Some years later, after the village had moved, we sat in one of the new "stick" houses, under bright electric lights, the oil stove purring warmly. Television had just come, and a group of neighbors were gathered around the set, watching "Charley's Angels," beamed in directly from Los Angeles, complete with Southern California commercials. Paradise?

Once we were weathered in at Point Hope, waiting for two days for a plane. Even the phones were out. The RCA technicians had been notified, but of course they couldn't get in. I walked out with Fr. Wilfred Lane to the little building that housed the telephone equipment. Wilfred jiggled some wires, gave the big metal case a masterful kick, and the phones came on. Back in touch with the outside world, we could at least find out when a plane might be coming.

I was on a visit to Tanacross soon after the new village had been built on the highway side of the river. Brightly painted houses stood in neat rows, in sharp contrast to the friendly disarray of log houses in the old village. We planned to have a service in one of the homes, but first a guy from the BIA, taking advantage of the gathering, gave people instructions on how to take care of the plumbing, clear plugged drains, and so on. In the middle of his presentation, the lights went out. We sat for what seemed a long time in the dark silence, while someone went to try to find a candle. A man asked, "What happens if the electricity don't come on until tomorrow?" "Well," said the BIA man, "the truth is, things will begin to freeze up. With no heat out in the water station, and the pumps not working, your water will freeze. Your oil furnaces can't burn properly. It'll get cold." "Oh..." People began to think of their cozy cabins across the river. But at last the lights came on again. A technician had kicked something into action.

We had a clergy conference at Juneau, and Dale Sarles, rector of Holy Trinity and master winemaker, presented each of us with a bottle of his dandelion wine. I wrapped mine securely in my sleeping bag. When I got home, a delicious smell came from the bag, along with lots of broken glass. Thanks, Wien Airlines, for the memory!

Bishop Cochran confirms a young man presented by the Rev. Jean Dementi, St. Jude's, North Pole, 1979.

The ordination of women and the revision of the Prayer Book were the hot issues at the 1976 General Convention in Minneapolis. In his first ACS Hosannah cartoon in *Alaskan Epiphany* shortly before the Convention, Scott Fisher anticipated the furor with a reassuring philosophy. After the Convention, Bishop Cochran commented on what had transpired in Minneapolis:

General Convention is over, and it looks like A.C.S. Hosannah was right. In the cartoon he said that the church was like the Yukon River: it "just keeps going the way God wants it to do. He made it. He keeps it going...and nothing stops it." Some hard and painful decisions were made...in Minneapolis...but even those who were most strongly opposed to the ordaining of women as priests and to the new Prayer Book have remained loyal to the church which made these decisions....I am confident that, like the Yukon, the church will keep "going the way God wants it to go."

...If we are going to help in this...we need to realize that His Spirit is at work out on the far and dangerous edges of life, as well as in our more traditional church ways. We must not have...a "closet theology" — neatly put away in a small, safe place among the treasures of the past. We need a theology that is as big as "all outdoors." ...As St. John reminds us, God's breath — the Spirit — blows where He wills, and we don't always know where He is coming from or where He is leading us. There's lots of breathing room in the church here in Alaska. Let's keep it that way.

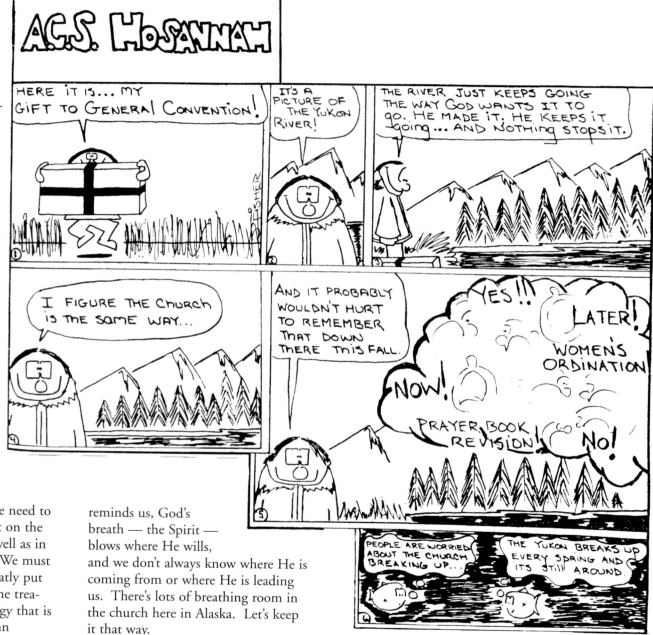

Right: David and Mary Cochran — it is hard to think of one without the other

Far Right: Teaching, preaching — the great strengths of a devout and devoted leader

Continued from page 61

Alaskans remember Bishop Cochran as a private, gracious man with a great sense of humor, who handwrote thank-you letters, who was able to make hard decisions, whose strength lay in pastoral ministry. He is also reputed to have been a cutthroat "Hearts" player! Most important, he led the Diocese through a rough passage with grace, skill and integrity.

One cannot write of Bishop Cochran's sojourn in Alaska without mention of his wife, Mary, as they were harmonious partners in ministry. Mary was known not only for her hospitality, her positive outlook on life and her compassion for persons and creatures in need, but also for an underlying firmness and determination, for looking reality in the eye. During a testimonial at their farewell banquet, the rector of St. Matthew's, Fairbanks, the Cochrans' home parish, observed that while church committees made plans, Mary Cochran just went out and did what needed to be done.

David and Mary Cochran settled in Tacoma, Washington, where they became involved in ministry to a group of Cambodian refugees. The group grew and thrived and eventually formed a parish of their own. Bishop Cochran is currently preparing six Cambodian men for lay or ordained service in the Church.

~ Anne Wenrick

✝

GEORGE CLINTON HARRIS
FIFTH BISHOP OF ALASKA

Born in Brooklyn, New York, Dec. 19, 1925, son of Clinton George Harris and Meta Grace (Warner). B.S., Chemical Engineering, Rutgers University, 1950. S.T.B., 1953; S.T.M., 1953; D.D., 1983, General Theological Seminary. Ordained to the diaconate, May 1953; to the priesthood, Dec. 1953, by Bishop Donegan. Married Mary Jane Shotwell, June 27, 1953; they have six children. Curate, Church of the Heavenly Rest, New York City, 1953-55; Chaplain, Easter School; Assistant, Epiphany Church, Baguio City, Philippines, 1956-62. Hartford Seminary Foundation, 1962-63. Principal, St. Francis High School, Upi Cotabato, Philippines, 1963-69. Rector, Lower Luzerne Parish, Hazelton, Pennsylvania, 1970-74. Director, Dakota Leadership Program, 1974-81. Deputy, General Convention, 1979. Consecrated Bishop of Alaska, June 7, 1981; served as Bishop, 1981-1991. Volunteers for Mission, 1991-92; and Visiting Fellow, College of the Ascension, Selly Oak, Birmingham, England. Member, Curriculum Revision Committee, Leadership Academy for New Directions (LAND), 1993. Staff Theologian, XXV Session, LAND, 1994-95. Member, Board of Directors, New Directions Ministries, Inc., 1994-present. Episcopal visitations, Diocese of South Dakota, 1993-94. Conference speaking and consultations in various U.S. and Canadian dioceses, 1993-present. Evaluation Team member, Living Stones Diocesan Partnership, 1994-present. Now resides in Aberdeen, South Dakota.

*For every high priest taken from among men is ordained for men in things pertaining
to God, that he may offer both gifts and sacrifices for sins...*

- Hebrews 5:1

VI

THE BISHOP HARRIS YEARS
1981 - 1991

Like his predecessor, David Cochran, George Clinton Harris was Director of the Dakota Leadership Program when he was chosen in 1980 as Alaska's fifth bishop. He brought with him perspective and experience that were cross-cultural, global and ecumenical. It is interesting to note that he, like Bishops Gordon and Cochran, had also been strongly influenced by the writings of Roland Allen, missionary to China at the turn of the century. Harris had discovered two of Allen's books in 1954 shortly before he and his family left for the Philippines, where he put some of Allen's ideas to work.

The diocese's Bishop Search Committee had already done some careful research to identify the most urgent needs the new bishop would have to address, and Bishop Harris "happily accepted their analysis as a starting point." The principal challenges, the Committee said, were 1) Communications between Bishop Rowe House (the diocesan center in Fairbanks) and the deaneries and congregations; 2) the ongoing development of Total Ministry and local leadership in every congregation; and 3) Stewardship education.

In addition, Bishop Cochran and others had written a mission statement in the late 1970s to keep Alaska's ship on course; the four-part statement read: a) Partnership with the rest of Christ's Church; b) Building the Church in Alaska; c) Reaching out in Mission; and d) Strengthening our unity and identity. Bishop Harris wrote: "I accepted this statement as my own, with a special remembrance on my part of the logistical, cultural and economic considerations that related to such a vast area, our multicultural membership, and the fragile environment and economy." The importance of the last component—the environment—was dramatically underscored by the Exxon Valdez oil spill which occurred during his term of office.

Bishop Harris immediately tackled the communications problems in Bishop Rowe House by having a multi-lined, coordinated phone system installed, and an answering machine for 24-hour coverage. He put the diocesan newsletter on a regular monthly schedule and asked the *Alaskan Epiphany* editor to maintain dependable quarterly publication. Rural telecommunications advanced rapidly during the decade, but it wasn't until the mid-eighties that the diocesan office had telephone access to all clergy and congregations.

Perhaps the most critical work lay in the development of Total Ministry and leadership in every congregation, a vision Harris shared with the two previous bishops. At the time of his consecration, about fifteen of the forty congregations lacked resident clergy and depended on occasional visits from diocesan staff or neighboring priests. Harris addressed himself to this concern with vigor, and recalls:

This work went slowly....But, in time, the new vision was increasingly accepted. Through the decade we did succeed in ordaining a number of persons (among them the Rev. Anna Frank, first Native American woman to become a priest) and preparing others with the skills for lay ministry in their local churches. We also inaugurated a diaconate program with good results and growing numbers of vocations and ordinations.

When Harris began his episcopate Alaska was receiving more than 50 percent of its financial support from the National Church through Coalition 14. It was clear that, in order to survive, the diocese needed a strategy toward becoming self-sufficient. "Happily, during these years the National

Church came to a consensus on the biblical tithe as a standard for our giving," he wrote, and with the backing of a strong committee, stewardship education became a hallmark of the Harris administration. "As a result of all these efforts, and in spite of an economic downturn with the collapse of world oil price levels in the mid-eighties, our local giving showed significant growth." The seeds for "planned giving" were also planted.

Harris's stewardship program included Alaska's participation in Venture in Mission, a National Church call to all dioceses to raise funds for missions worldwide. Alaskans gave $600,000 to this effort, the largest external grant going to the Diocese of Pusan, Alaska's companion diocese in South Korea. The largest internal grant went to the diocese's Development Loan Fund, enabling the church "to shift from a grant to a loan system, thus preserving the principal and helping congregations to become less dependent."

Because of its vastness and the isolation of many of its congregations, the diocese had always been difficult to administer, and ideas for dividing it were discussed periodically. The membership was always reluctant to take such a radical step, however; so Bishops Cochran and Harris put much effort into strengthening the diocese's regional structures known as Deaneries: the Arctic, the Interior, Southcentral and Southeast. Under Harris's leadership, full or part-time resource persons were placed in each deanery by mid-decade, regular annual meetings were enriched by teaching and program development, and diocesan funds were made available to implement deanery programs.

When Harris assumed office, the diocese was governed by a Standing Committee, chaired by an elected priest or layman and charged with carrying out the plans and programs approved at annual conventions. This arrangement had a number of drawbacks, so in mid-tenure Harris began to explore the possibility of changing to a Diocesan Council model of government, in which the Bishop is the Chairperson with the authority and resources to follow up on the Council's decisions. The idea gradually gained support and became a reality in a final vote at the 1990 Diocesan Convention. Bishop Harris recalls with satisfaction, "I was delighted, and felt we had thus passed on to Steven Charleston, my successor, a more efficient and workable instrument for diocesan government."

Harris's ecumenical endeavors included a term as President of the Alaska Christian Conference, under whose auspices he and Neil Munro, Presbyterian executive of the Anchorage Synod, planned and held the first New Pastors Orientation Conference in Alaska, attended by some 35 pastors, spouses and families. Internationally, he and others conceived the Pacific Basin Conference which was held in Hawaii in the summer of 1983 and was based on the ministry development ideas of Roland Allen. The 150 persons in attendance represented more than 50 nations and/or dioceses. Finally, Bishop Harris and his wife,

Outlining the program at a meeting of the Arctic Coast Deanery

Bishop Harris at his consecration, June 7, 1981, with his predecessor approving in the background

Catching up on the omnipresent paperwork at the diocesan office

Bishop George and Mary Jane Harris at the time of their 40th wedding anniversary, June 1993

Mary Jane, were present at the 1988 Lambeth Conference in Canterbury, England, which he considers "the high point of our experience with the international Anglican Communion."

As an administrator, Bishop Harris looked for framework, took seriously the canons on bishops' duties, paid attention to rubrics, and used a "hi-lighter" liberally. His tenure was an evaluation in progress—of himself and of programs—and he often paused to test the structure of his Church-building. He was, and is, a literary man, enjoying both reading and writing. He likes to tell, and be told, a good story. Others remember his humility and his faithfulness to his calling.

While Bishop Harris attended to diocesan matters, Mary Jane was earning a degree in music at the University of Alaska Fairbanks and teaching piano students at home. She was principal organist at St.

Matthew's in Fairbanks for two years and part of the volunteer staff at Jo Scott's Summer Arts Festival for nine summers. Bishop Harris wrote: "In the middle of the eighties Mary Jane got interested in bee-keeping (a hobby which continued for about five years). I (would take) a day off in late August to help with the harvest of honey— sometimes as much as 100 pounds from our one hive!"

Together they enjoyed the outdoors, cross-country skiing, running or taking walks, bicycling, and participating in the "Holy Roll" bike trips organized by his administrative assistant, Andy Fairfield (now the Bishop of North Dakota).

In various reflections on his time in Alaska, Harris has written: "Especially in the villages, a visitation involved home visits, meetings with the vestry or church council, and a potluck meal with the congregation, as well as the Sunday morning liturgies.

I almost always stayed with the local priest's family or lay member's home, both in village and city visits, and this led to close friendships with the clergy and people as the years went by. These weekend visitations were certainly the most enjoyable part of my work."

In an article in the *Fairbanks Daily News-Miner* shortly before his retirement, he said, "My wife and I leave Alaska to a rising generation of leadership, confident that the spirit of Christ will be evermore visible working through God's people in this beautiful, fragile and challenging 'last frontier.'"

A few months after retirement in 1991, Bishop Harris and Mary Jane left for a year's work with Volunteers for Mission at College of the Ascension in Birmingham, England. They now live in Aberdeen, South Dakota, near their oldest son and his family.

Upper right: The athletic Bishop was a familiar sight running or biking around Fairbanks. Staff, family members and assorted ambitious communicants joined in the "Holy Roll" bike trips organized by Bishop Harris during the '80s.

Upper left: Are we having fun yet?

Lower right: The diocesan van tempts bikers to grab a rest along the route of the "Holy Roll," 1987.

Lower left: The Bishop in mufti

Bishop Harris, 1987

Bishop Harris "Quotes"

From a brief article in *Alaskan Epiphany,* Volume III, 1987, "Honoring the Past With a Faithful Present":

All of us honor the apostles and prophets, the missionaries and elders who, in preceding generations have nurtured the faith, served in the name of Christ, and spread the Gospel by living it in their communities.

The day will come when future generations will look back upon us, however, and will be moved, perhaps, to honor the work we have done for the Lord.

...What will be said of us when an assessment is made of our contribution to the ongoing life of the church? Will it be perceived by future generations that we arose to the occasion in a turbulent and rapidly changing age to produce the energy, leadership, resources and the vision that made a significant contribution in our time to the life of the church? What will be said of us?

I would like to suggest that the best commemoration of the past is a living, dynamic and responsible present.

On the 1988 Lambeth Conference:

From his "Autobiographical Notes" — At this conference the bishops of color from the Third World outnumbered those from England, Canada, the U.S., Australia and New Zealand. In many ways this gathering deepened our confidence in the vitality and inclusiveness of our worldwide church.

A concelebration of the Eucharist at St. David's, Wasilla, with priests Sue Hewitt, Norman Nauska and Chuck Eddy

From "The Bishop's Log," *Alaskan Epiphany,* Volume IX, Number 3, 1988 — What I particularly wanted to share with you was the part of the Lambeth Conference experience that most of us found to be moving and memorable: the daily small group Scripture study....My group...included bishops...from Scotland, England, Ireland, Africa, South Africa, Japan, Canada and Australia....There, on a daily basis, we encountered the Lord and each other in an atmosphere of growing trust, openness and candor....The Lambeth experience confirmed all my earlier experience in this area: that God, speaking through Holy Scriptures, can draw us powerfully together, enriching our individual lives with all their troubles and hurts as well as their joys, and forging that deeper community on which so much of the mission and ministry of the church depends.

Frustration

From "The Bishop's Log," *Alaskan Epiphany,* Volume IX, Number 4, 1988 — Writing about the 1988 Diocesan Convention:

A view from the chair is one of real privilege and responsibility. The fact that I crushed my cup and broke my gavel in Minto does not mean that I did not fully enjoy leading the proceedings. I did! But...I invite your ideas and cooperation in the months ahead as you reflect upon ways in which our diocesan gatherings can be made more effective and more satisfying for every participant.

"Total ministry" was a catch phrase during the tenures of Bishop Cochran and Bishop Harris, emphasizing the involvement of lay people in the outreach work of their missions and parishes. Once again Scott Fisher took up his pen and put his unique stamp on the concept.

The Bishop with the Tuzroylukes of Point Hope: Claudia and her husband, the Rev. Seymour Tuzroyluke, stand beside Seymour's mother.

On the Exxon Valdez Oil Spill

"The Bishop's Log," *Alaskan Epiphany*, Volume X, Number 2, 1989 -
If there is to be a Christian perspective on this (the oil spill) it must not be trivialized in righteous anger at the most obvious and tragic figures in the drama: the ship's captain; the oil companies; complaisant legislatures and ineffective officialdom.
...If a Christian voice is to be raised, let it be a voice of prophecy and contrition. We are all citizens of the global village, locked together in the commonality of human existence, meant to share in the fruits of the earth as well as in its care. Those who believe in God and acknowledge the lordship that God exercises and shares with us, must acknowledge our blindness, greed and apathy. We can then, out of trust and hope in God, call our fellow human beings to become better stewards of planet Earth.

On Visitations:

"The Bishop's Log," December 1989 —

I lost my voice over Saturday night with a bad case of laryngitis, and on Sunday could barely croak the Eucharistic prayer and a short sermon after some home remedies. The congregation (St. Bartholomew's) responded with a gracious luncheon.

"The Bishop's Log," same issue —

My weekend trip to Anchorage for a visitations had to be aborted because of volcanic ash from the eruption of Mt. Redoubt.

"The Bishop's Log," Saturday, May 6 —
Flew to Beaver for my visitations. The community had been up all night on a flood watch due to the ice jammed in the Yukon River. Scott Fisher and I visited in the community, and the next morning we had Eucharist followed by a sandwich lunch in the sunshine on the shore of the ice-clogged river. Returned home (via Episcopal Airlines) and spent the next week in the office answering mail and preparing for my Pentecost visit to All Saints, Anchorage.

On Retirement

"Bishop's Corner," Alaskan Epiphany, Volume X, Number 4, 1989 —
I find...it is more difficult to carry out a decision than it is to make one! This past year or more during which the planning for my retirement and the election of a successor has been going on I have had strong feelings of ambivalence about the whole matter!
...However, I invite all of you to support the search committee in its work with your prayers and sound advice and keep an open mind and heart as we move into this transitional year in the life of the Diocese of Alaska. Mary Jane and I love you all very much and we want this as much as we have ever wanted anything to be a creative and helpful transition in your life and in ours.

✝

STEVEN CHARLESTON
SIXTH BISHOP OF ALASKA

Born in Duncan, Oklahoma, Feb. 15, 1949, son of Gilbert Mike Charleston and Billie Louise (Burns). Enrolled member, the Choctaw Nation of Oklahoma. B.A., Trinity College, 1971; Master of Divinity, Episcopal Divinity School, 1976; D.D., Trinity College, 1992, and Alaska Pacific University, 1994. Native American Theological Association. Married Susan Flora Shettles, July 28, 1978; they have one son, Nicholas Tecumseh. Ordained to the diaconate, 1982, by Bishop Wantland; to the priesthood, Mar. 1983, by Bishop Walter Jones. Executive Director, National Commission on Indian Work, New York City, 1980-82. Director, Dakota Leadership Program, 1982-84. Director, Cross-Cultural Studies; Associate Professor, Systematic Theology, Luther Northwestern Theological Seminary, St. Paul, Minnesota, 1984-90. Vicar, Holy Trinity/St. Anskar, St. Paul, late 1980s. Consecrated Bishop of Alaska, Mar. 23, 1991. Author: *Reflections on a Revival: The Native American Alternative; Respecting the Circle: Sharing in Worship with Native Americans; Good News from Native America.*

...for yet the vision is for many days...
                              ~Daniel 10:14

VII
THE BISHOP CHARLESTON YEARS
1991 - PRESENT

The Mission Wheel. An elegantly simple construct that could have a profound impact on the Diocese of Alaska. The wheel is a model of ministry on a diocesan level composed of a minimum of four segments: Stewardship, Evangelism, Leadership Development, and Christian Learning. Each of these areas is integral to the whole: If one is missing the wheel will not roll.

To date the episcopate of Alaska's present bishop, the Rt. Rev. Steven Charleston, has been a concentrated effort to give life to the Mission Wheel. It has not been an easy birthing. Only in a fictional television series can the captain of a starship say, "make it so," and a thing is done. From our experience together as members of the Body of Christ we have learned that only God is capable of such an action. And so, here in Alaska when a "blue jeans and bunny boots" diocese and its bishop make a commitment to change, to grow, to make things better, a vast number of people prayerfully set about to make it happen in the face of many obstacles.

Another thing we have learned as Christians is that only God can create something out of nothing. It should not be surprising then that in the Diocese of Alaska

the effort to give life to the Mission Wheel has been undertaken in the midst of certain tension-producing "givens."

These include a state that is struggling to gain its financial balance in the face of depleted oil revenue and a diocese that must overcome numerous problems produced by the enormous distance it encompasses; substantially decreased national church funding; the ongoing need to be sensitive to the spiritual needs of a complex, diverse, cultural matrix; and the characteristic tension that is evoked when a renewed commitment is made to total ministry in all levels of diocesan life.

On a regional level the Diocese has a partially developed deanery structure that has suffered from lack of funding. On a local level, congregations hindered by a long history of limited access to local training and the pastoral consolation of a sacramental ministry strive to spread the good news of the gospel in the face of unrelenting social problems.

In the midst of this situational landscape, the Mission Wheel has emerged as a viable model of how ministry could be done in Alaska. At the same time, because of this tension-filled environment, the model that has come to life is endowed

with certain incongruities.

Limited funding has forced limited staffing of the model. Instead of four staff positions—one for each mission area—the Diocese has had to settle for one: the director of Leadership Development. In order for the wheel to roll, the other three areas are being covered by unpaid volunteers on a part-time basis. Compounding the lack of personnel is the fact that since its birth the wheel has been amended to include a fifth area of equal importance: Communications. This new area has been recognized as the hub that connects all of the parts. At present it exists only because the present staff has been willing to shoulder increased responsibilities.

Lack of funding dictates that the program must use grant money since the diocesan budget has been unable to provide funding for program or travel. As a consequence, the diocesan staff must continually develop new ideas because only innovation opens up the possibility of new outside money. In order to maintain and support the ongoing objectives of this new ministry model, the Diocese finds itself locked in a "Catch-22" situation. When funding is dependent on new initiatives, financial support is all but impossible to find for many older ideas of merit which, if allowed to mature, would ultimately eliminate this dependence.

Recognizing this dynamic at work, the Diocese, early in Bishop Charleston's tenure, implemented a capital funds campaign, Faith into Tomorrow, designed to raise money for an endowment fund that would provide ongoing income for the support of the five central areas of ministry, each critical to the long-term health of the Diocese. The response to this campaign exceeded all expectations, and the projected goal of $1,000,000 was surpassed by a healthy margin. Faith into Tomorrow marks yet another step by Alaska's Episcopal community into the tension between a problematic "now" and a brighter "not yet."

A final tension needs to be acknowledged. There is no question that, in electing Steven Charleston to the episcopate in Alaska, the Diocese consecrated a spirit-filled pastor, evangelist, teacher, and visionary. To some extent this selection has proven to be both a blessing and a curse to the Diocese as well as to Bishop Charleston. Such a talented individual does not go unnoticed by the larger church. As a consequence, we find that the individual obviously chosen by God to lead the Diocese of Alaska to a brighter future finds himself torn between the heartfelt desire to be a faithful servant to his diocese and the incessant

The Very Rev. Charles A Perry, Dean of the Church Divinity School of the Pacific, the graduate seminary for the Eighth Province, visited Alaska in the summer of 1992. He and his wife traveled with the Charlestons throughout the Arctic Coast Deanery, as well as to Fairbankss and Tanana, where Dean Perry participated in services, taught, and met with clergy and lay people. He is shown here (left) with Bishop Charleston and the clergy of Point Hope: Elijah Attungana, Seymour Tuzroyluke and Patrick Attungana.

demands for his leadership and vision by the larger church, not only as a spokesman for native peoples throughout the Episcopal Church and the Anglican Communion but also as a leader of national prominence and stature.

As we enter our second hundred years as a diocese, we find ourselves in the midst of a great tension between a future that occasionally produces glimmers of hope and a present that is uncertain and fraught with prob-

lems. Perhaps that's the way it should be.

For if we have learned anything in the past hundred years it is that nothing is certain in this world except the enduring love of God, incarnated in our Lord Jesus Christ and present to us today in the power of the Holy Spirit. Amen.

– The Rev. Canon Luis Uzueta

✝

Left: The Charleston family in December 1993: Susan, a talented artist; son Nick, then age 15, and Bishop Steven

Bottom left: The Bishop at confirmation service at Holy Spirit, Eagle River, 1994, with acolyte Stephen Hill

Bottom right: At St. Paul's, Grayling, Donovan Deacon is baptized by Bishop Charleston.

From "Bishop 2000: A Native American Working Paper" (1986)

A Look at Episcopal Leadership After the Year 2000

...the Church of the next century will begin a journey in witness that will challenge many of the old icons of the 20th Century. It will be saying that "big" is not better. It will also be saying that "fast" is not always best....The example set by the 21st Century Episcopal Church will have a great impact on the social/ political condition of American society because it will offer that society a clear alternative....By the mid-21st Century, as many Western societies have strained to the limit to maintain a status quo of luxury and affluence, the Church will reach a breakthrough point where its own message of sharing communities takes hold in the popular imagination. The relationship among North-South Christians will emerge, not as the old "have and have-nots" of the 20th Century, but as fellow Christians living in common cause for a balanced global community.

Above: Bishop Charleston preaches during a visitation at Tanana, 1993

From Diocesan Meeting of Episcopal Church Women: Los Angeles (March 1988)

We've become accustomed, grown accustomed to, slumbering in the church as an institution. And what we're hearing around us is the plaster falling off the walls of that institution. And what we're beginning to see emerge is the Church as a witness, a living witness, a living word. Not as a structure, not as a program, not as an institution, but as a living community of faithful people who are going to be giving the world a hopeful new message. So I am not at all worried about the institutional breakdown of this Church. I am grateful to see the rise of the witness of the Church as it speaks to the world in a new way.

...That's what we need in this Church: leadership with virtue. And obedience? Yes, a servant with authority. To speak with authority, sure. To proclaim justice. Absolutely! To exercise compassion, undoubtedly. But to do so always remembering that you are a servant, that there is One greater than you. One, to whom you have given all of your loyalty, all of your devotion and all of your love. To the depth of your being, you have committed yourself to this one we call Jesus of Nazareth, and to be obedient to his Word in all that you do.

From "'Bishop 2000' Revisited - The Episcopacy in the Second Reformation" (1994)

To Be Or Not To Be: Still on the Tightrope

In the church to come, we will redesign the episcopacy by starting with what we want bishops to be, not with what we want them to do. Their relationship to the people will be decisive, not the amount of work we can cram into an already overloaded calendar. And in the end, with any individual we call on to be the visible embodiment of episcopal leadership, we will have to decide which is more important to us: ideology or community.

The Second Reformation: Finding the Future All Around Us

I realize that in our church we have grown accustomed to thinking of our problems as incredibly tangled and complex. We believe that there are no easy answers. In fact, many of us have believed that there is no way out of our predicament. Consequently, the Native response can seem strange, even absurd because it is so simple, so basic, so human. And yet, as a Native theologian, I would continue to say that the solution to our struggles is simple. It is so simple that it can be expressed in a single word: love.

The surprising option which we must embrace is to rebirth the episcopacy by taking the bishop off the tightrope and placing him or her gently in the midst of the loving community of God. The reform of the episcopacy will begin when we decide to shift

the balance, the fulcrum of the episcopacy from time to relationship. Then we can bring the bishops down from their imaginary high wire act and put them in the living context of the community. The ministry of the bishop, therefore, will become less of a job description and more of an interdependent relationship to the tribe of Christ. In "Bishop 2000" I suggested that we might want our spiritual leader to be a

"pastor, dreamer, counselor, prayer leader, and planner." To be a pastor means to be a person of love. To be a dreamer means to be a person of vision. To be a counselor means to be a person who listens. To be a prayer leader means to be a person who lives in prayer. To be a planner means to be a person who searches for the future in the world around them.

The Bishop and Owanah Anderson, Columbus Day, 1992, at the "500 Years of Survival" Eucharist, National Cathedral, Washington, D.C. At this great commemorative service Bishop Charleston preached of God's healing and redemptive power and of his own vision for the people of God in the years to come.

Good News from Native America

The time has come for this tribe to accept the responsibility of the gospel God has entrusted to it: to become the true alternative to a society coming apart at the seams through fear and hate, greed and exploitation, despair and a loss of faith. We are to be the eye in the midst of the storm. We are to be the sanctuary. We are to be the new community where people of all walks of life can come and begin moving in a different direction together. And let me be clear about the nature of that direction: it is toward the total reformation of both the church and the society. Our destination is the Promised Land. We will settle for nothing less. Those who embark on this journey are in it for the long haul. They accept the fact that it will not always be easy or pleasant, but they also believe and trust that it will be holy and loving.

Above: Bishop Charleston speaks at a Reconciliation service at Tanana in July 1993.

Right: Convention secretary Caroline Wohlforth reads and Bishop Charleston studies resolutions at the 1993 Diocesan Convention in Anchorage.

Native American bishops celebrate the Eucharist in National Cathedral, Washington, D.C. on Columbus Day, 1992. More than 3,000 participants, representing 35 Indian tribes from throughout the Western Hemisphere, met to observe 500 years of survival by Native Americans. Pictured left to right are: the Rev. Martin Brokenleg (Sioux) of South Dakota; Bishop Harold Jones (Sioux), retired suffragan of South Dakota; Bishop Steven Plummer (Navajo), of the Navajoland Area Mission; Presiding Bishop Edmond L. Browning; the Ven. Philip Allen (Sioux) of South Dakota; Bishop Steven Charleston (Choctaw) of Alaska; Bishop William Wantland (Seminole) of Eau Claire; and host Bishop Ronald Haines of Washington, D.C. (Episcopal News Service photo by James Solheim)

DR. OWANAH ANDERSON

Dr. Owanah Anderson, Staff Officer for Indian Ministry, at the Diocesan Convention in Anchorage, 1993

Dr. Owanah Anderson, national director for Native American Ministries of the Episcopal Church, and herself a member of the Choctaw Nation, preached the sermon at the consecration of Steven Charleston on March 23, 1991. Following are excerpts from her charge to the new Bishop:

...A heritage we share...is a lineage of ancient orators and wise counsellors ...wisdom of the past handed down by sages departed, along with knowledge gained by the living....We share a lineage of fiery preachers and patient teachers. Such men were your great-grandfather, Martin, and your grandfather, Simeon — steadfast preachers...of the Good News of Jesus Christ. Yours is a challenge...to reinforce

bridges that span the cultural chasm of a bicultural diocese....Acknowledge and honor this cultural diversity, but craft a model for the whole Church, which lives in full and equal cultural partnership...with neither dominant over the other....You, yourself, by bloodline, embody the diversity of this diocese.

(Speaking of white and Native strengths throughout the diocese of Alaska): *To these Native people, the Episcopal Church had been the center of the community...the heart of community life...the core around which circled all activity. The church was the magnet. The Native people of our country have 'turned over' their son to all Alaska, since they cannot all go with him.* Dr. Anderson charged the new Bishop to use *his God-given gifts"* — *"to restore the Episcopal Church* to the very center *of community life.*

Bishop Charleston after his consecration in Anchorage, March 1991. See color section for description of the symbolism of the episcopoal vestments. (Photo by Evolyn Melville)

Above right: Bishop Charleston and Madelyn Stella of Wrangell, with members of Wrangell's Inquirers' Group for high school teens, Richard Petticrew and Cerrina Bower, displaying Treasure Bear at the Diocesan Convention at Fort Yukon, October 1994. Treasure Bear symbolizes the Treasure Kids project active in at least ten parishes in the diocese; the program is designed for the recognition and education of children within the church community.

Right: The Bishop examines the portable organ carried by Bishop Rowe during the early years of this century. The organ is part of the traveling exhibit honoring the centennial celebration of the Diocese. The photo was taken at a reception at the Heritage Museum, Anchorage, in March 1995.

Above left: The Bishop flips burgers with John White and Ed Thielen at the Southcentral Deanery meeting at Meier Lake, June 14, 1994.

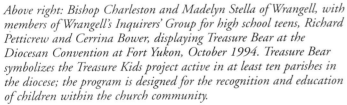

The ordained ministry in Minto, June 1974: left to right, Luke Titus, Kenneth Charlie, Anna Frank, Bishop Gordon , and Berkman Silas

Tinjuhnut tunnyitgitichooe, Vittekwichanchyo: aha tinjihnut tutthug tunnyigitchooe.
Let the people praise thee, O God; let all the people praise thee.

- Psalm 67:3

VIII

ALASKA'S NATIVE LEADERS
BUILDING THE CHURCH THROUGH TIMES OF CHANGE

In 1861 when the first shots of the American Civil War were fired at Fort Sumter, another kind of history was being made quietly at Fort Yukon, Alaska. An English missionary, the Rev. William W. Kirkby, visiting the trading post settlement of Fort Yukon, was the first representative of the Anglican Church to meet with Alaska's Native people. He was followed the next year by Robert McDonald, who served in the Yukon and Alaska for over fifty years. The long relationship between the Church and the Native community had begun.

Through all of the years to come, that relationship would grow as the Anglican, and, later, Episcopal Church expanded its mission throughout the territory of Alaska. The ministry of the Church could never have been carried out at all without the dedicated work of countless Native people.

Many of these people have become familiar names in the history of the Alaska Church, but many more are remembered only in the stories told by family and village. From the very beginnings, men and women from Tlingit, Haida, Tsimshian, Athabascan, and Inupiaq communities served the Church in a wide range of ministries. Some were guides and interpreters. Some built churches, hospitals, and schools. Some pro-

William Loola of Fort Yukon, a pupil of Archdeacon McDonald, was the first Athabascan ordained to the diaconate (December 1903) and served until his death in June 1918. (From a portrait)

vided transportation and food for the new missions. Some taught Sunday school and Catechism. Many became mission leaders and planners. A celebrated few became the ordained leadership of the Church.

Telling all these stories, of course, would fill this entire book. At best, we can highlight the crucial Native contribution to the Church, letting that be a testimony to the much broader involvement of Native people from all across Alaska.

Nine years before Alaska even had an Episcopal bishop, Native people were helping to establish an Episcopal mission at

Anvik. Their labor and support made this first foothold of the Episcopal Church possible in 1886. Later, other Native people helped to create missions in Point Hope (1890) and Fort Adams and Tanana (1891).

In a very literal way, the Episcopal missions of Alaska were built by Native people. St. John's in Ketchikan, for example, was raised by the hard work and dedication of the Tsimshian people. Like so many of the early church structures, it remains as visible testimony to the devotion of the Native community in bringing the Episcopal Church to Alaska. Examples of these Native-built church buildings can still be seen throughout the state. Each one is a tribute to the men and women who created them and supported them through the long years of Episcopal missions.

In 1895, when Peter Trimble Rowe became the first Episcopal Bishop of Alaska, the partnership between the Church and the Native people quickly took on even deeper meaning. While Rowe had expected his primary ministry to be with the Native community, he soon discovered it was complicated by the flood of European-Americans rushing into the gold fields of Alaska. The Church confronted all the social problems that came with a gold rush, both within the

NATIVE MINISTRIES IN ALASKA

When I arrived in Tanana in 1953 it was the end of an era when the ministry of the Episcopal Church was largely carried out by centrally located mission compounds consisting of a church with a seminary-trained priest, a hospital, school, and/or children's home. This would be the center of ministry for the village and surrounding villages. The doctor, priest, and nurses would make periodic visits to villages within a 100-150-mile radius. The school and hospital started by the Church had closed down in Tanana and were now in the hands of the government. Hudson Stuck Memorial Hospital was still functioning in Fort Yukon when I moved there in 1955. Fortunately, within a few years tuberculosis was under control, cutting down drastically on the number of patients. In 1960 that hospital was closed, with only a small clinic remaining in Fort Yukon. Seriously ill patients were flown to government hospitals. As the institutions were closed, teachers and doctors departed the mission field, leaving behind the memories of previous longtime missionaries such as Dr. and Mrs. Burke, Miss Hill and Miss Kay, and countless others.

Thanks to the dedication of pioneer missionaries of the Anglican Church of Canada and the Episcopal Church, the Gospel had spread throughout the upper Yukon area. By 1910 nearly all Native people in Alaska were members of a Christian Church; all Indians in the upper Yukon were Episcopalians. The early missionaries were dependent on the Native people to teach them how to live in Alaska's challenging environment, and many Natives worked alongside the missionaries in their pastoral

work. The Rev. Paul Mather, a Tsimshian, was Bishop Rowe's capable Native worker. Walter Harper, an Athabascan, was Archdeacon Stuck's indispensable assistant and traveling companion.

As the social institutions were established by the government to meet the educational and health needs of the village people, more and more professional personnel were recruited from Outside. Tony Joule, an Eskimo, was the only Native I know who was a teacher in charge of a village school. Thus, the Church had fewer Native people in leadership roles than at an earlier time. As diminished funding resulted in closure of the social institutions, Bishop Gordon worked to have seminary priests and professionally trained lay workers in most villages. Many villages had church buildings but no resident missionary. Fortunately, a few villages did have dedicated Native lay leaders.

As I began my ministry I observed Native men and women who demonstrated responsible leadership in their families and communities — people like George Edwin, Isaac Tritt, David Salmon. David and George were able to stand up and be counted as they dealt with the depression caused

Fr. Walter Hannum works with a happy group of Fort Yukon kids.

by loss of jobs in their home areas: no longer did they cut wood for the steamboats that had converted to oil; the dog teams were replaced by mail planes; the fur market collapsed. George went to Fairbanks to get work; there he ministered to village men who had a tough time living away from home. David went to work to pay off village debt.

I chose people such as these proven leaders in order to train the best possible church leader for each village. I also chose people who knew the saving grace of God. When I asked David Salmon why he wanted to be a layreader, he said, "The white man has some good ways, and he has some bad ways. The Indians have good ways and bad ways. Only through Jesus do we know what

Donald Oktollik and David Salmon study at the Yukon Valley Training Center, circa late 1950s.

is right and wrong before it is too late."

I began discipling these men and women by using models from the Bible: Moses and Joshua, Elijah and Elisha, Jesus and His disciples, and Paul and Timothy. The training took place in the context of my ministry in the villages. They would observe my role in ministering to the people, then would minister alongside me. Next I would observe them in pastoral roles, and lastly they worked by themselves and we then evaluated the fruits of their ministry. We spent three hours each morning in prayer and teaching. We studied the ministry of Jesus, St. Paul's writings, the liturgy, etc. Twice a week we had evening Bible studies for adults of the community, giving the trainees opportunities to teach what they had learned. Afternoons were devoted to

pastoral ministry, visiting people in their homes, ministering to the sick, to the troubled, to those in jail. Sunday School teachers and village council members were trained in similar fashion. Informal times together were an important element. This training was not designed to meet the standards set up by National and Diocesan Commissions on Ministry, nor was it just to benefit the individuals in training. I tried to equip the leaders to be able to bring people into a personal relationship with Christ, to lead the congregation in meaningful worship, to teach the Bible so it relates to people's lives in a way that makes a difference, and to carry out ministries that improve the lives of individuals, families, the Church fellowship and the community.

When I left Alaska in 1973, many Indian and Eskimo people were carrying out effective ministries in their churches and villages as deacons, priests, layreaders, church school teachers and village council members.

~ The Ven. Walter W. Hannum

boom towns themselves and within the Native culture as it sought to adjust to the invasion of newcomers.

A key to this challenging ministry was the support of Native people to the ministry of persons such as Hudson Stuck, an English-born missionary who became the legendary Archdeacon of the Yukon during the early Rowe years. In turn, Stuck was a strong champion of Native rights all during his untiring ministry here.

The protection of Alaska, and of its indigenous peoples, was a major part of the ministry of the Episcopal Church. Working with the missionaries, the Native community leadership rallied to support the traditional family life of the people. The Church became an active opponent of the use of alcohol and encouraged people to maintain their traditional lives as independent, healthy, and caring communities. Native people helped build schools and hospitals during these years, bringing education and medical care to the Interior. As instructors in their own right, they taught the Episcopal priests, deaconesses, nurses, and teachers how to live and travel in the demanding climate of central Alaska. They were guides and interpreters. They assisted in translating the Gospel into Native languages. In all these ways, Native leaders helped to withstand the negative aspects of the gold rush years and to preserve those unique qualities of Alaska life that have remained a source of pride for future generations.

By the 1940s, when Bishop Bentley became Alaska's second Episcopal Bishop, the Native communities of the state already had a significant history of leadership within the Church. In the Arctic Coast they had expanded the mission of the Church from Point Hope to include active congregations in Kivalina, Kotzebue, and Point Lay. Dedicated Inupiaq men and women worked tirelessly beside American clergy to express the Gospel in the language and values of the people. As volunteers, they kept the Church growing even during the troubled years of World War II.

After the war, Alaska changed dramatically. A new highway connected the Interior of Alaska to the "Outside." Military bases brought in new people and new technology. Aviation had become firmly established as a primary means of transportation. Communications were greatly improved. The realities of the larger world had come to Alaska to stay.

These major shifts in the life of Alaska impacted the Native community in profound, if sometimes subtle ways. The 1950s were an era when colonialism began to recede as post-war nations began to claim their sovereignty. A similar movement began in the Church. Building on the principles of visionaries such as Roland Allen, who was an Anglican missionary to China, the older missionary model of European "leaders" assisted by Native "helpers" began to be replaced throughout the world. In Africa, Asia, and Latin America local communities increasingly began to raise up indigenous leadership to replace what had once been a Church of colonial times. The moment was right for Native people to claim their place as equal partners in the life of the Church.

Blind Moses and Blind Paul, layreaders at Nenana and Tanana during the 1900s (Archives of the Episcopal Church)

Charlie Jensen and Chester Seveck served as layreaders at Kotzebue for many years.

Alaska was fortunate in this time of change to have a Bishop like William Gordon who embraced the new international vision of indigenous leadership. He supported Native people in their determination to gain access to all levels of leadership in the Church, including ordination.

Today we celebrate the names of these first Native pioneers who became priests and deacons of the Church: William Loola, Paul Mather, David Paul, Milton and Clinton Swan, David Salmon, Titus Peter, Donald Oktollik, Patrick Attungana, Raymond and James Hawley, Isaac and Albert Tritt, Philip Peter. These are the men who first extended the range of Native leadership into all Orders of service for the Church. They not only became the active leaders of the churches in their own communities; they also began the critical work of carrying the voice of those communities out into the larger Church. Because of their visibility, the whole Church began to recognize again the importance of the Native presence in the Episcopal Church of Alaska. Along with Native laity, they brought a powerful witness to Alaska as the Territory became a State. Their ministry was born in a time of transition, and it carried the Church through times of change as Alaska rapidly entered

Father Norman Elliott preaches at David Paul's ordination to the diaconate, May 1957, at St. Timothy's Mission, Tanacross. Paul was the first Alaska Native ordained in more than 30 years.

An ordination at Point Hope, 1984: front row, left to right: Fr. Mark Boesser, ordinand Seymour Tuzroyluke, Bishop Harris, and Fr. Donald Oktollik; back row: Frs. Tom Taylor, Andy Fairfield, and Patrick Attungana.

In May 1971 Philip Peter of Fort Yukon was ordained to the priesthood. Shown here outside St. Stephen's Church are Bishop Gordon, Fr. Isaac Tritt, the ordinand, and Fr. Titus Peter. In back row are Frs. Chuck Eddy and Don Hart.

Raymond Hawley leads a discussion at a meeting of the Arctic Coast Deanery at Point Hope, June 1984.

David Salmon – First Athabascan Priest

When Hudson Stuck died at Fort Yukon in 1920, it was said that one of his great regrets was that he did not live to see an Athabascan Indian — the people to whom he devoted much of his life — ordained to the priesthood.

Forty-two years later, on October 6, 1962, the soul of this consecrated pioneer missionary must have looked down with great pride on St. Stephen's Church in his old Yukon Valley home as Bishop Gordon ordained David Salmon, an Athabascan born in 1912 on the upper reaches of the Black River, as a priest in the Church. Six men, representing the scattered Indian tribes of the vast Interior, have been ordained as deacons in the hundred years that the Church has been at work in Alaska, but David Salmon is the first to go forth as a priest to serve his own people and to interpret through Word and Sacrament the living truth of the eternal God.

Father Salmon was born at Salmon Village near the Canadian border in a community founded by his father, who served as its chief and leader. The life of the Salmon family was a transient one, following the game with the seasons. Only a very few weeks of each summer were spent at Fort Yukon, so David and the other children had little opportunity to attend school. Except for two years during his teens when David lived with Dr. and Mrs. Burke at St. Stephen's Mission, he had no formal schooling; his almost spectacular development academically and spiritually has come through the determination of this man to teach himself and his willingness to make use of any opportunity to better prepare himself to serve his fellow men.

When David grew up he and his wife Sarah settled in Chalkyitsik on the Black River, about one hundred miles, by river, from Fort Yukon. They adopted two children, William and Sally, and David supported the family by trapping, hunting and fishing, while at the same time continuing to study and to teach others, using the Native Takudh Bible as a source of nightly teaching sessions in his home. Here in Chalkyitsik he also served for many years as chief.

Fr. David Salmon preaches the Word at the meeting of the Interior Deanery in Tanana, 1986.

The Episcopal clergy at Fort Yukon in the early and mid-fifties (Richard Lambert and Walter Hannum) encouraged David in his desire to give his time and talents in any way possible to serve his own people. He was promised that the Church would stand with him in every way, but the basic initiative and hard work would have to come from him, and that full-time service in the Church would not come easy.

During the winter of 1955 Walter Hannum and David Salmon studied together, and David served as a layreader in the ministry of the Fort Yukon mission. He showed such promise that he was sent for three months' concentrated training at the Parishfield Center at Brighton, Michigan in the fall of 1956.

During 1957 work and training continued with Fr. Hannum. Finally, after many months of study and devoted service to the Church, David was found prepared and worthy to be ordained Deacon. He was ordained to that office at Fort Yukon in May 1958 and assigned to serve the Church at Chalkyitsik.

To qualify for advancement to the priesthood would require a great deal more study as well as passing examinations before the Board of Examining Chaplains; however, when a man is willing to work hard to prepare himself and determined to serve his people, there are no insurmountable barri-

David Salmon and Bishop Gordon following the Oct. 1962 ordination of Fr. Salmon to the priesthood

the first man of his race in Alaska to be ordained a priest of the Church.

On October 6th many people came to Fort Yukon. They came from David's home at Chalkyitsik; almost half the village of Venetie on the Chandalar came to witness the ordination service. Fellow Indian deacons Isaac Tritt and David Paul came from Arctic Village and Tanacross, as well as forty persons in a chartered C-46 aircraft from the family of the Church in Fairbanks and nearby areas. Most appropriately, David Salmon was presented to the Bishop by Fr. Hannum, who by encouragement and direction and prayer and teaching had brought his fellow minister to this momentous day.

We are not proud that it took a hundred years to bring a Native priesthood to Interior Alaska. Whatever the reasons, we look forward, not backward. Surely our Lord will richly use Father David Salmon to speak in English and in Takudh in revealing his great truths to the family of God in the Yukon Valley. We look with certainty to others like him who will follow his example and rise up as priests and servants to lead us of all races along the trail that guides us to the kingdom of God.

– Excerpts from *The Alaskan Churchman* December 1962, Vol. LVII, No.4

ers. For four more years David studied and worked — alone, with Fr. Hannum, with Fr. Murray Trelease, at several sessions of the Yukon Valley Training School, and with the Examining Chaplains. Finally, this year, the examinations were given. Again, David Salmon was found prepared and worthy. A letter was written by six members of the Church in Fort Yukon and by two priests stating that David was worthy to serve God and His Church as a priest. These statements and a letter from the Bishop were presented to the Council of Advice of the Missionary District of Alaska. Permission was given to the Bishop according to the canon law of the Church for David Salmon, Athabascan Indian from Black River, to be

the modern age of the 1960s and '70s.

The demands on Native leadership during these decades should not be underestimated. If ministers in the time of Bishop Rowe faced challenges because of the sudden social pressure of a gold rush, then the ministers of the '60s and '70s faced even greater pressures as Alaska society evolved under statehood and the "oil rush."

Within one generation, Alaska's Native communities were transformed. Once relatively isolated and self-reliant, the Native communities suddenly became front-page news as a result of oil and land settlements. Native corporations came into being. Snow machines replaced dog sleds. Satellite communications linked mass media to even the most remote village. State and federal programs proliferated. Drugs competed with alcohol as a new source of pain and suffering. Cultural values were rocked by the influx of "outside" images, ideas, and inventions. Native languages declined as Native education opportunities increased. Across a huge spectrum of change, the Native people grappled with transitions that seemed to accelerate at a faster and faster pace.

Riding these waves of change were the Native men and women, including the new ordained leadership, who kept the Church on course as a reliable center for the village communities. As in the days of Hudson Stuck, the Episcopal Church stood for traditional values and for the protection of the people against addiction or exploitation. Against increasing odds, Native clergy and laity

✝

Left: Bishop Harris and Fr. Trimble Gilbert discuss plans for a service at Arctic Village, June 1985.

Above: Henry and Dolly Deacon present Archdeacon Andy Fairfield with a gift from the Grayling village corporation for the use of the diocese in training Native ministry.

maintained a proud witness of hope for their people, and many of the later successes in preserving land, culture, and health can be directly traced to their determination and inspiration.

As the Church entered the 1980s the tides of change had brought the Native community to new realities. In 1983, the Rev. Anna Frank was ordained as the first Native American woman priest in the Episcopal Church. The levels of leadership within the Church were now completely open to all Native people. This ordination was symbolic of an even deeper trend in the development of Native mission in Alaska. Behind the scenes, in countless meetings of church committees, commissions, and conventions, Alaska's Native people were exercising their gifts in shaping the new

Episcopal Diocese of Alaska. Native planners had helped to design the diocese even as it became a reality in 1971. Then, through the years of Bishop David Cochran and Bishop George Harris, the foundations of Native lay leadership began to expand and deepen. With an emphasis on local training, more and more Native people entered the ministry as decision-makers, teachers, layreaders, and counselors. This broadening on the base of Native leadership, while not always as celebrated as the more visible ordinations, quietly established a network of strong lay people across Alaska who would be prepared to guide the Church into the 1990s and beyond.

With the coming of Alaska's first Native Bishop, Steven Charleston, the role of Alaska's Native people turned the corner to a

second century of growth and development. Today, Native men and women serve the Church in every capacity as co-creators of the ministry with other Alaskans from many walks of life. Once again, more Native men and women are stepping forward to become ordained. Meanwhile, lay leaders not only work close to home in Alaska, but represent the Church in national and international forums.

And yet, just as has always been true for the Church in Alaska, we face new times of change and challenge. As the high tide of missionary support for Alaska has long since withdrawn, and as the oil boom of the 1970s and '80s slowly dries up, the Alaska Church faces the aftermath with serious issues of financial, structural, and spiritual need. How can the Church become self-

MILTON SWAN
WRITTEN BY BISHOP GORDON AT THE TIME OF SWAN'S DEATH

The Anglican Communion's first Eskimo priest, the Rev. Milton Swan, died in Kivalina on Feb, 2, 1982. His funeral and burial service were held there that week with the Rev. Donald Oktollik of Point Hope officiating. Survived by his wife and faithful co-worker, Martha, and three children, Fr. Swan served the church as layreader-in-charge, deacon and priest for more than fifty years. I ordained him priest in Kivalina in 1964.

The Milton Swan I remember:
Aug. 1943: Meeting Milton and Martha first at 4:00 a.m. as Shirley and I arrived by small boat from Point Hope where we had been arctic missionaries for less than a month and finding he had ministered faithfully as an unpaid lay reader although he had not seen a priest in three years.
Oct. 1944: Working with Milton (and Daniel Norton and Daniel Lisbourne) against time and an arctic winter for three weeks of ten-hour days erecting the first church building in Kivalina, knowing Milton should have been upriver fishing for his winter food supply.
Nov. 1945: Arriving in Kivalina on my first dog team trip from Point Hope alone with a frozen parka, pants and boots as a result of falling through the ice of the Arctic Ocean rounding Cape Thompson, and having Milton accompany me on the trip back (a four-day round trip journey for him). He said he had business at Point Hope, but about ten years later I realized that he was too caring and sensitive of another's feelings to tell a young missionary that he might yet be too inexperienced to travel alone by dog

Fr. Milton Swan of Kivalina, first Eskimo priest of the Episcopal Church

team under difficult conditions.
Numerous times when stormbound with Milton and Martha in their igloo: After his special sourdough hotcakes, playing Bible quizzes which I most often lost.
Any service in Kivalina: Great singing that made Kivalina famous throughout the Arctic, initiated by Tony Joule but carried on and deepened by Milton (a self-taught organist and accordionist) and his brother, Clinton.
Any confirmation class he presented: Clear responses and obvious commitment from a class well prepared.
May 1967: A flight in the "Blue Box" 3500 miles to Michigan where I showed him his first "ice igloo" (traditional Eskimo homes are made of sod blocks) and where he is still remembered as a marvelous, committed and deceptively simple witness to Mission.
Any Diocesan Convention in Alaska: The unanimous demand that Milton be celebrant at a Eucharist where he read the service better than any of us and you knew he was talking to God.
June 1981: Dropping out of the sky on our way back from Point Hope and surprising Milton and Martha as they sat in the sun outside their home. I'll never forget the look of surprise and delight on his face.

Milton Swan, after seventy-eight years here, has gone to be with the Lord, but it won't be any different for him because they've been together all the time.

Fr. Milton Swan outside his home at Kivalina.

The Fire Cannot Go Out

I am not worthy to tie the strings on the moccasins of these people, but I would like to recognize and honor them and the work they have done in blazing the trail for us. I think of William Loola, a deacon in Fort Yukon, and Arthur Wright of Nenana, and Paul Mather of Southeast Alaska. There were many more throughout the years, many Native people who helped the bishops and early missionaries in their work. Our people guided them and taught them survival skills which enabled them to carry out their ministry in the harsh environment of the Alaska wilderness. Without this help, missionary work would have been hazardous and slow. Translators were a critical part of ministry: without them we would not have services in the languages of the people.

There are a few people, like Moses Cruikshank, still alive today who traveled with the bishops and archdeacons and who can recall those days of the early Church in Alaska. The trail blazers gave us the courage to step forward and minister today. In the fifties it was Albert Tritt and David Salmon, David Paul, Titus Peter, Isaac Tritt, Philip Peter, and the Arctic Coast people who received training at the Yukon Valley Training Center. Having our own people taking part in the ministry of the Church brought encouragement, self-determination, and the knowledge that our people could preach and teach themselves.

Lay men and women have been active in ministry for a long time, but development of leadership roles is a more recent step. Traditionally, Native leaders were picked by the communities and taught community ways and values as their personal strengths were recognized; a lot of our young men were chosen in this manner.

Anna Frank leads devotions during the meeting of the Interior Deanery at Tanana, 1986.

Things have changed in this day and age. We have integrated various cultures, traditions and values, making it harder to recognize leadership. Women have moved into leadership roles, in both community and Church, a difficult step for traditionalists to accept. Being ordained to the diaconate sets apart people as acknowledged leaders, even though the responsibilities may remain the same as before: cleaning the church, building the fire, washing the linens and sacred vessels, visiting people, providing pastoral care. With leadership came responsibility as people looked to us as examples and spiritual leaders of the churches.

We need more committed people to take on the leadership roles. What our grandfathers started we cannot surrender. We cannot let the fire go out — the fire of the Holy Spirit.

– The Rev. Canon Anna Frank

✝

sufficient? How can it respond to the secularization of Native life? How can new forms of leadership emerge that will inspire and strengthen the Native community? How can better partnerships between Native people and their brothers and sisters from other racial communities be created to serve the common good?

Answers to all of these questions are, of course, the ongoing work of the Church, and of its Native leaders. And while the future always seems challenging to those living in the present, the lessons of the past give us more than sufficient reason for hope. Since that first tentative encounter in 1861, the Christian Church, as it finds expression in the Episcopal tradition, has relied on the Native community of Alaska. Not once, in all those years, has it found its trust to be misplaced. Generation after generation, Native men and women have arisen to meet the challenge and change of their time. They have led the Church through a transition from dog sled to the space shuttle. They have defended the tradition of their people while advancing the frontiers of the Christian faith. They have served almost unnoticed in the quiet, life-giving ministries of the Church just as they have stood in the most public arenas of international leadership. The history of the growth of Native missions in Alaska is the history of a people's ingenuity, perseverance, and ability. It tells us that the future of the Episcopal Church in Alaska will be in good hands because those hands are held steady by the faith and wisdom of Alaska's Native people.

– The Rev. Canon Anna Frank
The Rt. Rev. Steven Charleston

✝

The youth choir, crucifer, and acolytes prepare for the service at St. Timothy's, Tanacross, Ascension Day, May 30, 1957, when David Paul was ordained to the diaconate. (Photo by Dick Kezlan)

COLOR PLATES

1   Illuminating the Yukon landscape like a benediction, the winter day's last light is matched by the glow from within the little log church. We hurry through the snow to take our places before the liturgy begins. The shadowed forms of other worshippers can be seen through the frosty panes. This is a blessed place, this little church, storing the joys and sorrows, the tragedies and victories of our village. It will be warm inside, surrounding us with the truth and beauty of our faith, the Good News of Jesus Christ, and the love of family and friends. Listen, hear them singing!

Christ Church, Anvik, 1894
First church built in Alaska
Watercolor by Byron Birdsall, 1995

2   The beadwork of Alaska's Native women is widely recognized and admired, and many churches of the Interior are beautified by this artistry. Here are the moosehide frontal and superfrontal created by beadwork artists of St. Stephen's, Fort Yukon to commemorate the end of World War I. The inset photo highlights details of a familiar Christian symbol, and the moosehide bears the watermark of the 1948 flood on the Yukon. (Photos by Phyllis Fast)

3   In his Log in late June 1965 Bishop Gordon wrote: "Loaded with 800 pounds of supplies I flew 650 miles to Point Hope (delivering) the essentials for the Diamond Jubilee celebration...an amplifying system, 30 dozen eggs, 90 pounds of margarine, yeast for bread, 100 pounds of ham, ingredients for a gigantic potato salad, 1000 paper plates, cups and eating utensils...in expectation of feeding 500 people." More than 500 ecclesiastic and civic officials, diocesan clergy, and lay people crowded Point Hope in July for the 75th anniversary of the mission. The work begun by the sacrificial ministry of Dr. John Driggs 75 years earlier laid a strong foundation for the modern life of this far north community.

   Pictured here, left to right, are the Rev. John Phillips of Nenana; Bishop Gordon; the Rev. Milton Swan of Kivalina; Governor William A. Egan; the Rt. Rev. John Hines, Presiding Bishop of the Episcopal Church; and the Revs. Roland Cox of Princeton, New Jersey, formerly of Point Hope, Bob Jones of Kotzebue, and Keith Lawton of Point Hope. Services, feasting, Naligatuk (blanket toss), visiting, prayer, praise, and worship marked the two-day celebration. Dr. Driggs would have been proud!

4   St. Matthew's Church, Fairbanks, was dear to Archdeacon Hudson Stuck, and it was from its doors that he and a group of fellow adventurers set off to attempt a feat unrelated to his many achievements for the Church. With Bishop Rowe's permission for a leave of absence to pursue his dream, the Archdeacon put together a team which, on June 7, 1913, conquered the south peak of Denali (Mt. McKinley), North America's highest mountain. Dr. and Mrs. William R. Wood of Fairbanks presented this stained glass window to St. Matthew's parish in 1994, in honor of the Archdeacon's role in the founding of St. Matthew's and his work for the Church throughout the North. Designed by Seattle artist Lisa Valore, it was created in glass by Debbie Matthews of Expressions in Glass. Here the Archdeacon steps into history as companions Harry Karstens, Robert Tatum, and Walter Harper follow. Harper, a Native Athabascan, was the first person to stand on Denali's 20,320-foot summit. (Photo courtesy of St. Matthew's Church)

5   The well-tended grounds of St. Mary's Church are screened by trees and terrain from the turmoil of one of the busiest intersections in Anchorage. The original building, now housing the chapel and the parish offices, is shown here. Recent construction, at right, has expanded the church's ability to fulfill its versatile ministry to parish and community. The bell in the tower, left of the church, was a gift from Trinity Church in Buffalo, New York, where a new church was being built and their bell was no longer needed. Thanks to a remark made by Roger Waldron to a priest visiting St. Mary's, the bell was obtained; "All we had to do was pay the postage," the late Marcie (Waldron) Trent told us. "Postage due, $44.00." She added, "Roger never saw the bell in place, but after his death in 1962 his Dad brought a crew out and erected the bell tower. The dedication of it, in Roger's memory, was held in May 1963, with the congregation walking to the tower through six inches of freshly fallen snow!" (Photo by Jane Slisco)

6   The cope and mitre presented to Bishop Charleston at his consecration in March 1991 were gifts from the Native American community of the Episcopal Church. Purchased through contributions of Native people throughout the United States, the episcopal vestments were designed and created by artist Phyllis Lehmberg of Minneapolis.

The design of the cope is a celebration of the beauty of Alaska. The border at the bottom edge represents the oceans that touch Alaska; the rivers of Alaska move along the back of the cope. The forests, tundra, and mountains are symbolized; the Northern Lights are visualized as bursts of light from heaven. A raven embodies a tribute to Alaska wildlife, relating to the traditional creation stories of Alaska's Native community. The personal vision of the Bishop himself, as the first Indian bishop of Alaska, is contained in the four colors on the mitre and the sun and moon symbols rising above the snow.

The crozier, or shepherd's staff, is a sign of the Bishop's pastoral care for all the people of the Diocese. This was a gift from the Bishop's former parish in Minneapolis and was made by an artist in his home state of Oklahoma. It is fashioned of oak and adorned with otter fur and beadwork. One design on the crozier represents the Bishop's son, Nick. The feathers, gifts from his parents, are reminders of the humility befitting a servant of the Lord. The small circle from which the feathers hang is a symbol for the traditional "four sacred directions" of God's creation, indicating that God is Lord of all life. (Photo by Evolyn Melville)

7   It is fitting that these whalebone palisades enfold the earthly remains of the man who considered his years at Point Hope "the happiest of my life." Bill and Shirley Gordon spent five years in service, ministry, and spiritual abundance at Point Hope before his election as Alaska's third bishop (and at the time the youngest man ever to be elected a bishop). Scenes are shown here from the June 1994 interment of Bishop Gordon's ashes, as family, clergy, and numerous friends gathered in St. Thomas' Church and at the dramatic gravesite to pay final tribute to this revered leader. (Photos by Lee Davis)

8   The gold nugget cross presented to Bishop Rowe on July 26, 1903 by the first confirmation class of St. Mary's Mission, Nome, became the prototype for the cross of the Missionary District and later the Diocese of Alaska. The silver cross presented to all persons confirmed in Alaska (and coveted by many who are ineligible to receive one!) duplicates the basic design of the original Bishop Rowe cross. Elders who become members of the honorary Society of St. Simeon and St. Anna are recipients of a gold cross of similar design. (Photo by Chris Arend Photography)

BYRON BIRDSALL · 1995

Many women have done excellently,
but you surpass them all.
- Proverbs 31:29

IX
WOMEN IN THE CHURCH

For more than a hundred years women of the Church have been keeping the faith throughout Alaska. Evidence of their work is everywhere: churches begun and maintained, children taught, funds raised, altars cared for, the Gospel translated, lives influenced, communities strengthened, the Eucharist celebrated, the Good News preached, the hungry fed, counsel offered, wisdom shared. Accomplished quietly and behind the scenes, the work of women has nurtured and sustained the Episcopal Church in Alaska.

From the very beginning, women took an active part in missionary efforts. Nurses and teachers, some of them deaconesses, came to work in Alaska's missions. As early as the 1860s (while Alaska was still a Russian territory), Anglican missionaries from Canada brought the Christian faith to the people of the Yukon River valley. Archdeacon Robert McDonald translated the Bible, prayer book, and hymnal into Takudh, relying heavily on the language skills of Native women, traders' wives, Takudh speakers Eliza Boucher and Maria Flett. Later, McDonald's wife, Julia Kutug, helped with further translations which are still in use today.

Another source of early and continuing

Archdeacon Stuck considered Deaconess Clara M. Carter of Allakaket the "model of a perfect missionary woman" and the "guardian angel of women church workers."

support came from women who would never see Alaska. The Women's Auxiliary of the Board of Missions in New York City provided much-needed money and materials, as well as encouragement. The first Episcopal church in Alaska, Christ Church in Anvik, was built with funds from half of the first United Offering.

In the late 1800s, Episcopal women became increasingly involved in missionary and social service work. Training facilities opened in the 1890s in New York City and Philadelphia to prepare women for work in domestic and foreign missions, and many women workers who came to Alaska in the early years received training at these institutions.

The first Episcopal women missionaries to reach Alaska arrived in Anvik in 1894: a health worker, Dr. Mary V. Glenton; a teacher, Bertha Sabine (later a deaconess); and a clergy wife, Mrs. John Chapman. Interestingly, these are the three main roles filled by the more than two hundred women who came to Alaska over the next sixty years. Even without counting unpaid clergy wives, there were more women workers than men during Bishop Peter Trimble Rowe's 47 years as the first bishop of Alaska.

Women were usually stationed at the most remote mission sites in the territory's interior. In 1911, the Reverend John Chapman, longtime priest at Anvik, wrote in The *Alaskan Churchman*, "Their (the women's) success has been such as...to make it appear that the Church is in some danger of taking the position that the care of missions in the wilderness properly belongs to women, and not to men." In 1907 Deaconess Clara Carter and Clara Heintz went to Allakaket, as a nurse/teacher team,

Daily Vacation Bible School (DVBS) teachers with children at Tetlin in the 1950s

followed by a similar pair, Amelia Hill and Bessie Kay. It was not until 1953, when the Misses Hill and Kay left after 30 and 21 years respectively, that St. John's-in-the-Wilderness was "manned" for the first time by a resident priest.

Bishop John Bentley said he had once wondered why Bishop Rowe had not just stationed a man at this remote site who was able to deal with a pioneer situation, but Bishop Rowe had explained that he knew "the Indians and Eskimos would respect those two women...and protect them ...when, had a man been put there, the attitude might have been quite different." Forty years after establishment of the Allakaket mission, Miss Hill wrote in an *Alaskan Churchman* article: "We (she and Miss Kay) always know absolutely that if we have any emergency, any great need, we can depend on our neighbors to help and advise us. We are not alone in any sense of the word."

Women doctors and nurses ministered to people's medical needs at the mission stations and hospitals. In the early years they dealt with epidemics of smallpox, diphtheria, measles, and influenza. Tuberculosis was an ongoing scourge. A 1948 *Alaskan Churchman* article described the importance of the nurse in the village: "often the only medical person in a wide territory," and her advice and attention were critical.

Teachers started schools for both children and adults. They ran day-schools in villages and towns and operated boarding schools in Anvik and Nenana. Women ran the missions when a priest was not available (sometimes for years), doing everything in the church except those functions reserved to priests. In addition to their work as

Deaconess Bertha Sabine at Circle City, circa 1911; tall man near right of photo is Joseph Minister, lay assistant.

Deaconess Sabine and the Circle City branch of the Woman's Auxiliary, circa 1911. The deaconess also served at Anvik, arriving there in 1894.

In their book, *A Woman Set Apart*, William and Ellen Hartley tell the story of Harriet Bedell, a deaconess who in 1916 traveled from her home in western New York State to serve for 15 years in Alaska, first in Nenana, then in Stevens Village, and finally in Tanana (refer to Suggested Readings). Chapter 15 is of particular interest, not only describing a dramatic event in Deaconess Bedell's life in the Interior but also shedding light on the personality and character of other leaders of those days.

The Deaconess was visiting Fort Yukon in the spring of 1918, staying with Dr. and Mrs. Grafton Burke. The erudite and always controversial Archdeacon Stuck was present, as well as an internationally known explorer who was a patient in recovery at the Fort Yukon hospital. Vilhjalmur Stefansson had just completed a five-year experiment in living under primitive arctic conditions when he was struck down by typhoid, pneumonia and pleurisy. "Dr. Burke had raced north to meet (Stefansson) at Old Rampart on the Porcupine River.... Archdeacon Stuck and Walter Harper, his trail assistant, had also launched a rescue dash from the Arctic coast (they had been on an extended tour of the northern missions), finally reaching the sick man and Dr. Burke between Old Rampart and Fort Yukon."

The story notes that Deaconess Bedell found dining with these men "a memorable if somewhat disturbing experience." Stefansson, an outspoken atheist, met his match in the equally uncompromising Christian devotion of Stuck. Despite heated discussion which "thundered on" until late evening, as Mrs. Burke's "excellent meal

grew cold," the men maintained mutual respect even as they exploded at each other's convictions. (In his book, *Discovery*, Stefansson later expressed appreciation for the care and companionship he received at Fort Yukon.)

This was a strong scene in the opening pages of this chapter, and the pace was sustained throughout the next twenty pages by the story of Deaconess Bedell's 160-mile winter trip from Stevens Village to Fort Yukon to transport a seriously ill young girl to the hospital. The girl, stricken around the Christmas season, grew continually weaker despite the tireless care of the Deaconess. Her symptoms suggested poliomyelitis, but there was no way to treat it nor to validate the diagnosis. Despite the terrible weather conditions — "the winter had been unusually severe with deep snow and intense cold" — it was obvious the child must be taken to a hospital. The nearest one was at Fort Yukon, 160 miles upriver "over rough terrain. For a few miles out of Stevens Village, a trail of sorts connected with a deserted lumber camp. Thereafter, no trail existed."

The Deaconess asked her trusted assistant, young Henry Moses, if the trip was possible. He replied it was "possible... but it is dangerous." He added bluntly, "I didn't say I would go...but I will." Another man, Benjamin John, noting that the journey was a crazy idea, also volunteered to go. The party started out in early March with 11 dogs, a sled loaded with provisions and trail equipment, and the sick child warmly layered in a second sled. The men had to break trail on snowshoes ahead of the dogs most of the way; the Deaconess also took

her turn at this exhausting duty. The description of the harrowing trip details the extreme trail and weather conditions, the numbing fatigue, and the highlights of meeting the kindly, colorful Yanert brothers at their cabin at Purgatory (the Deaconess was the first white woman the brothers had ever seen on the trail in all their years in the wilderness), a hospitable Japanese trader at Beaver, and an unexpected proposal of marriage from an elderly trapper who offered the group shelter one bitter night.

The welcome sight of smoke rising from the cabins of Fort Yukon met the party's eyes after twelve days on the trail. Knocking on the door of the Burkes' new house near the hospital, Harriet Bedell found herself looking into the face of Archdeacon Hudson Stuck. "That usually imperturbable man literally gasped in amazement" as the accomplishment of this small group made its impact. With the sick child safe in the hospital (the Deaconess's tentative diagnosis of poliomyelitis confirmed by Dr. Burke), the travelers enjoyed the warmth and hospitality of the Burkes' home. Deaconess Bedell was able to share her concerns about the work at Stevens Village with the Archdeacon who, in ill health himself, was residing with the Burkes at that time.

Annie Cragg Farthing founded St. Mark's boarding school at Nenana in 1907. Despite her tragic death three years later, the school grew and influenced many children from Nenana and other Interior villages in its nearly fifty years of operation.

Gladys Shreiner came to St. Mark's Mission, Nenana as the mission nurse in the late 1940s, married into the Coghill family and remained an active member of the mission and the community until her death in 1980. She is shown here with, left to right, Donny Moses, Teddy Luke, Tommy Justin, John Starr, and Percy Joseph, circa 1949. (Photo courtesy of Marilyn Coghill Duggar)

teachers or nurses, they cared for the church buildings, held services, led choirs, and instructed lay readers and altar guilds. They distributed clothing to those in need and visited the ill and the elderly. Many women dedicated their lives to this work.

Women at remote and often under-staffed stations were often called upon to perform unfamiliar work. They mastered new skills — using snowshoes, handling a dog team, shooting a rifle. They learned to deal with isolation in places where transportation was by dog team in winter and boat in summer and where mail and visitors might arrive only a few times a year. Occasionally they faced privation, as in 1913 at Tanacross, when Margaret Graves

and Celia Wright lived for months on a diet of rabbits as repeated resupply attempts failed. They fought epidemics: Lizzie Woods coped alone with a diphtheria epidemic in the upper Yukon area. They braved fire and flood: Deaconess Kathleen Thompson experienced both within a single year at Nenana in 1948.

The remarkable women serving in Alaska were both gutsy and innovative. Deaconess Harriet Bedell, who ran the mission at Stevens Village alone for ten years, poled a boat to summer fish camps to extend learning and health care through the summer; once mushed 160 miles to the hospital with a sick child (see sidebar).

The women workers assumed positions

of heavy responsibility, facing dangers and handling emergencies, but more significant than their responses to dramatic events were their daily interactions with the people. For decades these teachers, nurses, and deaconesses were a continuing influence in the villages. They lived among people they cared about and whose welfare—spiritual, physical, and intellectual—was the focus of their days and years.

After the closure of St. Mark's boarding school in Nenana in 1955 and the Hudson Stuck Memorial Hospital in Fort Yukon in 1960, women's names virtually disappeared from the rolls of church workers in the missionary district. During the next 20 years, however, women continued to do the work of the Church as clergy wives, missionary nurses in remote villages, and Vacation Bible School teachers. They kept their churches functioning in the absence of a priest, and they trained for leadership roles.

Bishop Gordon often insisted that "Women are the heroes." He meant not only the women who staffed the missions, but also clergy wives, who dealt with the isolation and hard work of village life while supporting and enabling their husband's ministries. In 1959 he wrote in *The Alaskan Churchman*, "All too often they [wives] receive little or no credit; little of the glamour of the work falls their lot, but quietly and lovingly and effectively they witness to the cause of Christ in their village and town communities and thus preach the most effective sermon of all—the example of the Christian family at its best."

It had been feared in the early years that women workers would be "lost" to the work of the church through "committing matrimony." But, in fact, many of them married clergymen, remained in Alaska, and continued to serve the Church. Perhaps the first such marriage was that of Clara Heintz and Dr. Grafton Burke in 1910. After their wedding in Allakaket they moved to Fort Yukon, where they worked together for many years serving the medical needs of the area and welcoming the villagers to their home.

Clergy wives were an important source of support to their husbands. The Rev. Murray Trelease wrote in *The Alaskan Churchman* in 1963, "My greatest personal blessing is a loving, understanding, and highly mobile wife." Often stationed in remote sites, with their husbands away from home base caring for other villages or

Miss Lizzie Woods, one of the earliest of the missionary women, worked at the Fort Yukon mission circa 1906. Archdeacon Stuck, with whom she had many thorny disagreements, is shown in center of photo.

attending meetings, some clergy wives found their roles difficult, others met the challenges without noticeable stress. Like other women in their communities, they were busy gathering wood, hauling water, baking bread, and caring for their children. Some taught Sunday school or started Girls Friendly Societies; others were nurses who ministered to the health needs of their communities. Their homes were public—open for recreation for children and for drop-in visitors of all ages.

In September 1964 Bishop Gordon flew 24 women to Anchorage for the first Clergy Wives conference. One wife recalled "the moving voices of several of the wives testifying to the depth of the faith which sustains them in the roles to which they've been

called, their stories of the life and work in the villages, their great moments with the saints who cross their daily paths."

Many young women came to Alaska as volunteers with the Vacation Bible School (VBS) program. After training sessions in Fort Yukon (for which Mrs. Louise Hannum was largely responsible), they were dispersed in pairs to a succession of villages. Some volunteers continued to work for the Church in Alaska following their VBS experience; a number married clergy. Joyce (McDonald) Sarles of Juneau and Deacon Teresa Thomas of Fort Yukon originally came to Alaska as VBS volunteers. Joyce Sarles says, "We were richly blessed by our time spent with the people in the villages. We received much more than we gave."

Above left: Deaconess Marilyn Snodgrass at Venetie, 1967

Above center: Clergy wife Sally Fairfield dishes up soup in the kitchen of the mission house, Fort Yukon, 1974.

Above right: Deaconess Kathleen Thompson devoted many years to the children of St. Mark's Mission, Nenana.

Left: Deaconess Thompson with "her girls" at the Alaska Railroad depot in Nenana, circa 1941

Improved communication and travel opportunities made it possible for the Episcopal Church Women of Alaska to provide forums for Churchwomen from widely scattered towns and villages. The Episcopal Church Women (ECW) met annually in two convocations: the Denali Convocation for Cordova northward, and the Southeast Convocation for Juneau southward; both met together every other year. According to Mrs. Billie Williams, the ECW expanded women's horizons beyond their own churches to others in Alaska and states "outside," and around the world. Convocations featured nationally known speakers and focused on communication. Partnerships were established between parishes in Alaska; for example, between St. Barnabas, Minto, and St. Mary's, Anchorage. The Mutual Responsibility and Interdependence program linked Alaska with the dioceses of Michigan and Zambia in Africa.

Monetary contributions of Churchwomen from around the country provided vital tools for the ministry in Alaska, notably the airplanes that Bishop Gordon used to visit far-flung village congregations and to transport church personnel. The United Thank Offering provided two of these planes——the "Blue Box" and "Blue Box II", and the women of Western New York provided a third, the "Episcopalian."

In the 1970s the Episcopal Church's General Convention provided for new roles for the Church's women. For the first time, women could be ordained as deacons and priests. On February 23, 1972, in Shageluk, Jean Aubrey Dementi became the first Alaskan woman to be ordained as a deacon

Above: Clergy wives at All Saints, Anchorage in 1964 for the first Clergy Wives' Conference. Left to right, first row: Ann Files, Margaret Hall, Martha Swan, Charlotte Cleveland, Stella Elliott, Joan Wilcox, Dorothy Mendelsohn, and Barbee Hodgkins; Second row: Margy Zabriskie, Sharon Carrington, Carol Walker, Phyllis McGinnis, Mariette Trelease, Carol Phillips, Judy Jones, Bishop Gordon, Evelyn Bullock, Mildred Boesser, Marilyn Caum, Polly Simmonds, Clover Jean Ward of the Diocesan office, Sarah Salmon, Betty Hart, Shirley Treadwell, and Naomi Tritt.

Left: DVBS team at Allakaket, 1967. In center of back row is Lynne Davenport, later the editor of Alaskan Epiphany. The Jim Bills family is at center and right in front row.

Above: Women of the Altar Guild of Good Shepherd Mission, Huslia, discuss their activities around the kitchen table at the vicarage, 1963. Left to right: Shirley Attla, Lorna Vent, Alda Henry, Emily Sam, and Connie Keller, with two-year-old Christina Keller in the foreground. (Photo courtesy of Connie Keller)

Right: Diane Tickell, accepted as a priest in good standing in Alaska at the same service at which Jean Dementi was ordained, later served as pastor at St. George's, Cordova for twelve years before retiring to Juneau.

after she had served the Church in rural Alaska for more than twenty years. At the time of her ordination she was interviewed for the June 1972, *The Alaskan Churchman.* When asked if she thought "it was about time" women could attain this rank in the church, Mrs. Dementi shook her head and said gently, "No, I think, rather, the time has come." Five years later, in January 1977, the Reverend Jean Dementi was ordained by Bishop Cochran as Alaska's first woman priest and continued serving the Alaska Church until her death in 1988. (See story on next page)

The Rev. Diane Tickell's route to the priesthood was quite different. She had been a social worker in Juneau for a number of years, then attended the Episcopal Theological School (now the Episcopal Divinity School) in Cambridge, Massachusetts. Graduating in 1973, she was ordained to the diaconate the same year. In September 1975, she was one of four women ordained to the priesthood in an irregular service in Washington, D.C.; these ordinations came just over one year after eleven women were ordained in Philadelphia. Both of these groups were ordained by retired bishops before ordination of women was permitted by the Church. At the 1976 General Convention it was voted to change the canons to allow ordination of women to the priesthood.

On October 8, 1983, in Minto, Anna Frank became the first Athabascan woman to be ordained to the priesthood. In addition to her secular job as a mental health counselor, she has continued to work as a priest, traveling extensively to serve at many altars and facilitating workshops and semi-

Continued on page 108

ONE GOOD WOMAN

Although no reliable measure exists of the impact one person can have on the lives of others, there is no doubt that Jean Dementi was a strong influence on the faith and character of many who were fortunate enough to know her.

This was a special kind of woman. Missionary nurse, hospital administrator, deacon, first woman ordained priest in Alaska, strong feminist, dedicated wife and mother, straightforward preacher, caring pastor, devout Episcopalian, Christian saint.

From her early Alaska days as a nurse caring for the children of St. Mark's Mission in Nenana, to the well-deserved honors of her final years, Jean's practical goodness and pure gold sense of humor traveled with her like an aura throughout her numerous and varied assignments.

When she was in charge of Hudson Stuck Memorial Hospital at Fort Yukon: "I was chief dietician, doctor, head of nursing staff, and ordered supplies. We ran out of flour in January of that year but still had 16 cases of peanut butter." Which may have been a sign of things to come, for the story is told of how, while about to celebrate Communion many years later, she glanced down and noticed there was no bread on the paten. Leaning down to the young acolyte beside her, she asked him to run home and bring back some bread, which he did, returning promptly with — peanut butter sandwiches.

With no doctor at Fort Yukon, Jean became an expert at minor surgery, delivering babies, dental work and diagnosis, noting dryly, "nearly everything we did was illegal, but it worked."

Next stop, Shageluk, as nurse-evangelist, to be translated: "Jean, you do everything."

In a talk presented during the farewell banquet for the Gordons in 1974 Jean said, "When the Bishop dropped me off at my bush assignment and I looked over the facilities, I finally knew what the Litany means when it talks about 'privy conspiracy'!" And how her eyes twinkled when she claimed her favorite hymn to be: "Drop kick for Jesus through the goal post of life."

She took care of all medical needs of Shageluk, preached the Gospel, taught, and made many friends. Here she met and married her husband Jim. The idea of an ordained ministry had so far never occurred to her, but Bishop Gordon suggested ordination when the Church voted in 1970 to allow women to become deacons. She wasted no time in pursuing this step and, after five years as a deacon, serving at Christ Church, Anvik, she became the first woman ordained as a priest in Alaska, in January 1977. For several years, until cancer claimed her strength and forced her retirement and eventual death in 1988, she served

St. Jude's Church at North Pole, edited diocesan publications, and did chaplaincy work in hospitals and jails in the Fairbanks area.

Jean's sermons were always Christ-centered, personal and practical, her insights and humor all-encompassing. Labeled "liberal" because of her empathy with and acceptance of others and her demands for equality, Jean countered: "'Liberal' is a political word. 'Inclusive' is scriptural. Jesus was fully inclusive." She was born a liberated woman but had to devote a lot of time to helping the rest of male-dominated society catch up with her thinking. She was not afraid of what others would say, for her conscience and convictions were forever clear and always strongly defined.

Preaching just prior to her retirement, Jean talked about the biblical woman who anointed Jesus with precious ointment shortly before His death. "She broke open

One of Jean's friends said, "She poured out her life in service and she finished it rejoicing."

Jim and Jean Dementi

an alabaster jar full of an expensive perfume and poured the contents over His head. I do not believe that this was the 'done thing' in Jesus' day any more than it would be today. What if one of you women were to try to show your love for your church and your Lord by drenching your bishop with Chanel #5? You would be seen only as a crazy lady, an embarrassment....But Jesus saw what was in her heart....Jesus not only validated what she did, He saw it as a prophetic action. Jesus knew love when He saw it."

Jean's exemplary life and work earned her an honorary degree of Doctor of Humanities from the University of Alaska in 1983. One year earlier she had a brief audience with Pope John Paul when he visited Fairbanks. She slipped him a small piece of paper with the message: "Your Holiness, we women priests bring a new dimension of wholeness to our Lord's ministry." His Holiness looked understandably startled at facing a woman who wore a cassock and clerical collar, and her message obviously had no influence on his subsequent encyclicals!

Reserving the right to criticize whatever she considered unjust, even when it occurred within her own beloved church, Jean always tempered criticism with fairness, constructive thinking, and her loving view of mankind and his relation with his maker. She outlined marks of excellence for the church and believed the Episcopal Church, as a "gifted" church, was truly headed toward this excellence. In 1985 she wrote: "I think the next 12 years of the Church are going to be the most exciting of any so far, as the church now is more interested in doing God's will than in worrying about the opinion of others....And we are set to do something about the terrible human needs of the world because it is God's will, not worrying about who is worthy, or how it is going to happen. No outcasts...all children of God. Not perfect... but going in the right direction."

Once when someone told her they wished they possessed as much faith as she did, Jean said, "Faith is a gift, a spiritual gift. It isn't something we crank out by ourselves—it's given to us."

"The mercy of God is such that for the sake of one good man the human race is granted a second chance," Jean once said in a sermon related to Noah's survival of the Flood. "God deems mankind worthy of extinction, but he makes a new beginning possible by means of one good man....And," she went on, "the ultimate saving of the human race is done by the one perfect human who totally reflects the image of His heavenly father in all that He does."

This was one good woman.

Jean considered her ministry "a two-way street," saying, "I am always being made whole by the very people I am called upon to serve."

107

Continued from page 105

nars. Currently she is Canon to the Ordinary assigned to develop Native ministries in Alaska.

Other Alaska women have been ordained as deacons or priests and are serving in a variety of capacities in urban and rural churches, some of them also holding secular positions in their communities. Alaska churches are led by women priests: St. David's, Wasilla—the Rev. Dyana Orrin; St. Michael and All Angels, Haines—the Rev. Jan Hotze; and St. Augustine's, Homer—the Rev. Paula Sampson.

The Reverend Canon Anna Frank emphasizes that, in recognizing women for their contributions to the Church in Alaska, credit should be given not only to ordained women, but also to laywomen in the villages. She says, "They are the ones who have kept the doors open."

Bishop Steven Charleston said recently, "Contemporary women are active in all aspects of our Church and their service should be celebrated." Episcopal women throughout Alaska are involved in many ministries, and this has been true traditionally, as well. According to Anna Frank, over the years the women have played an important role in the Church, strengthening church life through the work of altar guilds, Sunday School teaching, and the whole social fabric of their churches and communities. If the community had a priest, he would say what was needed, and the women would carry it out. When Anna was growing up in Minto, women taught Sunday school; if they had their own families, they brought their babies along. They hauled water and cleaned the church and built the fires. They provided encouragement and support to the young people.

Symbolic of the Episcopal Church in Alaska are the beautiful, intricately beaded altar cloths made by Athabascan women earlier in this century. This art continues today. In Venetie, an elder noticed that the altar cloths were getting old and needed to be replaced. Elizabeth Cadzow took her words to heart, organized a community-wide design project, and started raising funds to purchase beads and skins. The submitted designs were incorporated into an elaborate master design, and the entire community was invited to work on the cloth. The completed altar cloth was dedicated in a special service in May 1994. Just as Native women helped Archdeacon McDonald with his translations in the late 1800s, women have been assisting Wycliffe Bible staff in recent years, translating the Gospel into the languages of their communities. Among them are Judy Erick of Venetie, who has done major work in translating the Gospel of Luke into Gwich'in; Addie Shewfelt of Fort Yukon, who was involved in translating several New Testament books into Gwich'in; and Mary Dick of Tanana, who has helped translate the Gospel of Mark into Koyukon. Mary Dick emphasizes the collaborative nature of the project, recalling that she and Virginia Newby, also of Tanana, and Hilda Stevens of Stevens Village worked closely together to determine the most accurate wording for the Bible passages.

Women throughout Alaska have helped establish churches in their communities. They have campaigned for churches to be built and priests to be assigned to them,

The Rev. Anna Frank offers the chalice to her husband Richard during Holy Communion following her ordination. (Photo by Wilson Valentine)

Left: The Rev. Dyana Orrin (right) reminscences with Elna Barrington at a meeting in Anchorage. *Right: Lillian Jensen worked in the diocesan office for many years as secretary to Bishop Gordon and resident manager of Bishop Rowe House. This efficient, personable woman typifies the many women who have served the Diocese in supporting roles throughout the years.*

raised funds for church construction, and even helped in the building process. When the St. Elizabeth's Ladies Guild of Ketchikan petitioned Bishop Rowe for a meeting hall, he suggested a church instead, and St. Elizabeth's Church was built in 1927 with Tsimshian priest Paul Mather as its spiritual leader. Rae Sowle recalls that her mother, Louise Bradley, talked about pounding nails along with the men to build St. Philip's in Wrangell, as well as cooking for the building crews. Women care for the churches, cleaning, polishing, washing the linens, arranging flowers, and assuring that the church is ready for services. Clara Joseph of Beaver lights the fire to warm the church for services on cold winter mornings.

Women raise funds to buy the necessities to keep their churches functioning: in Point Hope, oil to heat the church; in Kivalina, expenses for travel to diocesan or deanery events; in Ketchikan, a new organ to replace one damaged by rain. Fund-raisers are organized not only to meet current needs but also to support projects that will carry the Church forward: in the words of Elsie Pitka of Beaver, "for the future of our children." Women—-priests, deacons, and trained layreaders—-hold regular services in their churches. They train and guide acolytes and are actively involved in Christian Education. They reach out to those in need. A sewing circle meets in Fairbanks to make winter outerwear and footgear for people whose belongings were lost to floodwaters in Allakaket, Alatna and Hughes. Women in Anchorage visit Episcopalians from rural villages who are hospitalized in the city, far from family and friends.

Many women have become members of the Society of St. Simeon and St. Anna, an elders' "council of advice" for the Bishop, for which they must be nominated by their churches. Bishop Charleston says it is a strength of women in Alaska that there are so many to lift up as role models.

Women keep parish offices and the diocesan office running smoothly. In the March 1963 issue of *The Alaskan Churchman*, Margaret Merrell wrote about busy days in Bishop Gordon's office when she and Clover Jean Ward handled a dizzying variety of tasks. She added, "We pray for ourselves also that we may, day in and day out, remember that typewriters and accounting books and telephones and magazines are instruments through which God may choose to speak and with which we may serve Him."

Our women carry their faith into their family lives and into their work lives—as wives and parents at home, as volunteers in the community, and as workers in secular jobs. These, too, are forms of ministry. The voices of today's Episcopal women bring important messages on the Alaska Church's 100th anniversary. Winona Hawley of Kivalina emphasizes the importance of praying for one another: "Prayer has no distance." Ginny Doctor, missionary in Tanana, says, "People need to realize the extent to which the work they do is ministry." Maudy Sommer of Huslia speaks about the elders as a strong part of the church: "They keep us going. We remember how they used to encourage us." Margo Simple of Venetie says, "We need to hear God's call over the noise in our lives."

Bessie Titus, current president of the Standing Committee of the Diocese, likens the Church to a beadwork altar covering in which many individual designs are joined together to form a beautiful overall pattern—a work of art that has the power to inspire and to bring people to God. In the beadwork pattern, each part is essential to the whole; in the Church, the ministry of each man, woman, and child is vital.

Through their many ministries, women have woven their gifts into the fabric of the Episcopal Church in Alaska, building and sustaining it in the past century and nurturing and strengthening it for the next.

~ Janine D. Dorsey

Above: The Rev. Paula Sampson is applauded by Bishop Charleston, the choir, servers and congregation following her ordination to the priesthood, April 1995, at Holy Trinity Church, Juneau.

Right: In April 1995 the Bishop accepted an award from Soroptimists International of Anchorage in recognition of the Diocese's role in advancing the status of women. The awards banquet, at which the Rev. Canon Anna Frank spoke, was attended by many Episcopalians from the southcentral area. (Photo by Winnie Nowak)

...and a book of remembrance was written before him of those who revered the Lord and thought on his name.

- Malachi 3:16

X

STORIES FROM THE MISSIONS

THREE-YEAR HONEYMOON ON THE KOYUKUK

Diary entry from Anita Miller's first day in Allakaket: "Wednesday, July 8, 1953. Evening service — 47 in attendance. We had supper with Miss Hill and Miss Kay. I did the weather report for the first time, and we practiced working the Delco pump machine. We met Mr. Durand running the tractor for the new airfield. Johnson Moses cut Dick's hair. Discussed delivering babies with Miss Hill. Mosquitoes as bad as ever."

Anita and I had arrived to be the nurse and the first priest assigned to Allakaket and Alatna. Alatna was the Eskimo village on the south side of the Arctic Circle. The former was the post office on the north shore (north of the Arctic Circle) where I began as postmaster and the only white person living nearby.

For a combined total of 50 years Miss Hill (a registered nurse) and Miss Kay (schoolteacher for the parochial school) had ministered in Allakaket. Now Bishop Gordon had placed me, a deacon right out of General Seminary, along with my recent bride, in their place. The school was to become a territorial school.

Nursing duties were assigned to Anita. A 24-volt gas-operated radio with transmitter, which occasionally worked, was the only help Anita had for emergencies. In a closet were most of the medicines distributed by the Alaska Department of Health for use in isolated villages at the discretion of the medical authority. These could be administered — generally after a doctor prescribed them over the twice-weekly radio contact with a hospital 90 miles away. Frequently they were administered without authority if radio contact could not be made.

That first month, at Bishop Gordon's suggestion, we left for a 500-mile trip southward by river in an outboard motor boat to take census of our church families. We traveled with Joe Williams and learned a great deal from him. Whenever the boat had used five gallons of gas we dropped off ten on the shoreline for use en route home. We stopped at each fish camp and in the village of Hughes, 90 miles south. Worship services were held. Anita administered any needed first aid and began prenatal care where necessary.

Anita's diary, August 12, 1953: "Near Little Henry's fish camp Dick had a narrow escape: He put his pipe in the same pocket as his .22 bullets. A bullet caught in his pipe and it went off; broke his pipe in half,

missing him." I well remember the shock of the explosion. I threw the pipe into the river, as if it was the cause of the trouble. We gave thanks to God!

Census was taken at each fish camp and in the village of Huslia, 250 miles south. Nearly everyone was an Episcopalian, except for a few Roman Catholics who had moved upriver to Huslia from the Yukon. At Huslia we met Barney Sackett and his parents, Jack and Lucy. Jack was about eighty years old and his son about eight. (Barney had been at the Nenana mission school when I was there as a seminarian in the summer of 1951. He was quoted as asking the mission nurse, Miss Aubrey [later to become the Rev. Jean Dementi], "Miss Aubrey, you ever seen an Indian?" Nurse Aubrey laughed and said, "There are Indians all around us here at the mission, including yourself!" Replied Barney: "No, no, I mean a real one with fedders.") Jack and Lucy had run the outfitting stores in Cut-Off Village before the town was moved to higher ground and called Huslia. Jim Huntington, a great dog musher, ran another trading post.

Very seldom had there been exposure to the Episcopal way of life south of Allakaket on the Koyukuk River, except for annual visits by the bishops. Within a year a cabin

Upper left: Dick and Anita Miller talk with Abraham Oldman and a young resident of Hughes, circa 1956.

Above: Miss Amelia Hill, R.N., "The Angel of Allakaket," 1955 (Photo by Shirley English)

Left: The old church of St. Johns-in-the-Wilderness, Allakaket, "manned" by women for 46 years

was built at Huslia for visits by deacons, priests, summer seminarians, vacation Bible school teachers — and, of course, the Bishop!

Allakaket had no store; it was 100 miles to the nearest one. Ordering food was done by mail and air freight for everyone in the village. The Bishop gave me a thousand dollars to buy stock for a food store, which was named the AK Store, short for Alatna River's Kaket (junction with the Koyukuk River). I trained Simon Ned, Matilda Bergman and others to stock, sell, add, bill, and all the other intricacies of operating the store. It soon became a $2,000 a month business. Within a year the villagers constructed a log building with IOUs to the builders from the assets of the store. The IOUs could not be cashed except on certain months in the future. Before long the store acted as a bank, giving loans and even borrowing with interest payments.

Hunting became a time for fellowship, pastoral relationships, and a source of income in-kind for us and the villagers. Once, on a trip upriver with Simon Ned and Oscar Nictune, we cut several cords of wood, shot a bear which had come into camp at dawn, and even found a moose swimming in front of us as we pulled the wood and bear meat downstream. After helping cut up the moose I arrived home late at night, cold, wet and tired. Anita's only comment as I climbed into our warm bed was, "Get away from me! Your feet are frozen!"

I was to be ordained priest on November 30th in the church of St. John's-in-the-Wilderness, Allakaket. A great deal of work went into preparing choir robes and the hymn, "Come, Holy Ghost." School was to be dismissed for the ceremony until Miss Schlosser, the territorial school teacher, said that public schools were not be let off for religious ceremonies. Bishop Gordon appealed, but she stood firm! On the 29th the Bishop arrived with only one priest, Dick Lambert. Weather was so bad he couldn't stop anywhere to pick up another priest. Ordination was held the evening of the 29th. On Tundra Topics at 9:30 that night came the radio announcement: "The superintendent of the territorial schools informs Miss Schlosser that she should allow the school the day off for 'a reorientation service.' The next day was snowy, with no chance of the Bishop's plane leaving, so we had a 'reorientation' service. Later, while waiting for better flying weather, Bishop Gordon gave me a haircut.

Months became years. In the summer of 1956 we went on furlough and, due to some serious medical problems involving Anita's pregnancy with our second child, we did not return to the Koyukuk. But we will always remember the many things we loved during those three years we spent on our honeymoon on the edge of the Arctic Circle.

~ The Rev. Richard S. Miller

MEMORIES OF TANANA AND ALLAKAKET

North to Tanana
(Dorothy Mendelsohn has written extensive memoirs addressed to her five children. The following stories are excerpts from her Alaska collection.)

In the year 1955 a woman going alone to the Territory of Alaska from the Lower 48 was looked on as pretty adventurous and maybe of questionable judgment. My parents and siblings were sure I would never be seen or heard from again.

I came to this dramatic change in my life while reading the tales of Jack London and other authors. Their experiences in such a remote environment, their challenges in setting up comfortable, satisfying lifestyles despite obvious hardships, intrigued me. At that time, having finished nursing school, I was receiving recruitment notices from the U.S. Government, Alaska Native Service, to consider applying for a tour of duty at one of the BIA hospitals. I sent in an application and considered the employment prospects. The terms were good, and, without much difficulty, my decision was made. I packed my belongings, had an emotional farewell to family and friends, and boarded an Amtrak train in Florida, where my family was living. I had no idea what lay ahead.

What lay ahead, after the long, cross-country train ride and a flight to Juneau, was assignment to Tanana. I was flown in to Fairbanks. It was September, and the gold of autumn highlighted the endless miles of twisting rivers and scrubby spruce trees. An occasional, isolated cabin was the only sign of human life.

Fairbanks seemed rugged, a little primitive, with its log-cabin homes and few paved streets. I stayed in a hotel in the middle of downtown, with a neon-light sign flashing in my room all night and the boisterous sounds of arguments, fist fights and bodies hitting walls punctuating my rest. Apparently others who were in town were not there to sleep.

Flying to Tanana next day we were

again over unpopulated territory. I had always read references to "the mighty Yukon," and after my first glimpse I realized how apt that description was. The restless, churning water stretched for miles both in width and length, echoing the restless activity back in Fairbanks and reflecting vitality as river boats and barges deposited people and cargo in the villages along the banks.

At the Tanana airfield a red jeep station wagon (the hospital ambulance) and several white-uniformed nurses were waiting for me. I don't know why the uniforms surprised me except that by then I wasn't expecting anything traditional. Everyone was informal, welcoming, eager to answer questions and provide information. We drove to the hospital complex, a simple, two-story, white frame structure housing 40 patients in semiprivate and ward rooms, with dining room, kitchen and delivery room and quarters above for some of the staff. Nearby were a building with private quarters for hospital personnel and several maintenance outbuildings. I was pleasantly surprised by both the hospital and my own comfortable quarters. All the nurses and the medical director, Dr. Persons, a tiny, young, vivacious woman, lived in this facility. Our close contact in living and working together made the staff seem more like family than fellow workers.

(At the time of Dorothy's arrival in Tanana, the Rev. Randall Mendelsohn had been vicar at St. James' Church for three months. They became good friends, sharing in the spiritual, social and medical life of the village. The following year, 1956, they were married at St. James by Bishop Gordon.)

As a new bride my domestic skills left much to be desired. Bishop Gordon visited from time to time. That poor man was, thankfully, a very understanding one, considering the meals he ate with us. And the time I decided to press his rochet (the full, flowing vestment worn by bishops at services of the Church). I used a friend's flat-iron, heated on the wood stove. I put it down on the synthetic material of the rochet sleeve and it went right through! With horror and embarrassment I sewed up the hole, tucked it into the folds of the full sleeve, and then showed Bishop Gordon the damage. He said generously, "That's all right, Dorothy; no one will ever tell the difference." But he and I knew.

Bishop Gordon was always ready to pitch in, washing up, drying dishes, or lending a hand at the stove. He told us about Randy's predecessor at Tanana, a bachelor named Walter Hannum. It seems Walter was somewhat inexperienced when it came to ordering groceries, which had to be ordered sight unseen, by the case and boatload. Walter once ordered a case of Drano for a house with no plumbing. Unaccustomed to cooking a full meal for himself and usually relying on a peanut butter sandwich when he was not invited out, Walter prepared some nourishment for the Bishop, who had arrived tired and hungry after several hours of flying. He served him a bowl of peas and a bowl of Wheaties!

As my year's contract at the hospital neared expiration, the Bishop approached us about a move to Allakaket, where both clergy and medical help were needed. We said "yes" without much hesitation and so moved on to a very important chapter of our life.

Life in the Wilderness

At Allakaket we lived in the mission house, a two-story log cabin situated along the river bank and in the village center. Keeping warm in winter was a challenge. We often hung blankets over the front door and huddled near the stove. We always wore long woolen underwear and heavy socks and slacks. We never ventured outdoors without fur boots, two pairs of socks and mittens, fur parka with hood, and a scarf to protect our faces. The cold was a respected foe and one did not challenge it; but one could live with it and be compatible.

We joked that we had running water, and in a manner of speaking we did: water running from two 50-gallon drums placed upstairs in one of the bedrooms with hoses ending at the kitchen sink. The drums were kept full by hauling water obtained by chopping ice in the river, packing pails of water up the high bank to a waiting sled and dog team, and then hauling it to the house, up the stairs and to the drums. On wash days the ice chunks were heated on a woodstove in the kitchen. The water was always used for two or more purposes, such as laundry, scrubbing floors and, after the babies came, boiling diapers.

Because of winter's long hours of darkness it usually was necessary to carry a lantern as we moved about the house doing chores, but at night a lantern sitting on the table allowed us to read and was comforting and cozy. We cooked on a propane stove until the temperature dropped below minus 40 degrees (the temperature at which propane freezes); then we cooked on a small auxiliary woodstove. Anything to be kept

Randy Mendelsohn conducts services at a fish camp.

frozen needed only to be placed in the unheated storage room or on the floor in a corner of the kitchen. Wood was obtained by floating cut trees from the forests further upriver and then continually cutting and splitting these each day with a chainsaw. Each night Randy would carry in enough green wood to stoke the stove full. About two o'clock in the morning all this would "take off." We would have a roaring fire for about two or three hours, then when we woke in the morning we could see our breath in the living room. One felt one always had to beat the elements, but there was much satisfaction in doing this.

The radio was most important to us because at 4:00 p.m. four days each week the doctor at the Tanana hospital would make a round-robin call to all villages within his jurisdiction to inquire and offer advice about medical problems. His contact and concern were most reassuring when he came in loud and clear; when his voice became distorted or did not come through due to poor signal conditions, it was devastating. The same held true for attempts to make plane contacts in emergency situations. We were very dependent on that outside link and were often cut off from it. Those were the times our isolation was hardest.

In summer it was pleasant to get out and travel the river to visit people at their fish camps and watch the wildlife and the rugged beauty of the country. The day of arrival of the barge that came once a year to deliver supplies was a high point of the year. In summer, also, the plane schedule increased to sometimes three times a week, bringing in frequent visitors, mail and news from other villages. Since we rarely left the village, except when Randy visited other villages for services, we were always delighted when someone from Outside paid us a visit. We were the only home with extra sleeping accommodations, so an assortment of people bunked with us: a government anthropologist, guides, an occasional pilot either weathered in or diverted off course by the weather, a Cat skinner building trails for some government agency. Air Force personnel on furlough from a remote Distant Early Warning installation base a few hundred miles away sometimes stayed in our little Bishop's cabin next door to hunt or fish for a recreation break.. We hosted teams of physicians, fellow priests, the Presiding Bishop of our Church, Arthur Lichtenberger, our own Bishop Gordon, and Amelia Hill, former missionary who had been stationed in Allakaket in earlier years. It was always fun to talk with people, solve all the problems of life, and hear what people Outside were doing.

Besides regular clinic visits and services at the church, the village people would drop in daily to visit us. Although not talkative, they liked to socialize with us, ask questions, read magazines, and observe the children. Sometimes they would talk a little about how their lives had changed since the missionaries had come. We would invite a family in for turkey dinners on Thanksgiving and Christmas. Their children liked my "beaded" cookies (decorated with sprinkles).

Our food usually came from the cans in our pantry which had arrived by boat with our yearly order or consisted of fresh or frozen caribou, moose and mountain goat which your father or our Native friends had hunted. Cold-storage eggs and fresh lettuce, vegetables and fruit were luxuries we enjoyed only a few times a year when Bishop Gordon flew in to visit, having shopped personally before he came. He had lived in a remote village and knew how one longed for these fresh tastes. He never forgot us or anyone else when he visited.

It was impossible to have a garden or dig a well in Allakaket or in most other Interior villages, because the ground was permanently frozen six inches below the surface. Sometimes lettuce, carrots and potatoes could be planted for the short, intense growing season. We managed quite nicely and did not feel deprived. We had our taste cravings, though, and certainly could not satisfy them by running out to the nearest corner store.

Amelia Hill

Amelia Hill and Bessie Kay must have been very unusual women. We had an opportunity to meet Miss Hill, but never Miss Kay. We were told about them by other Church staff and village people. Everyone who talked about them referred to them as Miss Hill and Miss Kay. Both had come to Alaska after applying to the Church to become missionaries. Miss Kay was a schoolteacher and was sent directly to Allakaket in 1936 to teach in the Church-supported grade school. Miss Hill was a graduate nurse. After applying for U.S. citizenship (she was from Ireland), she found that the several months this involved would delay her planned intentions to do missionary work in China. The Church suggested she serve temporarily in Alaska. Once there, she decided to stay, plans for China put behind her. She had been there for several years before Miss Kay arrived.

The women lived together in the mission house in Allakaket and both were enmeshed in the lives of the village families. Miss Kay taught while Miss Hill tended to everyone's health needs. They and the villagers were a true community.

The stories told about these dearly loved but powerful and authoritative women include those of Miss Hill traveling by dog team 70 miles to the nearest villages, Bettles and Huslia, visiting in camps along the way, ministering to the people. The physical toll was great, as it was no small task for a woman to travel such distances caring for her dog team and herself in all kinds of weather and environment. She kept a journal of medical problems. Apparently she took in those who were so sick they needed personal care, and these women usually lived right in the mission house as long as necessary. She wrote of one dramatic story when the village came down with an epidemic of botulism. They had shared an obviously tainted wild game carcass, moose or caribou. One by one the young and infirm became very ill. Three children died. Miss Hill sent for a physician downriver, via Morse code wireless, but it was several days before he could get there. While she waited for him she tried to tell the village men of her suspicions about the meat, but couldn't convince them. When the doctor arrived the two of them poured kerosene on the meat and set it afire, exposing themselves to the wrath around them, and nursed the many inhabitants to recovery.

Although she was a woman, and a white woman at that, Miss Hill's wisdom and abilities commanded respect, even outside her domain of medicine. The story was told about how some men were making moonshine and had a rather rowdy party in one of the cabins. The women and some of the children became very fearful. In the early hours of the morning Miss Hill was awakened by a young man and his mother knocking at the door; they came in and related their anxiety about the goings-on. Miss Hill got dressed, hurried to the cabin, picked up the washtub of moonshine, carried it to the door, and emptied it on the ground. This was followed by a directive telling everyone to go home to bed. The next morning she was told by a sober male resident, "Don't ever do that again if you value your life!"

Once during our time in Allakaket Miss Hill visited the village and spent a few hours with us. It was a highlight of our experience there. She sat so composed, so commanding yet unpretentious, so in charge of herself, telling us her experiences and memories of life there. We took the boat upriver and picked berries at one of her favorite spots. She visited with the people, walked through the village and reminisced. Then she asked us a very significant question: "Do you ever hear or see anything unusual around the church or the mission house?" Our answer was "no," but she went on to tell us why she had asked the question.

The Ghost of Hudson Stuck

When Miss Hill came to Allakaket in 1922, the only way to get to the village was by river boat and barge. Because she was a young woman traveling alone, the boat personnel set up a tent on the floor of the barge to offer her privacy. The boat stopped at many little villages as it made its way up the river, letting off and taking on passengers, and there was a varied assortment of people traveling, mostly men. This was summer, it was daylight 24 hours, and she slept through the night in the tent but in full light. About 2:00 a.m. one morning she woke up and looked out to see a clergyman walking up and down the barge, pacing. As he noticed Miss Hill awake he came over to her tent and said, "You are Miss Hill, are you not?"

She replied, "Yes." He said, "You're going to Allakaket?" She said, "Yes." There was a pause and then he said, "Well, you're going to find life hard there but stick it out and you will also find it worthwhile." He walked away and she went back to sleep. Although she had not seen this man among the passengers the day before and did not see him after getting up the next morning, she assumed he had disembarked at one of the villages. She thought no more of the incident until she reached Allakaket and the people met her and escorted her to the mission house. Just inside the front door, hanging on the wall, was a picture of the man who had spoken to her. When she asked the people his identity she was told, "That's Archdeacon Hudson Stuck. He died two years ago."

A practical individual, Miss Hill had never believed in ghosts, but she was so overcome by this experience that she told no one until a long time later.

The presence of Hudson Stuck was confirmed by two other stories. In Fort Yukon a clergyman once entered the empty church to practice on the organ. After playing for about thirty minutes he looked up in the darkened church to see the vision of Hudson Stuck celebrating the Eucharist in the sanctuary. It is said that the clergyman quickly left the building.

Back at the mission house there was another incident. Miss Kay and Miss Hill had been living together for some time, and Miss Kay had never been told of Miss Hill's "ghost story." The original small cabin, attached to a newly built addition by a passageway, was used to store supplies and staples. One day Miss Kay went into this stor-age area while Miss Hill remained in their living quarters. Suddenly the door to the passageway opened and Miss Kay came through hurriedly, visibly shaken, her face ashen. She told Miss Hill that in the dim light of the old cabin she had seen a clergyman, his white collar visible. His head was bent, hands clasped behind his back: it was later learned that this, along with the pacing, was a characteristic pose of Stuck's. He appeared to be giving a blessing. After hearing this account, Miss Hill shared her earlier experience with Miss Kay.

While talking with us Miss Hill recalled not only these incidents but two or three "spooky" ones when they heard footsteps outside the front door, a knock, a rattling of the doorknob, but upon opening the door found no one. Was the presence still there? We never doubted her word, were even convinced by her story, but could truthfully claim no unusual events in what was for us a different house and a different time from those the women had lived in.

But these two women, true pioneers, also exerted a lasting presence. Bishop Bentley described them as: "Saintly, courageous women. Had to be." Can you imagine young women with so little life experience leaving their homes for such a remote area to teach and care and minister among strangers? Even though six years had passed between their departure and our arrival in Allakaket—with the Millers there for several of the years in between—the spirit, the presence of these two pioneer women was still vitally alive in that village during our time there.

~ Dorothy Mendelsohn

"BUT OUR CHURCH IS STILL STANDING"

"For waters shall break forth in the wilderness..." Isaiah 35:6

With tired, shocked eyes, the man sat in the Carlson Center in Fairbanks on the last night of August 1994. Normally a hockey rink and community center, this night the Center was filling up with makeshift cots. Mothers moved slowly, sleepwalking with children and small handbags toward the cots. In the center of the rink, Red Cross officials held pieces of paper and made lists, directing families toward the cots.

Oscar Nictune, 93-year-old Inupiaq patriarch, was already stretched out sleeping on one of the cots, a small bag on the floor beside him. Carefully he had placed uneaten cake in his bag when the evening meal ended. When you've lived that long in the Country, you learn to save what comes your way — one never knows what the future might hold and, this night, that small bag now contained everything Oscar Nictune owned after 93 years.

The man with the tired eyes sat at a table, sipping coffee in the darkness. He had just returned from a 500-mile round trip flight north to his community. "It's gone," he was explaining. "It's just gone." "Devastated," echoed his companion, who had flown with him. "Total devastation."

From its headwaters high up in the lost mountain valleys of the Brooks Range, the Koyukuk River flows for 500 miles before it meets the Yukon River in northern Alaska. Flowing clear and cold across graveled bottom, twisting and turning around the hills and through the spruce and birch forests, the Koyukuk River is home to four isolated, scattered communities. Northernmost of the four, some 200 miles northwest of Fairbanks, located on the Koyukuk as it crosses the Arctic Circle with the Alatna River emptying into it from the west, are the communities of Allakaket and Alatna.

Long an historic trading ground between the coastal Eskimo people and the Koyukon Indian people, Allakaket was established in 1907 when Episcopal Archdeacon Hudson Stuck built a mission and school at the confluence of the rivers. Soon people gathered, forming Allakaket on the bank, around the mission, and the smaller community of Alatna on the opposite shore. Staffed by deaconesses and missionaries through the years, until Bishop Gordon ordained the Rev. Joe Williams of Allakaket in the early seventies, the mission of St. John's-in-the-Wilderness grew and thrived. Sunday after Sunday the great bell, originally hoisted by Archdeacon Stuck and inscribed "O ye Frost and Cold, bless ye the Lord" called Koyukuk people to worship. When the most recent church was built in the community several years ago, the last action was moving the bell over to its new tower. The old church was left standing, out of respect for the years of prayer and faith it contained.

As August 1994 was nearing its end, the people of the region were busy. Life along the Koyukuk has always been life based on the land, the river, and the great cycle of the seasons. Fall is the time to get ready for the coming winter, and the winters are long and hard and cold along the Koyukuk. Temperatures are often colder than fifty below.

This August most of the young men of the village were away in Montana and Washington fighting forest fires, to gain money for trapping and winter supplies. At home in Allakaket the women, children and elders caught the last of the summer's fish, picked berries, thought about cutting wood, and talked about the coming moose season. Overhead, the ducks and geese were leaving. Two men were somewhere upriver prospecting (for this is historic gold mining country) and scouting out possible hunting sites.

The August rains had finally stopped, the birch trees were turning yellow, and the chill in the night air meant winter was coming. Northern lights moved overhead as the Allakaket sled dogs slept. They are legends in Alaska, these sled dogs of the Koyukuk, and winter's coming meant their time was coming too.

Eighty miles downriver, squeezed against the bottom of the hills in the smaller community of Hughes, church volunteers from Chattanooga, Tennessee worked with village residents building the first Episcopal church in the village. Over the year church services had been held in schools, homes and stores, but now Hughes was finally getting its own church. Joe Beatus, 79 years old, smiled. It was about time.

While Joe smiled at the emerging church in Hughes, and Allakaket people carefully put away the fish they were catching and the berries they had picked, the rivers to the north, swollen with rain water, were flooding south through the Brooks Range. Sunday evening, August 28th, as parents and children prepared for the next day's opening of school, the swollen rivers hit the Koyukuk.

Twenty-four hours later, Allakaket and Alatna would no longer physically exist, and almost all of the residents would be wandering shell-shocked around an army barracks outside of Fairbanks. Evacuated during the night by army helicopters, they now sat in the sunshine of a Fairbanks afternoon and wondered what the flooding waters were doing to their homes. "I ran through water up above my knees," recalled Rhea Williams, widow of the late Rev. Joe Williams. "I was holding my little girl. That's what made me cry — she was scared."

"The last time," elders remembered, "the last time it flooded was 1938, but that was nothing like this." Oscar Nictune recalled a flood when he was a small boy: "I lived in a cache for a week, but it wasn't as high as this one was." Someone brought photographs taken from the air that day over the communities, and the reality of the destruction began to hit. "My house!" cried one young mother, "my house is gone!"

And it was, as were most of the houses.

Tony Moses looked at the photographs and reached into his pocket, pulling out his skinning knife. "I'm 70 years old and this is all I have left in the world."

As the Red Cross made plans to move people to a more permanent shelter at the Carlson Center, warnings were telephoned to Hughes about the high water pouring their way, and diocesan officials worried about the Chattanooga church volunteers. Later that night power went out in Hughes, and all communication stopped. The waters had hit.

Back in Allakaket, church committee member Lydia Bergman and her husband

Lindberg paddled through the community trying to rescue more than 200 sled dogs. Later in the week, when they finally came to Fairbanks, Lydia explained why she'd stayed behind. "My grandmother warned me when I was a little girl that this was going to come sometime. She told me what to do and she told me to be ready and really try. I remembered that, so I did." Lindberg echoed her thoughts, "That's my ground. I didn't want to leave it."

By Wednesday evening, August 30th, the population of Hughes, including the Tennessee church volunteers, had also been evacuated into Fairbanks, joining Allakaket and Alatna in the Carlson Center. As he left Hughes on one of the first flights, Joe Beatus had warned the volunteers to run a line from the church still under construction to one of the village telephone poles. "Maybe it won't float away," he told them. It didn't. But Joe had seen all of his own belongings swamped by the raging river, when the raft he'd constructed overturned. "Well," he said later, "I don't worry about us, my wife and I. We're old and we're going to die soon and we don't need a house. We can live anyplace. It's the young people, the young families I worry about."

By August 31st the first flights back to survey the damage in the three communities were confirming what air photographs had revealed. Buildings, houses, city offices and out buildings had all shifted, been destroyed, or disappeared in Allakaket and Alatna. Five houses sat now on the runway. and the new, eight-sided, 40' by 60' log community hall of Allakaket sat three miles downriver in the middle of a forest, surrounded by other houses that had floated

away. Rhea Williams's house, where she and Joe had hosted Alaska's bishops over the years, had totally disappeared, along with most of the older section of the community along the river. Many sled dogs that Lydia and Lindberg had not been able to reach in time, had drowned, disappeared or were missing. By the end of the next week, wolves would be prowling the edges of the ruined village, finishing off any loose dogs foolish enough to venture too far. Fuel tanks had fallen and split open, spilling over 60,000 gallons of diesel onto the ground, along with overflowing sewage. In Hughes, many of the houses remained on their foundations, but all had been damaged by flood waters.

Red Cross officials classified the Koyukuk floods as a Type 4+ disaster (the last major hurricane that hit the southeastern United States was a Type 5+), and federal officials estimate over $40 million in damages. Federal, state, city, private and Alaska Native organizations raced to organize relief and cleanup efforts in all three communities. Floods, though comparatively rare along the Koyukuk, are not uncommon in the interior of Alaska, but they usually occur in the spring with the breaking up of the rivers. The summers then allow a time of rebuilding. The Koyukuk flooded on the edge of autumn, when leaves were already falling in Allakaket. Soon the surrounding hills were capped in snow and the north wind that blows down from the Brooks announced that winter was near. How long that small window of time would last, before the hard freezes came and the snow covered the debris, was the unknown question. What would happen next spring, when it all

melts again, is another unknown.

The people of the Koyukuk resided in the hockey rink until the middle of September before scattering to apartments throughout Fairbanks. Though many of the younger residents returned to aid the cleanup efforts, along with elders like Lydia and Lindberg, most remained in Fairbanks, waiting to see what would happen next. Relief organizations, Native organizations, the diocese, and St. Matthew's Church in Fairbanks coordinated efforts to help preserve some sense of community for these displaced people.

Three weeks after the flood the last missing house from Allakaket was found. The river had carried it 70 miles, abandoning it behind willows only 10 miles above Hughes.

At the Sunday Eucharist at St. Matthew's on Labor Day weekend, most of those Koyukon people were there, for all three villages are exclusively Episcopalian. Bishop Charleston was there, having rushed back from General Convention to be at the service and announce emergency relief contributions sent by the National Church.

"It's good to be here," Joe Beatus announced during the open forum that developed during the service. "It's good to be here with you, my people. I was baptized Episcopalian and raised Episcopalian and you are my people. We have lost everything. All our moosemeat, all our fish, all our berries, all our winter clothing. All we had put away for the winter is gone. But we can still pray together, and that's good."

Is Allakaket destroyed? Ask Johnson Moses, layreader, chalice-bearer and elder in Allakaket. "People say Allakaket is gone," he says. "But Allakaket isn't gone. Allakaket is here." And he points to his heart. "And have you noticed," he says, "that the only building not shifted or destroyed is our old church? Our church still stands, and God is still with us."

– The Rev. Scott Fisher

(UPDATE, June 1995: As this book goes to press, the people of the Koyukuk have returned to their villages, and recovery and rebuilding are progressing well. The church at Hughes has been completed. Allakaket and Alatna are relocating to higher ground. Roads are being put through, and the Allakaket community hall is being rebuilt. Both old and new churches will be moved, and the original church building may be declared a National Historic Site. Assistance from the National Church and outside dioceses has amounted to about $50,000.)

MEMORIES OF THE MISSION NURSE

Sept. 1949: As I stepped off the train from Anchorage last week I realized that St. Mark's Mission was "en masse" on the platform to greet me. Their welcome was a warm one in spite of a four-day-old Mission tragedy. Father Robert Reid, priest-in-charge, and two of the Mission boys had drowned on the treacherous Tanana River when their small motor-powered boat had capsized 80 miles from Nenana. It happened on the first day of a two-week hunting trip for moose and caribou meat for the winter. A third boy miraculously survived

to report the accident. Two floods, a fire, and now this, most tragic of all, have hit the Mission within the last two years, yet the good work goes on, as it must.

There are 35 children, Indian and Eskimo, in this Mission boarding school, with more expected soon. Deaconess Thompson, petite and conscientious, does unending hours of selfless work for the children and people in this community. She teaches all the grades in the modern, one-room school building. Miss Webb and Miss Watts are the housemothers, both splendid people with great humor and the patience of Job.

Bishop Gordon flew in to visit and then to take Suzanne Reid in to Fairbanks. My first meeting with him — he is a fine-looking young man of 31 years. He brought me some precious Depo-Penicillin, which I used on a patient half an hour later.

Oct. 1949: I have just done some tooth-pulling, a sideline of my medical work here. Consulted with Deaconess Thompson about my technique, to be sure I had gotten the whole root out; she offered me reassurance, as always. I cannot overestimate the tremendous amount of support and wise knowledge that she has given me in all my many "first experiences" here. She has probably brought more wee nubbins into the world, treated more illnesses and pulled more teeth in her 20 years at the Mission than I shall ever see — and this in addition to all her other million undertakings.

Our little "atom bombs" are wearing the staff down to nerveless entities with their obsessive tastes for kitchen cleanser and toothpaste. Last week one little girl discov-

ered Old Dutch Cleanser and proceeded to taste, enjoy, and ultimately devour the contents of the entire can before being spotted. We spent the afternoon retrieving. The hard lesson was soon forgotten, and she has since admittedly repeated the tasting. I wonder what scouring powder contains in the way of a daily minimum requirement!

It is Sunday now, and the children are shedding the scarves, coats and boots they wore to church. In the absence of a priest, Deaconess takes the 11 a.m. services, leading the Mission folk and Native people from the village in Morning Prayer. An occasional white person from town joins the congregation, and the Native people often number 24 or so. When Father Reid was here he held Sunday evening services downtown in the Church Door Canteen, but right now there are no regular services of any kind for townspeople who do not care to walk out to the Mission.

The Alaska Native Service has limited funds with which they do as much as possible for all the Natives of Alaska. It is to them that we appeal for funds to cover expenses of our Native charges, both in and outside of the Mission. The Mission is able to fill some of the great need for medical and social service among the people, but conditions frequently arise that make trips to Fairbanks necessary for X-rays, dental work, the advice and examination of an M.D., hospitalization, help with pensions for those unable to be supported otherwise, and other problems. At times when the ANS is unable to satisfy the need, the Mission reaches deep into its pocket. As the yearly appropriation, measured by the United Thank Offering purses turned in to

Deaconess Kathleen Thompson and her choir girls at St. Mark's Mission in the 1930s

Housemother Martha Webb and the St. Mark's kids carve the Thanksgiving turkeys, 1949. (Photo by Dorothy Vinson Hall)

the National Church by each parish, is barely adequate to keep the Mission — or any other church mission — above water, you can understand how often and how severely our hands are tied. Right now we have many children badly in need of dental work, tonsillectomies, and X-rays to check for tuberculosis. But, even with all the shortages and problems, the children are adequately fed and clothed, sheltered and instructed, and they feel secure here. They do not lack for affection either, and seem to keep in the normal curve of a happy state. The Natives outside of the Mission, for the most part, are thankful for whatever counsel or treatment we can afford, and it is only we who are here to minister who feel our inadequacies.

Dec. 1949: Eight more days until Christmas! All 39 Mission children are buzzing with excitement. The Christmas

tree has been gracing the middle of the main street for a week. Its base, several blocks of ice, was recently cut out of the Tanana by Mr. Fred Mueller, our Mission handyman, and hauled in the Farm-All tractor and sled trailer by our older boys.

This Saturday is "Shopping Day." The older ones and the stronger will poke through the stores downtown — Coggie's, Northern Commercial Co., and Fowler's, where the counters and shelves are well-stocked with toys, decorations, plaid shirts, levis, woolen socks, mukluk liners, white bread, canned goods, comic books, moose-skin, glue, and Mixmasters! The younger children will pick and choose from the "Mission counter" in the Big Room. Boxes of gifts sent to the Mission make this a great spree. After Saturday, the children will have difficulty holding themselves down until the pageant in the church on the afternoon of Christmas Eve. Each child shall have at

least one speaking line (thanks to Deaconess), and blue jeans and cotton dresses will lose their identity under shepherds' coats and angel wings. At 8:00 that night the village Native people will come to the Mission for the Christmas tree and to each hunt a small gift from beneath the spruce boughs. Bishop Gordon plans to be here for our Christmas service on the 25th, for which we are all very grateful. After the chapel service there will be a wild dash for the stockings which the staff will fill on Christmas Eve and hang in the Big Room. I am anxious to see the merriment of the children.

The weekend temperature held at 40 below, too risky for flying small craft, so Bishop Gordon could not be with us for the Christmas morning service. Deaconess led us in Morning Prayer. The excited children were spic and span in clean dresses or shirts. After the service they were overcome by the first sight of their stacks of toys and gifts. The unwrapping of presents took only a few minutes: paper and ribbon covered the floor, and 39 children were happy above all expectation.

Including the Mission folk, 87 people braved the cold to attend the Christmas service, just about capacity for the little log church. With the singing of "Joy to the World," the fragrance of spruce in every breath, and the happy faces, it was truly Christmas!

June 1950: Holy Week and Easter at the Mission were glorious. I wish you could have peeked around the chapel door during the early celebration of Holy Communion on Easter morning. Thirty-six happy youngsters in new dresses or pants and shirts, cowlicks subdued, bangs and braids neat, faces shining with joy and mischief. Later came all the fun that goes with Easter — the egg-dipping, table-decorating, Easter basket hunt, treasure hunt, and the Easter Monday dance. How everyone's feet did fly after the long weeks of Lent!

Miss Watts left on furlough shortly after Easter, and we miss her tremendously. But Mary Ann Hakes joined the Mission family to take her place as housemother. Few could have fitted in as she has. These housemothers have my greatest admiration.

Mission troubles have included the usual list, with a few additions. Miss Webb tangled with an ironing board a few weeks ago and is still willing to trade in one big toe. Mumps was added to the routine for the past several weeks: a faint knock on the door before breakfast, a little voice saying, "Miss Vinson, my neck feels…" and another bed is turned down for a ten-day occupancy.

Fred Mueller and the boys have worked hard to plow and plant the vegetable fields and gardens and to rake off the winter debris. Our birch and spruce add dignity and grace, and the Mission is beautiful in its fresh spring dress. The Mission boat is a bit wobbly and decrepit, but Fred is fixing it up for the fishing season. The fishwheels are ready for the Tanana when the salmon run starts next month; Deaconess has planted flower seeds along the Mission paths; and the children are now wearing holes into short socks instead of winter's long ones.

Tragedy struck the village two weeks ago when an old pilot house being using as a cabin burned to the ground, taking in the flames a mother and her eight-year-old son. Passing the smoldering logs the following day with one of the young Mission children, I realized, as so often, that great philosophies do not depend on age. "That boy was lucky," the little girl said, "He died with his mother. I hope I can die with my mother. You know, when someone like that dies, it's like he just went away. I don't feel sad."

~ From the letters and diary
of Dorothy Vinson Hall

REMEMBRANCES OF THE CHIEF

Paul George's mother, Belle George, who died in 1953 at the age of 90 years, told Paul the story of the first preacher that came to Nenana when she was ten years old, about the year 1873. Nenana had been a village for a long time, and people gathered there for fishing and potlatches. The man came in a boat, rowing up the Tanana River. He talked to the people in the village and tried to break his words down to help them understand. He came to give them names and to baptize them. Paul's mother and her friends Kitty John and Laura Charlie, later Chief Charlie's wife, listened to the man at the river. He gave them names and taught them a few English words. He said he wanted to teach the people to speak and write in English. He showed them how to write words on a paper and how to fold the paper and put it in an envelope to send to friends in other places. The people liked that idea.

The preacher promised to build a big building to teach children to read and write and count and how to live. He asked them to give him some land so he could put up a building and a church and make a garden to feed kids, so they gave land. He said when the people learned what he taught them the land would go back to the people. A promise was made and written down.

The first mission building was a log building that burned down. The next was a frame house. They built a sawmill at the mission, and the church of St. Mark's Mission is made of three-sided logs.

At that time the Native village of 5,000-6,000 people was getting overcrowded. Seventeen houses were built across the river. Paul's mother lived over there in the Native village. Chief Thomas was chief all during this time (this was around 1912-1915, before Old Minto started). The younger people, who spoke English now, said they would elect a new chief. It was decided that Chief Thomas would go on being chief but that other men were needed to help run the village. They appointed a cop and council members. No liquor was allowed to be sold, and bootleggers were fined. It was like that for a long time.

Paul learned from Peter John, traditional chief of Minto, that Chief Charlie went down and staked out Old Minto in 1917, in a location near the good hunting lands near Lake Minto and Goldstream.

About 1919-1920 a flu epidemic killed many Native people. Paul's mother was sick and stayed at a place at Rex; soldiers took patients there on the narrow-gauge line that went from Nenana to Healy. She saw the soldiers remove five bodies of flu victims from the house where she stayed.

When Paul was a kid, Bishop Rowe was here, and Miss Farthing, now buried under the big cross on the hill, worked at the Mission. Together they took care of the kids. Athabascans lived at fish camp all summer and trapped all winter. People in camp who came into town would dress up and go to church. Bishop Rowe sent word to the fish camps that he would make a potlatch and have everyone come up. The women made moccasins and boots for the men and children to wear to look nice for church. They all came in and had a big picnic after church.

Paul didn't go to the Mission school; he was raised in the woods. Mission kids cut and made dry fish to feed dogs. Paul's family had a hard time, and Paul did many odd jobs to help out. His mother told him it would make him feel good to go to church. He was working for Bishop Bentley at the time, chopping wood and working in the garden. He told the bishop he wanted to be a Christian, and he was confirmed in 1940.

Paul remembers they "ate good all that summer."

Moses Jimmy, known as Blind Moses, was often around St. Mark's Mission. He got only $15 a month relief check, and the mission gave him bread, sugar, tea and other staples. Boys from the mission would split wood and carry water for him. He'd tell them, "No noise, Onion (Indian)," and the boys who followed him around would laugh. Blind Moses held services in the church for his people in their own language. He died in 1936 and is buried up on the hill.

The Nenana people started a village in 1929 out at Toklat, 42 miles west of Nenana. Paul remembers going there to fish, make sleds, and haul logs with dogs. During the winter some visitors came from the mouth of the Toklat. When a baby died they decided to bury the child out there. It was too far to bring a preacher, so they held the service themselves. Two people read the Bible, and a funeral service was held for the baby. Paul remembers reaching up to hold his mother's hand at the funeral. He recalled how people made their own service by reading from the scriptures.

Before Bishop Bentley left he had the people elect a vestry. Paul is the only surviving member of that vestry: others were Frank Alexander, David Esau, Winifred Coghill and her son Bob. Everything changed after Bishop Bentley left. The Mission school closed. The main building was sold to brothers who used it for a bar and lodge. The school and the church, close to the river bank, were moved to safer locations. In 1961 or so, the large Mission building was swept downriver. The signifi-

cant years of St. Mark's Mission and school came to an end.

~ Paul George, Traditional chief of Nenana, as told to Dora Powell

THE FORT YUKON MISSION HOUSE

The following document presents an excellent description of the nature and importance of the work carried out at Fort Yukon in the early years of this century.

Fort Yukon Mission House - National Historical Site Nomination Application prepared in 1977

Fort Yukon's evolution from an isolated trading post to a regional center for missionary activity is exemplary of the emphasis given to the church-school movement of the early part of this century. A combination of secular and spiritual instruction, underpinned by a program of health care, was advocated for villages such as Fort Yukon both as a humanitarian gesture and as a move to facilitate the education of Native peoples in Christian teaching. Fort Yukon will always occupy a prominent place in church history because of the important contributions of the church to this community, and because of a long history and association with several exceptional men and women who served there and whose dedication to Native peoples and to the Church were substantial and lasting.

The first missionaries came to Fort Yukon in 1861 with the arrival of a priest from the Church of England's Mackenzie

Dr. Grafton Burke and the Fort Yukon Boys Club, 1909

River District Missionary Society, Northwest Territories. Thus, Fort Yukon became the first, and soon the most important, interior Alaskan center for religious instruction. A small church and mission house were erected in 1893 to become the first such establishment in the middle Yukon region. Missionary work continued under the auspices of the Canadian Church until 1899 when the first American clergy arrived to establish a permanent Episcopal mission. By the turn of the century the Episcopal Church had assumed all responsibility for what was known as St. Stephen's Mission on the banks of the Yukon River.

Within the next ten years two men came to Fort Yukon whose talents and dedication would gain for one international, and for the other local fame and admiration, as well as enhancing the position of Fort Yukon as an important regional center. The first was Archdeacon Hudson Stuck and the second was Dr. Grafton Burke. Under their leadership the Church-Mission House-Hospital complex earned for Fort Yukon the Church's praise as its most significant missionary work in Alaska. For years these facilities provided the people of Fort Yukon and the surrounding villages with spiritual, medical, and social services until air transportation made such luxuries generally available. Although the Hudson Stuck Memorial Hospital was closed in 1960 and the Mission House was converted into a clinic by the Public Health Service, the Mission House remains an important part of Fort Yukon, Alaska, for reasons supplementary to its medical services.

The history of the Episcopal Church at Fort Yukon chronicles three Mission Houses. Two were destroyed by fire, but the third, and present structure, built in 1924, still stands. After the second Mission House burned down in October of 1924, Dr. and Mrs. Burke and the people of Fort Yukon decided immediately to rebuild the Mission House; an indication of how important this building was to the village. With the help of the Department of Missions, the local

people, and two well-known Church-workers, N.J. Nicholson and Moses Cruikshank, the third Mission House was built and on the same site as the 1914 structure. It stands now, as it did then, a hundred yards from the Hudson Stuck Hospital, the ruins of which are still visible from Dr. Burke's old upstairs Mission House office window. Soon after the fire, Mrs. Burke noted in an issue of *The Alaskan Churchman* that the new building was to be an exact duplicate of the one which burned with the exception of two extra feet added to enlarge the kitchen. With great community effort and sense of purpose, the rebuilt Mission House opened its doors in 1925.

During the first three decades of this century, Fort Yukon shipped more fur to the outside world than any other place in Alaska, and nearly all families, both Native Athabascans and non-Natives, were heavily involved in trapping. With the establishment of the Mission at Fort Yukon, there was a trend toward village centralization. One result of this centralization was that it became less common for families to trap together as a unit. It became more common for the children to remain in town during the winter to attend school, and most of these children went to the Mission House where they were cared for while their parents were away. Then, in the late spring and summer, they would join their parents to go to fish camps or duck hunting. In return the church received whatever could be provided.

A child's tuition or "sponsorship" was often paid for with a quarter of moose or caribou, or so many muskrat or beaver pelts. However, this was not a formal agreement, because the church provided free services for orphans or children whose parents couldn't provide a reimbursement. Community members in general supported the Mission through handmade goods and services such as cutting wood and providing food. The Mission House became, in these ways, the center of a unique Indian-white relationship and served an important community function by providing for the children.

In addition to religious instruction, the Mission House offered a boarding-school environment where students attended classes and performed daily chores. Unlike the boarding schools in many other parts of the United States, the students remained in their home region and familiar environment.

The elders of Fort Yukon retain fond memories of when they were children and called the Mission House their home for much of the year. Johnny Thomas remembers that when he stayed there each boy had to bring in ten sticks (four-foot lengths) of wood every day and twenty on Saturdays, to feed the huge steam boiler in the basement. And he also recalls how water was hauled from the Yukon in the summer by wagon and during the winter by sledge. It was then poured through a hose, put down the wood chute, into a 10,000-gallon concrete cistern.

Adelia Williams remembers the four years she spent in the Mission House kitchen as the cook. One of the children's favorite meals was her beef stew which they all ate as one big family, gathered around six tables in a large room. All her supplies, except for a few vegetables, came by barge each spring at break-up. Special times were Halloween, Christmas, and the Fourth of July, because on those days Dr. Burke held huge parties for the children and staff.

The twenty or more children in residence at the Mission House were cared for equally whether they happened to be from Fort Yukon, a village several days journey away, or an orphan with no other guardian. Many of these same children are now the elders of Fort Yukon, and names such as Thomas, Carroll, Peter and Stevens can still be found on the old Mission House ledgers. Above all, there is a feeling that the Mission House is part of Fort Yukon and an important link to its past. Villagers expressed deep regret when the Hudson Stuck Memorial Hospital was torn down. There is now fear that one day the Mission House will also go.

This would be a shame, for St. Stephen's Mission was at one time the most highly endowed and energetic program sponsored by the Episcopal Church in Alaska. The structure serves as a constant reminder of that period of Church and community history. For the individuals who built and worked at the Mission as well as those who stayed there when they were children, the building has special meaning. It is a reminder of their particular history recalled in stories and the memory of years spent with dedicated church men and church women.

(Editor's Note: Unfortunately, the historic Mission House was destroyed by fire a few years ago.)

GROWING UP IN ANVIK

When my grandfather, the Rev. John M. Chapman, went to Alaska in 1887, he was not sure exactly what awaited him, so he left his fiancee, May Seely, behind. They did not see each other again for six years, and during that time, according to my mother, they had mail only once a year. She must have thought he was worth waiting for, because when he went out on furlough they were married. She returned to Anvik with him in 1894, and my father, the Rev. Henry H. Chapman, was born there the following year.

By the time I arrived on the scene, my grandfather had retired and the two of them had left Anvik, but my grandmother's legacy

Dr. John W. Chapman with baby May, daughter of his son and daughter-in-law, Henry and Susan, June 1930 at Anvik. (Photo courtesy of Hazel M.C. Huebner)

Left: Laura Chapman at Anvik, circa 1937 (Photo courtesy of Laura Chapman Rico) Right: Anna Chapman, age 3, 1941 at Anvik (Photo courtesy of Anna Chapman)

lingered on in the Anvik I knew as a child. She had created a garden near the river bank. The outlines of its formal design could still be seen in the earth, and her Iceland poppies, in which I delighted, were still reseeding themselves. Also, in the hall of our home stood her organ, which I was told had once been in the church. After my mother showed me how, I picked out hymn melodies, using one finger. The organ that was in the church at that time was played by my father, who had been instructed by my grandmother so that he could take over for her.

The legacy of my grandmother's skill as a painter can still be seen in the church in Anvik today. In lieu of stained glass windows, she painted reproductions of old masters to hang on the church walls. Among

them are Lerolle's "Arrival of the Shepherds," a picture of the supper at Emmaus, a picture of Christ blessing the children, and two angels, one on either side of the altar. There is also one of Grandmother's own compositions, showing Christ as healer.

When my grandfather retired in 1930 the work at Anvik was taken over by my father, who by that time had married my mother, Susan Smith. She had come to Anvik in 1921 to teach in the boarding school, having graduated from the Church Training and Deaconess House in Philadelphia. My father, who graduated from General Theological Seminary in New York City the same year, served a year as a deacon in Vermont before returning to Alaska as a missionary in 1922. This fact led to the family joke in later years that Mother was actually the senior missionary in Alaska, having arrived a year before him, although she had not been on the payroll since their marriage.

My parents met in Nenana in 1922 when she was accompanying a sick friend (Marguerite Bartberger of the Anvik mission staff) to the hospital, and he was returning to Anvik to supply there while his father went out on furlough. Thus far their memories agreed; interestingly enough, one recalled they had met on the boat; the other thought they had met in the town. In any

case, the meeting took place, and during the following year in Anvik they became better acquainted — well enough acquainted, in fact, for my father to propose marriage. (Other members of the mission staff during that year, besides Miss Bartberger, were Mr. and Mrs. John Bentley.) My mother, however, thought they hadn't known each other long enough, so when my grandfather returned from furlough, my father went off alone to Fairbanks to serve four years there. Upon his return to Anvik his proposal was more successful, and he and Susan Smith were married there in 1928. Mother was given in marriage by the only member of her family present, her sister, Adelaide Smith, also a Deaconess House graduate, who served in Anvik for a few years (later she became Sister Adelaide of All Saints Sisters of the Poor in Baltimore).

My mother, who originally went to Anvik as a teacher, continued to teach in the day school after the boarding school closed and the rest of the mission staff left. During my childhood there, my father taught the older children in the school room of the mission house and Mother taught the beginners in the hall in our house, but she did the lesson plans for both. She also conducted one Vacation Bible School that I remember with enjoyment, probably the year my younger sister Anna turned three, when Mother would have had more time to devote to the mission work.

In 1948 my father was transferred to Sitka, where the church had been closed for two years. Because of my mother's interests and training, he asked her to conduct the work with children and young people. During the eleven years they were in Sitka,

The Mission at Anvik

the Sunday School grew from seven children in three classes to over a hundred children in eleven classes, and junior and senior youth groups were founded. This work was one of the factors that led to her being named Alaska Mother of the Year in 1954.

The last three years of my father's ministry were spent in Petersburg, where my mother continued her work with children and young people and established a choir of older girls who sang for Sunday morning services.

Many people are familiar with my grandfather's memoirs, *A Camp on the Yukon*. My father has also written his memoirs, to be entitled *A Home on the Yukon*. The dedication reads: "To Susan, who made our home on the Yukon all that a home should be."

~ Laura Chapman Rico

ISAAC FISHER

During John Chapman's early years in Anvik it was essential to find assistants among the Native community to interpret for him. He regularly included this pressing need in the daily prayers that guided and strengthened his ministry.

One day his prayers were answered, although at the time he could not have known it. A young Indian woman arrived at the door of the mission with a ten-year-old boy in tow. The child was ragged, his boots stuffed with grass to insulate against the cold. His mother had died, and his sister asked Mr. Chapman if the mission school could take him in. Although the facility was already crowded, room was made for the boy, whose name was Isaac Fisher.

Isaac proved to be a bright student and, in time, became one of the best interpreters on the lower Yukon. In 1897 he was appointed lay assistant of the Anvik mission. When he was only 16 he helped Mr. Chapman translate much of the Scriptures and the Prayer Book into the Native language.

A well-known story about Isaac was recalled by Bishop Bentley and recorded on his tapes years later. It seems Isaac, then a young man in his late teens, went hunting one day and used up all his ammunition but one bullet. Just before he reached home, he went around a rock bluff on the Yukon and came face to face with a bear. It was springtime, and the bears had just started to come out of their hideouts where they had been hibernating all winter; at that time they are very mean and ugly. Fortunately, Isaac had saved one bullet. Dr. Chapman said, "Well, Isaac, what did you do?" In his careful, precise way Isaac said, "Mr. Chapman, I shot the bear." And Mr. Chapman said, "Well, Isaac, what would you have done if you had missed him with that one bullet?" Isaac replied, "Mr. Chapman, when you only have one bullet, you do not miss the bear."

As Isaac grew older, it was his dog sled that carried Mr. Chapman to the outlying villages, as Isaac was one of the best dog drivers in that part of Alaska. Eventually Isaac married and had a family, and his children attended the mission school.

One spring an epidemic broke out at Anvik. Most of the men were about to set off on their spring hunt, but Isaac stayed behind to help care for the sick. Contracting the disease himself, he died, one of many victims of the scourge of influenza. His memory and his dedication to the work of the mission live on in Anvik.

~ Excerpt from *Builders of the Kingdom*

THE EDGECUMBE EXPERIENCE

My first eight years in Alaska were spent in Valdez and Cordova. Then, in Sitka, Dr. Henry Chapman was about to retire (1959), so we Grumbines moved some 600 miles to Sitka at a time when the picturesque St. Peter's-by-the-Sea was in the early stages of a

Mt. Edgecumbe students at Sitka, circa 1960

Many students enjoyed the Saturday Open House at St. Peter's with Fr. Bob Grumbine and family.

complete structural renovation. Bishop Rowe had lived in the rectory and was buried in the churchyard. His seal appears in the stained glass window of the residence.

The small but exceedingly loyal congregation recognized that a large part of their missionary responsibility was among the more than 100 Episcopal young people who lived in dormitories from September to May pursuing their high school education at Mt. Edgecumbe School, operated by the Bureau of Indian Affairs. These teenagers came from villages throughout Alaska, communities too small to provide secondary education. The Episcopalians represented Eskimo and Athabascan Indian stock, coming from central, northern or northwest Alaska. From Southeast Alaska came the Tshimsian, Haida and Tlingit Indian groups, and Aleuts from the Aleutian Chain. Thus, the name of the Mt. Edgecumbe yearbook, *The Taheta*, had one letter for the name of each

group which made up the student body. Our Episcopal young people came from Point Hope, Point Lay, Kivalina, Allakaket, Fort Yukon, Arctic Village, Minto, Anvik, Chalkyitsik, Shageluk, Stevens Village, Tanana, Venetie, Beaver and many other villages. Students from the Interior were flown to and from Sitka by commercial flights each school year.

For years Dr. Chapman, his wife Susan, and daughter Laura had been providing Christian Education, choral work and fellowship for the students who attended church on Sunday morning, plus their normal parochial responsibilities to the local communicants. When they departed, our ministry was to attempt to augment and amplify their efforts, building upon their rock-solid foundation.

One of the more successful projects was a recreation program every Saturday in the parish hall, to which the Edgecumbe stu-

dents were invited for games, dancing, talking and refreshments provided by the parishioners. The students were issued passes to visit Sitka on Baranof Island from Edgecumbe's location on nearby Kruzof Island. The government operated motor launches on frequent schedules and accommodating from 20 to 30 people. From the landing dock it took about 20 minutes to walk to St. Peter's. Rain and snow — and there's a lot of each in Sitka — never deterred these young people from participating in the Saturday "open houses." I soon learned not to worry about ever winning at checkers with any of these young people. I never won a single game!

Another project developed during our tenure was more personalized than the crowded and noisy Saturday afternoon "open houses." We Grumbines now had four children, and the Edgecumbe students, both boys and girls, often coming from large families, missed their siblings. We invited different students to share weekend dinners with us. It proved to be 100 percent reciprocal in that our family learned a great deal about the culture and traditions of the students, their families, and their home villages; the students, in turn, enjoyed home-cooked meals away from the school.

Most of the boys had been trained by

their village priests to serve at the altar, and many wanted to serve at St. Peter's when the opportunity presented itself. The local Sitka boys also liked to serve and had been well trained by Dr. Chapman, so we never lacked for acolytes. The girls also had opportunities to serve in the choir and in the preschool nursery.

A highly successful program of Christian Education occurred every Tuesday night on the Mt. Edgecumbe campus. Mrs. Rose Skannes, now deceased, a communicant of St. Peter's, accompanied me on the shore boats across the water to the school, in foul and fair weather alike. Rose worked with the girls and I with the boys, occasionally switching groups and sometimes meeting together in one large group. Photographs of each of the religious groups were printed in the yearbook, such as Russian Orthodox, Roman Catholic, Presbyterian, Episcopal, etc. The Episcopal group consistently had the largest turnout, numerically, on these Tuesday night "released time" classes, although we were certainly not the largest Christian group. I think the credit for this goes to the village priests who encouraged their teens to participate regularly in Christian Education and weekly worship as well as the social activities. Rose also invited groups of Edgecumbe girls to her Sitka residence and was beloved by everyone.

One year, in the early spring, I received a phone call from the local post office demanding that I proceed to the post office pronto, at once, immediately, and claim a large package that had been sent from the priest at Point Hope in care of me, destined for his dozen students at Mount Edge-

cumbe. When I asked why I needed to pick up the parcel NOW, the clerk said I would smell the contents before I entered the post office. Obliging him, I found that Father Lawton had sent some oogruk which had thawed en route. Enough said!

A highlight each year was the visitation by Bishop Gordon to St. Peter's-by-the-Sea. When I learned his ETA, I would try to get together as many Edgecumbe students as were available, and we would commandeer a few automobiles of local parishioners and drive to the "turnaround." This is where the PBYs of World War II vintage and the Grumman Goose would land in the water, taxi up a concrete ramp and discharge passengers and cargo. When Bishop Gordon deplaned, we'd all yell greetings of welcome and then encircle him with shouts of joy.

I salute the Church in Alaska in its centennial year. I salute the late Rev. Dr. Henry Chapman, my predecessor, and I salute the late Bishop William J. Gordon Jr., who recruited me for Alaska service during his barnstorming visit to my alma mater, Virginia Theological Seminary, in 1951. And I salute each of the 129 Edgecumbe High School students, Indian and Eskimo Americans, who autographed my copy of their yearbook, *The Taheta*. God bless each of you, wherever you may be.

~ Fr. Robert Grumbine

LETTERS TO LOUISE

(These are excerpts from letters written by the Rev. Jules Prevost to his fiancee, later his wife, Louise, during his years as a missionary in the Alaska Interior, beginning in 1891.

28 July 1892: I am very much interested in the people here, and the interest is by no means unappreciated. I am now able to render part of the service in their Native language, and the singing of hymns is all in that tongue. An organ that is coming up this year will do much towards improving the service....Last winter I made a long trip up the Tanana River. It was during the coldest part of the season and the indica-

Fr. Jules L. Prevost served the Alaska missions for 15 years, arriving here in 1891, before the Episcopal Church officially began its Alaska ministry. He is shown here some years after he left Alaska. (Photo by Gilford Photography, Inc., courtesy of Joan Prevost Fortune)

tions on the thermometer danced between 40 and 60 degrees below zero all the while. Yet during all that time, notwithstanding the cold, the only shelter we had, excepting a few days with a cloth canopy overhead, were branches of the spruce laid on the snow for a carpet, and logs arranged at the back and side to protect us from the wind, and a tremendous fire in front which sometimes sent sparks on our canopy and made good-sized skyholes. Although I suffered a little from the cold, on my return I never felt better in my life.

18 Jan. 1893 from Fortymile: I have made a very long trip up the Tanana River, over the mountains, and down again on the Yukon, at the above place. I have met a large number of Indians, and baptized no less than forty during the trip, thus far. I started from St. James' Mission on Dec. 15th, and arrived here only yesterday, making the trip thirty-three days in length. I will rest here about a week and return by another route, which will be still longer. The distance traveled was about 700 miles, and before I reach the Mission the whole distance traveled will have been 1500 miles at least. I did not suffer at all from the cold, and most of the time we camped out in the open air with nothing to shelter us but our blankets. We had no snow, plenty to eat, and our dogs were in good condition. This was a far better trip than that of last year. I was not alone then either; a trader accompanied me, who is on his way out to the States. It is through him I am able to send this letter. We celebrated our Christmas in the open air. A large fire burned before us. A piece of canvas stretched on poles protected us from the wind. We stretched our-

selves out on green spruce boughs, cut for the purpose, and rested comfortably after the day's journey of twenty-five miles....We had besides a good Christmas dinner; the following is the Menu: Dried Salmon, Vermicelli Soup, Fricassee Rabbit, Plum Pudding, Slap-Jacks, Tea, Cocoa, and Snow water. Do you not think this a dinner fit for a king?

(After three years of service in Alaska, Jules Prevost returned to the States to marry, then brought Louise back to the residence at Tanana. In 1900, when his wife was "outside" for health reasons, Prevost wrote her about his first trip to Nome.)

27 May 1900 from Nome: The beach has been free of ice for over a week, and the first boat of the season came in on the 21st. Altogether four boats have come in and I am feasting on eggs at $1.00 per dozen which is cheaper than boarding out at $3.00 per day. Potatoes fresh are only 25 cents per 2 pounds. I am batching it so as to make my living cheaper. I have already secured two lots paid by contributions and hope to raise enough money to start building soon. At present lumber is very high, selling at 50 and 75 cents per foot. I have started a church organization with wardens and vestrymen, and have named it St. Mary's Mission.

11 June 1900 from Nome: I am well. Working hard to enthuse people in the church work. Everyone is up here to make money and has little time for anything else. The people here say the winter was delightful, and surely nothing more could be

expected of the lovely spring which has just passed. But the rainy season has just started in. Very little sickness at present in the camp.

(Addendum from *Cry in the Wilderness*: Prevost made the six hundred-mile journey from Tanana in forty-three days, and his first sight of Nome must have been something to be remembered. Nothing, other than gold, could have caused the building of a city on that spot. There was no harbor or roadstead, no shelter or protection of any kind, and yet Nome became the perfect example of how men of the north could conquer local conditions and bring comfort amid the bleakness and desolation of nature.

When Prevost first arrived, he found a few cabins made from drift logs, and a number of tents....The most colorful tent was made of blue and white stripes, and housed the inevitable bar. The Episcopal priest lost no time in buying lots and setting up a tent church.

Bishop Rowe himself was among the many thousands who came by boat in the summer of 1900, and he helped Prevost build a permanent wooden structure, the first actual church to be erected in Nome. It was closed a few years later, when the population declined. In his stories about the early worship services held there, the Bishop tells that in order to avoid the two feet of mud on the street and "sidewalk" he laid down several stout wooden planks leading to the church doorway. At the end of the service he discovered they had been stolen — wood was that precious a commodity in Nome at that time!)

A Tale of Two Churches

St. Thomas' Church, Point Hope

The first missionary who came to Point Hope in 1890 was Dr. John Driggs. He was a single man, a doctor, and he knew medicine. After living here for 13 years he was ordained to deacon. In 1908 he was sent to Seattle for retirement but later returned to Point Hope and made his home at Cape Lisburne. He died in 1914 and was buried at Cape Lisburne.

The Rev. A.R. Hoare took over Dr. Driggs's work in 1908. The son of an Anglican clergyman, Hoare joined the gold rush in 1898, but, attracted to the work of the Church in Alaska, entered the priesthood. He built the Point Hope mission house and Browning Hall for recreation in 1912. His plans were cut short when he was shot to death by a white man, a teacher.

Archdeacon Goodman arrived in Point Hope in 1925 following a five-year stint by the Rev. W.A. Thomas. The prayer book was translated into Inupiaq. Work in other communities (Kivalina and Point Lay) was thwarted by lack of funds. By 1943, near retirement age, the Archdeacon was in deteriorating health.

A young couple came to Point Hope in 1943, the Rev. William Gordon Jr. and his wife Shirley. Archdeacon William Goodman stepped out of the mission house with two small suitcases and boarded the return flight with Bishop Bentley.

The Rev. William Gordon and Shirley made many friends at Point Hope, also in other coastal villages nearby. He learned to be a dog musher during his stay at Point Hope, using a team of nine or ten dogs on many trips north as far as Point Barrow and south as far as Kotzebue, meeting with lots of people along the coast. In 1948 he became the third Bishop of Alaska, and his headquarters were at Fairbanks. That's where he learned flying an airplane called the "Blue Box" and flew all along the coast and Interior, meeting more friends, baptizing and confirming and having other services of the Church.

The Rev. Howard Laycock came with his wife, Agnete, as successor of Bishop Gordon in 1951. This priest also learned to fly, but the following year, after a visit to Kotzebue, coming home to Point Hope with three passengers, there was a crash landing and all in the airplane were dead.

From time to time a successor came. The Rev. Rowland Cox and his wife Mary took the work at Point Hope, and a young man named Page Kent came to assist. Later the Rev. Al Reiners and the Rev. Bob Jones helped with the services. In 1953 the Rev. Keith Lawton and his wife Jackie came. The local people started helping move St. Thomas' Church and the mission house closer together at the old town site.

The Rev. Walter Hannum and his wife Louise took over for a while, until Donald

Fathers Patrick Attungana and Wilfred Lane administer Holy Communion to Point Hope congregation. "Be not Faithless but believing" exhorts the dramatic reredos of St. Thomas' altar, which depicts Christ revealing His wounds to the apostle Thomas.

Oktollik was ordained deacon, with the help of the Rev. Milton Swan. Donald Oktollik and Clinton Swan were there and were ordained together at Point Hope. The Swans were from Kivalina but helped whenever they could with services at Point Hope.

Services were led by the Rev. Donald Oktollik, and two more men, Herbert Kinneeveauk and Patrick Attungana were ordained as deacons, with the help of Donald Oktollik and Milton Swan. All three were working together there at Point Hope: the Reverends Donald Oktollik, Herbert Kineeveauk and Patrick Attungana.

After the death of the Rev. Herbert Kineeveauk in the late 1970s, Seymour Tuzroyluke Sr. took training. In 1983 he was ordained a deacon, then ordained to the priesthood later in the year. His wife Claudia was a good helper while Seymour was training. After the ordination of Seymour Tuzroyluke, Elijah took training and in 1987 was ordained a deacon and later a priest.

I presented them both to the Bishop for ordination. Now we are looking for a young trainee, but have not had response of any kind here at Point Hope.

The Reverends Seymour Tuzroyluke Sr. and Elijah Attungana are serving at the present time, but Elijah Attungana will have the full work as missionary when Seymour Tuzroyluke retires at the time of our centennial this coming summer.

Sam Rock was the first interpreter and a student of Dr. Driggs, and he learned well, reading the Bible. The first visitor, Kinneevee(a)uk, later the father of the Rev. Herbert Kinneeveauk, was given food by Dr. Driggs, and suddenly the visitors multiplied until there were nine boys there. Sam's Eskimo name (Uuggahguk) means "the rock." He is the grandfather of the Rev. Seymour Tuzroyluke Sr.

Harry Killbear helped the Rev. Augustus Hoare as interpreter. During the Rev. William Thomas's time, interpreters were Harry Killbear, Tony Joule and Ebruluk Rock.

Then came Peel Tooyak, my dad, who, until his death at 43 years of age, served with Archdeacon Goodman and also with the Rev. William Gordon. Andrew Frankson also helped interpret, and Roy Vincent and the late David Frankson interpreted for the Rev. William Gordon. The late Donald Oktollik and the late Milton Swan also served as interpreters.

Milton Swan was ordained a deacon and served Point Hope whenever he came here. Donald Oktollik became a deacon at the same time with Milton Swan. Herbert Kinneeveauk, Patrick Attungana and Clinton Swan were trained as deacons and ordained at the same time. Nelda Werning, although ordained as a deacon, requested release from these vows by Bishop Cochran.

Then Seymour Tuzroyluke Sr. was trained and became a deacon. He has served since 1983 and his retirement is planned for early summer 1995 at the time of our centennial celebration.

Since the death of Patrick Attungana in early 1994, all of the priests, excepting Elijah and the Rev. Clinton Swan, have retired or passed away. Various men now serve St. Thomas' Church.

In the mid-1940s the late Peter Koonooyak and his late wife Annie founded the invocational services which are still held.

They both served God in founding these services, usually holding the services at their home, one of the biggest buildings in Point Hope. Since their death the services have been held at St. Thomas' Church on Sunday evenings.

~ Andrew Tooyak Sr., Layreader
St. Thomas' Church, Pt. Hope

St. Mary's Church, Anchorage

The first service of St. Mary's Mission was held on Nov. 28, 1954 in a garage in the Anchor Homes subdivision with 22 people present. Less than a year later, on property (six and a half acres) donated by Mr. and Mrs. Roger Waldron at the corner of Lake Otis and Tudor roads, land had been cleared and a basement built (Pillsbury Hall), and on Oct. 2, 1955 the first service in the new St. Mary's was held.

The National Church contributed generously, both in loans and outright gifts; many people from near and far away had a hand in making this mission possible, and under the watchful eye of Bishop William J. Gordon and the Rev. Philip Jerauld it was nurtured and it grew.

The church was built over the basement and finished for services by Oct. 12, 1958. A church school building, which was an army surplus Quonset hut, was purchased and moved onto the property, and a parishioner generously donated and installed a furnace in the building. We were now well on the way. A Boy Scout troop was sponsored by St. Mary's, and there was a Women's Guild and an Altar Guild. The Rev. Sandy Zabriskie took over from Father Jerauld in 1958.

Throughout the spring and summer of 1960 members of the parish explored every possible way to remodel, build or purchase a rectory more adequate for the needs of St. Mary's, and so, on the property, with the aid of a $20,000 bequest that had been given to Bishop Gordon for the Church in Alaska and an additional $10,000 from parishioners, a new rectory was built. In 1963 the bell tower was constructed in memory of Roger and Art Waldron.

In March 1964 the largest earthquake ever recorded in North America shook Anchorage. To all who lived here, it is referred to as "the Good Friday Earthquake." On Easter Sunday, March 29, 1964, St. Mary's Church was filled with worshippers from many denominations. Churches in the downtown area were closed due to severe damage, and so St. Mary's became a "meeting place," families and friends "found" each other that glorious day up on the hill at Lake Otis and Tudor. There was no heat in the church, but the warmth was felt, not only from our layers of clothes but from the hearts of people who rejoiced and were thankful.

As the years went by we left our mission status and became, first, an aided parish, then a parish in 1971. In 1967 the first floor of the Christian education building was built, with the second floor completed in 1974. In 1969 Sandy Zabriskie left us for Bethlehem, Pennsylvania, and the Rev. Charles (Chuck) Eddy became our third priest.

In 1972 we were proud of five of our own St. Mary's parishioners who were ordained: Larry Spannagel, Bob Thwing, Jurgen Lilliebjerg, Joe Aprill, and Don

View from St. Mary's sanctuary, 1995 (Photo by Jane Slisco)

Spafford. By 1979 we had grown to the point where a second priest was needed, so Father Bob Nelson joined the staff.

During the 1980s St. Mary's became sponsors of Laotian refugees and continues to be active in this service.

As the years went by we grew and grew. A magnificent new church was constructed in 1990 and dedicated in 1991. Our original church has become a chapel and also houses the administrative offices. The rectory, which has been our office since 1981, when our pastor and his family moved to their own home, will house our first sexton

and the refugee office.

This has all happened on the six and a half acres at the busy corner of Lake Otis and Tudor, a sanctuary whose matchless view allows us to "lift up our eyes unto the hills" as we worship, a beloved church we all call "home."

~ Winnie Nowak
St. Mary's, Anchorage

XI

OUR PEOPLE REMEMBER

This happened long ago. I was just a little girl. Things were different back then. During the summers at fish camp, we stopped the fish wheels Saturday nights, because we never did any work on Sundays. It was the Lord's day and the time to visit the other fish camps. We got word that Bishop Rowe was coming to visit. We walked from our fish camp up to the "Rapids," about 45 miles upriver from the present-day village of Tanana. We always looked forward to Bishop's visit, not only for "Service," but also because Mrs. Rowe would come with him. I remember her being helped off the *Godspeed*. In her arms she had a big pan of homemade cookies. All of us children would line up and we would each get two cookies, a real treat for us. During the service, Bishop Rowe would have all the children stand in a circle. Then he would lay his hands on us and bless each one of us.

Another time, during Bishop's visit, we were having an outdoor service on the bank. Bishop was preaching away when he noticed that people were pointing toward the river. He turned to look and there were caribou crossing the river. We never hunted on Sundays. Bishop Rowe stopped preaching and told us that for this time it would be

"okay" to hunt as long as a feast was made for everyone. Some men went out and killed a caribou. What a big feast we had that day!

~ Pauline Swenson
Tanana

Dolores Bifelt arranges the holy vessels as other members of the Junior Altar Guild observe at Good Shepherd Mission, Huslia, circa 1963. (Photo courtesy of Connie Keller)

The first church in Huslia was a combination school, community hall and church built with considerable financial support from Bishop Gordon in the early fifties. The village of Huslia was relocated from Old Town which was at the junction of the Huslia and Koyukuk rivers and which was regularly flooded out in the spring. The Bishop encouraged the village to move downriver and promised to provide a building if they did.

Arlene Chatterton, a nurse evangelist, lived in the original rectory before Pat arrived as the first resident vicar in 1956. George Glanders, a Church Army captain, did the cabinet work in it. He and Chat, as Arlene was known, were later married.

In the church itself the pole altar was built by Johnny Isaacs and used first in the multipurpose building before the church was built in the summer of 1959, then it was moved to the new church. The altar guild did the superfrontal of unsmoked moosehide with the Sanctus in beautiful beadwork. There are many still in Huslia who worked on it; Catherine Attla was the prime mover.

The new rectory was built in 1959, the church the following year. The United Thank Offering paid for the milled lumber, windows, and other things. The crew working on it was all local. There was a very active junior altar guild as well as acolytes, 1956-63. Visits by the Bishop were very important. He always brought a movie, doughnuts and pop for the village and fresh fruit and vegetables for the Kellers.

Our years in Huslia were very important for us then and now.

~ Connie Keller (Mrs. Pat Keller)

Parishioners of St. James the Fisherman, Kodiak, were puzzled on the first Sunday of 1993 when they arrived for service and discovered the processional cross was missing from its appointed place. Speculation was that it may have been taken for a scavenger hunt or a New Year's Eve prank. Senior Warden Susan Oliver and interim priest Fran Ray hesitated to say it had been stolen. It just wasn't there.

A frantic search was made throughout the church. The police were notified. Everyone was upset, as Bishop Charleston was to make his annual visit the following Sunday. There was a feeling of sadness and confusion that something like this could happen. A substitute cross was fashioned from an old altar cross. We could still rejoice in the services of baptism and confirmation with the Bishop.

But—blessing of all blessings — the following Saturday morning, there was the cross among snow shovels and brooms, upside down but unharmed. Only one small scratch was found. On Bishop Charleston's arrival, he was greeted with the good news: "The cross has been found!" It

was a happy visitation. It is presumed that someone "borrowed" the cross for a week. We were just happy to have it back.

~ Beverly Horn
Kodiak

Our daughter, Christine, was born in early May 1966. At the end of the month the Archbishop of Central Africa, Francis Oliver Green-Wilkinson, came with Bishop Gordon to visit us in Minto, and the Archbishop baptized Christine. That was when Zambia and Alaska were partners in mission, in the days of the Mutual Responsibility and Interdependence program in the Church. Meeting the Archbishop in Minto led to our visiting his diocese in 1970. Christine and her sister, Carole, were four and two and had many friends in the rural village of Chipili where we lived and helped with services and education in the church for three months. Shortly after our return to Alaska,

"Bishop Oliver" was tragically killed in an automobile accident. Joyce and I treasure our memories of him and of the people of Zambia.

~ The Rev. Dale Sarles

My mother told me this funny (but scary to her) incident. I was born in Hudson Stuck Memorial Hospital in Fort Yukon. One day she heard this commotion and the nurses whispering, "It's time to feed the babies and Irene is not in the nursery." They ran to Dr. Burke's office to report me missing, only to find Dr. Burke holding and rocking me. Mama said the nurses really scolded him.

The Hudson Stuck Memorial Hospital at Fort Yukon during high water in the late 1940s

I remember a time when Bishop Bentley arrived in Circle from Fort Yukon by boat; I believe it was his last trip. I was confirmed at that time. My grandfather William Moses presented Lena Joseph, William Joseph and my mother, Lucy Roberts. The Bishop said if we did not see each other again we'd meet again on the other side. A little boy thought the Bishop meant "across the river" and wondered out loud, "Why are we going across the river?"

And who could forget the story Bishop Harris told about people asking him, "How's the Bishop?" and Bishop Harris said, "I'm fine." The people said, "No, we mean Bishop Gordon."

~ Irene E. Roberts-Bogenrife
Holy Trinity, Circle, & St.
Matthew's, Fairbanks

Barrow, the most northerly village in the State of Alaska, was the beginning of my ministry in what was to become a lifelong friendship and commitment to the Natives of Barrow and other villages up and down the Arctic Cost.

On occasions when the Presbyterian minister was visiting neighboring villages, I was asked by the elders to conduct their services. This prompted a long-distance phone call to Bishop Cochran asking permission to preach, since I was only a licensed layreader. Over the course of a year Bishop had a sizable collection of my sermons. The Episcopalians and Presbyterians worshipped in the Utkeagvik Presbyterian Church in Barrow.

While there in Barrow under the direction of Bishop Cochran, Dr. Richard Wayne held a healing service every month. A confirmation class, with four girls dressed in their best jeans and white veils I had made for them, was presented to Bishop Cochran. The girls' grandfathers (two families) had urged their faithful attendance at the confirmation classes held in my home once a week.

When we left Barrow we were transferred to King Salmon. We found there were nine Episcopalians stationed in the area, so we started the first congregation ever in King Salmon, holding Evening Prayer and healing services twice a month, again at my home.

When my husband died I had to leave the weather service quarters, so I moved to Anchorage and seriously pursued my ministry. I was ordained a perpetual Deacon June 1, 1984. I continue to serve at the Anchorage Native Medical Center in Anchorage on 24-hour call with Father Norman Elliott. Included in my ministry is geriatrics, so I am the Episcopal Chaplain at Our Lady of Compassion Care Center, Anchorage, also on 24-hour call.

From Betty's journal: "Bush Wife" - June 14, 1977: Holding Holy Communion in the "Bush" is quite an experience. Father Keith Lawton from Kotzebue was in Barrow representing Bishop David Cochran at the Inupiat Circumpolar Conference. After being given many directions he happened upon my husband in the Stuaqpak and was sent to see me where I worked. He seemed a somewhat frail priest, in spite of his backpack and trapper's hat. It wasn't until he preached that Sunday that I saw his strength

as a person and the ease with which he spoke of profound experiences. Later, when we shared a moose roast and discussed the services still to come, I found him easy to talk with. We had a baptism too, and I assisted in the services, improvising the linens and vestments and holy vessels for communion. This service was very meaningful. Father Lawton knew the many Eskimos present as he traveled frequently among their villages. We also held a healing service with both of us and all the communicants participating.

~ Deacon Betty Lou Anthony

On Friday nights at the Nenana mission, the students were allowed to dance in the entrance hall of the dormitory, with 78 rpm records on a wind-up phonograph. The majority of the students were girls, so any boys visiting from town were welcome, but most of the time the girls danced with each other. The mission was in charge of Deaconess Thompson, a petite lady who supervised the teachers and a nurse. After I married, my wife and I were about the same age as the Episcopal minister, Robert Reid and his wife Suzanne, and due to mutual interest became involved in the young people's group that included the marshal, George Sullivan and his wife Margaret. Of course Jack and Bob Coghill were in the group too.

The mission had its share of tragedies along the way. Robert Reid drowned in a boating accident in the fall of 1947 along with Enoch Tooyak from Point Hope and Teddy, oldest son of the mission's maintenance man, Fred Mueller. One winter there was a house fire at the minister's house in which his family lost their baby.

The flood of 1948 was one of the worst in many years. During the flood the Tanana River changed its course and cut through what was known as the Mission Slough. The erosion was tremendous. As the point was going to wash away, the church building was moved in to the town of Nenana and the Bishop's House was dismantled with the idea of rebuilding it further inshore. Before that could be done the point had eroded away and taken the new foundation with it. In the summer of 1961 the erosion reached the dormitory building, and half of it was washed downstream.

~ Virgil Patterson

The article (in *The Alaskan Epiphany*) about the Koyukuk flood saddened me deeply. Many emotions and memories remain with me from the years I lived with the wonderful people of Allakaket and Alatna (1966-69). Everyone in town included my family as part of the community, treating us with warmth and respect. As a nurse, I can truly say that the best job I ever held was working as a volunteer R.N. in the village under the auspices of the Alaska Public Health Service.

Several memories of Allakaket stand out in my mind. The first involved Jim's many winter trips. I soon learned that one of the men in the village regularly checked my wood supply and quietly brought wood into the mission house to keep the wood box full. Someone else checked to make sure the boys and I had adequate water. These kind gestures spoiled me.

Another memory was the November day we brought our second son home from the Fairbanks hospital. We were met at the Allakaket airstrip by many people of the village. In the blink of an eye, Lydia Bergman bundled David (the new baby) warmly in her arms and, along with our first son, Tom, disappeared on a snowmobile. Jim and I walked home to find the boys in the house surrounded by our friends. The wood stove was going strong and the mission house was warm and comfortable.

One of my favorite memories of village life in Allakaket is the time I photographed the bell of St. John's-in-the-Wilderness. I used a short ladder to climb onto the church roof and then crawled up the slope to the bell tower. Perched in a rather awkward position and refusing to consider the possibility of falling, I snapped pictures of the bell. Since I was in a position to see the village from a different perspective, I also took photos of "uptown" and "downtown." I descended from the roof content with the snapshots taken but not understanding at the time the real significance of the bell photo in my life. To this day I carry the picture of St. John's bell in my Bible. Almost every Sunday I glance at this photo and remember. Regardless of the time of day, when Jim or someone would ring the church bell, everyone in town would gather at church. It is interesting that the old church was the only building to survive the water. There certainly is a message in this! Did this unique bell also manage to hold fast?

Allakaket people touched the lives of many individuals and will continue to do so as rebuilding occurs. Thank you, Allakaket and Alatna, for your love and my many memories. I still try to respond to Christ's bell when it rings.

~ Harriet Bills McClish

When Amelia Hill was in charge of the church at Allakaket, my parents went to church every Sunday. I remember when they were passing the offering pan I put

The renowned bell at St. John's-in-the-Wilderness, Allakaket. The inscription: "O ye Frost and Cold, Bless ye the Lord, Praise Him and magnify Him forever." (Photo courtesy of Harriet McClish)

money in and wanted to get change back, but my parents wouldn't let me.

As a little boy I was amazed at how the church worked in harmony. I learned to read the Bible from Pat Keller and the Bible school teachers. Everything was better when we had a priest in the village, which we don't anymore.

~ Thomas M. Henry

One Christmas in the early 1950² the young bachelor priest at Tanacross burned the old log rectory down while trying to thaw his water pipes. Bishop Gordon called Joe (Aprill) and said, "Go down there, get a list of all materials we'll need to rebuild it this spring. We have to get the building materials across the Tanana before the ice goes out." We had always gone to Tanacross as layreaders. The following May I went down with our two young sons and lived there during the last ten days of construction.

The women of the village often came by to visit and talk. The chief's wife always wore an orange coat, bright red scarf and deep fuschia dress, and we could see her coming. The bachelor priest was a jokester. He saved some July Fourth firecrackers until he knew all the old ladies were in the little wickiup they used for their steam baths. He rounded up some of the older boys and they sneaked up behind the sauna and lit the cherry bombs off. Naked female flesh rushed out and scattered everywhere. This same priest was later known to throw the Elliotts' wedding suitcases out of their sec-ond-story window, and was alleged to have

been responsible for cops showing up at St. Matthew's, Fairbanks, for the Zabriskies' wedding. How that priest would laugh and rock back and forth in his chair when he'd come home and tell us about his latest antics.

While Joe was working in Anchorage the Rev. Sandy Zabriskie appointed him sexton of St. Mary's. He had wanted to go into the ministry, but without college behind him he couldn't tackle seven years college and seminary. But then Canon 8 allowed training for non-stipendiary priests. Several fellows trained with Chuck Eddy, Don Hart, and Norman Elliott as their mentors. We met monthly with all the wives for potluck. What a wonderful family we became! Joe was ordained deacon in August 1972, with Jorgen Lilliebjerg, and we retired to Anchor Point, where he became the itinerant priest of the Peninsula. After his ordination in 1973 he was the priest in Kenai, Homer and Seward. For his ordi-nation, St. Mary's, Anchorage, chartered a flight and arrived with 21 people. Fifteen years later, Joe celebrated in St. Augustine's Church,

Homer. Homer and Kenai both had their own church buildings going. Joe carried his communion set, Prayer Book, Bible, etc., in a large satchel, along with cruets for water and wine and a small box of linens. I acted

Annie Vent of Huslia holds daughter Susie Ann following the baby's baptism at Huslia, 1953, with seminarian Don Gardner and Annie's ten-year-old son Floyd beside her. (Archives of the Episcopal Church)

as a one-woman altar guild. Our motto was "Have cup, will travel!" Joe served the Lord for 18 years.

We always enjoyed the bishops' visits so much. David and Mary Cochran slept in our house in the days when the bathroom didn't have a ceiling. Once, later, Bishop Harris, in a rented car, entered the curve of our driveway a little too fast and hit a tree. After that we always called it The Bishop's Tree.

~ Elisabeth D. Aprill

I was about 14 years old when Mr. Files came to our church in Huslia. We were up at Little Peter's Camp, and Mr. Files came in his boat and held services right on the beach.

~ Annie Vent
Good Shepherd, Huslia

It was a cold winter day in 1956 as I sat in my office at All Saints Church in Anchorage, waiting for Annie and Dick Demming to come in from Palmer. I was worried. The roads were covered with ice made more hazardous by freezing rain. The Demmings were a young couple then, driving in to have their baby son baptized because there was no Episcopal church in the Matsu Valley.

I had called their home — no answer. I thought, "Maybe they will turn back; the drive is too dangerous." In those days the road between Palmer and Anchorage was a curvy two-lane highway with the challenge

of the Eagle River hill to be climbed before you could make it into Anchorage.

In my mind were all sorts of dire thoughts: their car off the road or stuck — an accident, maybe. But to my relief I looked out the window and saw them pulling in. Even after the baptism I was still upset. "We've got to do something about this. You people in the valley need your own church," I said with some emotion. Annie replied, "There are other Episcopalians in our area. Maybe it is time we did something about it, but when?" I said, "How about next week?" They both responded with, "It's a deal!" And that is how St. Bartholomew's in the valley came into being!

~ The Rev. Malcolm H. Miner

I remember my Dad, Wilson Sam, leading the gospel singing with his beautiful voice. Carla (Vent) Saunders and I used to stand behind him and be his backup singers. I remember when everyone in town used to go to church and rejoice. I remember crying at friends' weddings and baptisms or saying goodbye to friends at funerals. When I think about it, almost all the important things as I was growing up happened to me in church. My earliest memory is when I used to take a hymn book or prayer book and pretend I could read it, when really I had memorized most of it.

My Dad taught me that as long as I trust God I'll make the right decisions in my life. He always made church exciting for me. I still love to listen to him sing and

pray. He's a wise man, because he's been through a lot and he believes in God.

~ Cesa Sam
Good Shepherd, Huslia

I remember visits of the Presiding Bishops of the Episcopal Church, beginning with Bishop Lichtenberger. And the visit of Bishop John Hines for Point Hope's glorious celebration of their 75th anniversary in 1965. During the feast and dancing at St. Thomas', the Rev. Donald Oktollik stood up and rapped on the wall for attention and said, "Listen, everybody! The plastic fork and knife we just gave you must last until you go home." I doubt Bishop Hines had ever had to keep track of a plastic fork and knife for two days and three more meals!

I remember the hushed audience as Tony Joule spoke during the celebration. He told of the early school and church and the people who were sent to live and be a part of his people's lives, when his aspirations were to be a teacher too.

I remember the group that went with me that morning in Point Hope as we walked out to the coast and moved a little ice aside and brushed our teeth in the Chukchi Sea.

The town was full of tourists from all over the states and England and Japan. We slept on any available floor. I came home late after the opening night of the feast and dancing, walking around the village in the bright sunlight of midnight and seeing people I knew from times they were in the hospital in Anchorage or attending meetings with me in other parts of Alaska.

Martha Swan

I remember a choir of Eskimo voices singing the "Hallelujah Chorus" a capella during the church service. St. Thomas' Church was full far beyond capacity. I remember the thunder of the voices as they praised God and gave thanks. I remember Milton Swan celebrating the Eucharist in his wonderful singing voice. To have attended a Eucharist celebrated by Milton Swan was to experience the presence of Christ. In the natural rhythm of the chant and with singleness of purpose he carried all others along with him.

I remember Martha Swan, the most remarkable woman I would ever know. I first met her at a Denali Convocation meeting in Seward. She was so tickled when they served delicious baked halibut cheeks, with the new plastic lemons. While squeezing the lemon a stream of liquid squirted in whatever direction she aimed it. She brought us all to a oneness in this moment

of her discovery and fun. She would bring a oneness many times in the years to come in the gathering of our Churchwomen.

Another time, Martha was staying with us during one of the clergy wives' conferences in Anchorage. A part of every meeting of that sort was an "evening out" with Bishop Gordon hosting the group for a movie. In town it would be at a local theater; in the bush it would be one he brought with him. This particular night it was Richard Burton in *Hamlet* at the Fourth Avenue Theater. Next morning when Martha was asked about the movie, she said, "It is a long show to tell a short story. Too many words."

Martha and Milton Swan were two of the most unforgettable people I have ever had the privilege to call my friends. Martha taught Milton to read and write; she taught him so well that he became our first Eskimo priest on June 17, 1964.

Once after Martha went back to Kivalina she wrote and told me she was making me a special gift. A year or two later Milton went in to Fairbanks for a Missionary District Convocation and was very concerned when he realized he had lost a package on the plane. Bishop Gordon had someone take Milton out to the Blue Box II where Milton found the package. It was a brown paper bag that had been rolled down so many times the top of the bag felt like velvet. Back at St. Matthew's he found me and gave me the bag. I was surprised, as I hadn't thought of Martha's letter since it had first come, and now Milton was smiling at me, waiting for me to open Martha's gift. I did and found inside a most precious article — a loons' neck purse of black and white

feathers, with white sealskin bottom and drawstring area, all lined in silk. Milton told me Martha shot the loons and cured the necks with the feathers intact. I have never before or since had such a wonderful gift. Then Milton told me the Eskimo legend of the whaling captain and the loon and the pearl necklace the loon wears until this day.

I visited the Alaska Native Service Hospital in Anchorage once a week for eleven years and met many wonderful friends. It is hard to think of these times and not remember Lewis Hodgkins, a priest at All Saints, whose ministry included the hospital pastoral care. His untiring visits and Eucharist services Sunday nights were well attended. Lewis prepared patients for confirmation and sometimes had baptisms. He always had a good congregation of Episcopalians, but if Bishop Gordon was there you could be sure the large room would be full and the conversations later on as long as each person wanted to offer greetings to the Bishop and hear any news he had of their village. I don't think you can mention often enough the rapport the peoples of Alaska had with the third Bishop of Alaska. Bishop Gordon was gifted and could speak with intimacy about each person's family and village. He could be trusted to deliver any message sent through him to families in whatever village. He rarely came to Anchorage that he did not call at the hospital, usually checking with Lew Hodgkins or me to see if there was anything he should know before visiting. I went on many of these visits, and the most remarkable part of the visit was the closing prayer — always very personal, including the concerns of the moment in the hospital and a comprehensive, loving and intimate prayer for the loved ones at home and the problems they were facing. Always a prayer off the top of his head and personal.

These were the heavy years of tuberculosis in the interior of Alaska. Nearly all families were touched by this disease and separated from families for months and even years. For us in Anchorage it was a time to serve the Church and a time to know our fellow Alaskans. Their stay was long enough that we could get to know them and their families. Their confinement to one shared room was such an adjustment for them, but their corner of that ward did become a home, containing the treasures they brought with them or had received while in the hospital.

I read *Time* magazine to Larry Mayo, a delightful young man who was blind and waiting patiently for corneal transplants. His situation was brought to the attention of the Alaska Democratic delegation and the presidential candidate, John F. Kennedy. When Mr. Kennedy kicked off the opening of his presidential campaign in 1961 in Anchorage, he sent the flowers from the head table to this young man in the Alaska Native Service Hospital.

I remember Ivan Titus, a patient for a long time after a terrible accident left him a paraplegic. The hospital did a wonderful job of rehabilitating this extraordinary man.

I remember when Tom Tull was in Fort Yukon, filling out grant forms and preparing the community for a large multipurpose community building that would house a gym, meeting rooms, a place for showers, and a coin laundry. Thinking of Tom, I remember his trip to Anchorage with the Fort Yukon Boy Scout troop. They traveled by plane to Fairbanks, train to Anchorage, and cars to the camping area in the Matanuska Valley. The boys lived in various homes or in the basements of churches as they traveled.

Walter Hannum and Murray Trelease always remind me of the Yukon Valley Training Center where many of the leaders in the Church in Alaska received their training. Walter was a hard master, seeking the best from everyone and usually receiving it.

I remember Elsie Pitka and her energy. She worked for the school in Beaver, was the village nurse, and the layreader in the church. She was and is one of God's shining lights. One can always meet Christ through Elsie. Once when I was in Beaver I met one of her Godsons. She had spent the spring teaching him to run a trapline. He was so proud of all she had taught him. She, like Martha Swan, is one of the most remarkable women I have ever known.

Elsie's husband Elman came to the Anchorage hospital with TB. He looked terrible, tired, pale, and surely not happy to be there. The following day Bishop Gordon came to town on business. He called me and I told him about Elman. He asked me to pick him up, which I did, and we went together to the hospital. Elman was so happy to see the Bishop and told us they were sending a plane for him to go home as his TB tests had come back positive. As soon as he landed in Beaver he went out with his dog sled to clear his trap lines, about an 80-mile trip. He made it back to the village just in time for the return trip to Anchorage. I saw him just after his return and, although he was absolutely exhausted, he already looked better for having taken care of his important business back home.

I remember the amazing story of Ida Edwards of Beaver, a story she shared with the Denali Convocation about 1963. She told of her journey in life which included a walk from Barrow over the Brooks Range to the Yukon River and Beaver. She was a young girl and had a child along the way. It was like a Jack London story of adventure, danger, catastrophe, and death, a story bigger than life. Alaska is what it is because of people like Ida who were here long before any of us cheechakos.

Many leaders came to Alaska as convocation speakers. I remember Estelle Carver, who introduced us to St. Paul, a man she knew well! I remember Reuel Howe, who met us in Juneau and led us in a discovery of communication and words. And Claxton Monroe from Texas, who led us in an awareness of who we were as individuals. And Bishop Ralph Dean, executive officer of the Anglican Communion. He spoke to us in Fairbanks about Vietnam and our role in the greater Church around the world. And Verna Dozier who challenged our knowledge of Christ in our lives. And the list goes on. In the years since I left Alaska I have come to realize what a difference those meetings made in my life.

I sat with the Rt. Rev. John Bentley in 1985 as he reminisced about his first trip to Alaska and his relationship with Bishop Rowe and the Rev. John Chapman in Anvik, where Bishop Bentley went as a layman. How he was ordained a deacon by Bishop Rowe in the church at Anvik. Here is a man who quotes Bishop Rowe, a man who knew him very well. He also knew and worked with the Rev. John Chapman, the Rev. Henry Chapman, Archdeacon Goodman and many others. It is good to have these memories of Bishop Bentley's on tape. (Editor's note: Billie shared transcriptions of her tapes with us, and Bishop Bentley's recollections form significant portions of this book.)

~ Billie Williams
(Mrs. Quin Williams)

I remember the days when the Rev. Don Hart and his wife Betty were in Huslia. The church was so full of life and worship. Lay people have kept our church active for about 20 years. Here in Huslia our hope is that one of us will be ordained priest.

~ Maudy Sommer
Good Shepherd, Huslia

When I was 12 years old and living in Stockbridge, Massachusetts, I heard wonderful stories of a faraway place which, unknown to me, was destined to become my home. These were told by Bishop Rowe, who in 1919 visited George G. Merrill, the rector of St. Paul's in Stockbridge. Dog sledding was not the style of transportation employed by Episcopal bishops in Massachusetts in 1919 and, indeed, it's not what is generally used by Episcopal bishops in Alaska circa 1995; but Alaska in the early 1900s was a different place. It was a place Bishop Rowe knew and I was able to imagine through the exotic stories he told.

He wasn't the only missionary whose influence I felt. As a young woman considering nurse's training, I met Gertrude Selzer, who had served in China and was instrumental in my choice of St. Luke's Episcopal Hospital in New York City for training. It was her alma mater and eventually became mine as well. While at the hospital, I attended the lovely chapel daily with the other students. Certain services, however, were held at the Cathedral of St. John the Divine, located less than a block away. So many years later, I can still visualize us in navy blue capes over nurses' uniforms marching down to our pews.

My husband Arthur and I lived in Hewlett, Long Island, where, during World War II, I taught nurses' aides for the Red Cross. One of the visiting lecturers was Mrs. Grafton Burke, whose husband was founder of the Hudson Stuck Memorial Hospital in Fort Yukon. Her reminiscences were so compelling that when I repeated them to my husband, we decided to move to Alaska.

After we had lived in Anchorage for two years, we moved to Homer back when there was no road. Living without a road out was a very new experience for me, but perhaps one that somewhat approached what Bishop Rowe had described to me all those years ago. Bishop Gordon had his first communion and baptism service in our living room in Homer in 1949. From my childhood

in Stockbridge until my retirement in Juneau, the Episcopal Church has always played a major role in my life.

~ Natalie Hewlett
Holy Trinity, Juneau

Although my father, Paul Mather, was always involved in church work in Metlakatla and Ketchikan, when he was asked by Bishop Rowe if he would accept the "call," he hesitated to respond until he had discussed it with my mother, Emma. With seven children still at home, his wage of $250 a month as a millwright at a local mill was hardly enough to support his family. He knew that ministers' salaries were even less. However, mother persuaded him to answer the "call," reminding him of the Bible story of Jonah and the whale. Father became the first Native deacon in 1927 and priest in 1932. He served St. Elizabeth's

St. Elizabeth's, Ketchikan

Episcopal Church for 15 years. He died in January 1942. During his charge, the church had the largest church school in Alaska; all-native council or vestry, Altar Guild, Ladies' Guild, senior and junior choirs, Acolytes' Guild, Ushers' Guild, Girls Friendly Society, Young People's Fellowship, Layreaders, and a Boys' Band. Paul Mather spoke the Tsimshian and English languages fluently. Bishop Rowe referred to St. Elizabeth's as his pride and joy.

~ Gertrude Mather Johnson,
St. Elizabeth's Mission, Ketchikan

I was born in Ketchikan and baptized in St. Elizabeth's there, where my grandfather, Robert Ridley, was a layreader, reading the Bible and speaking it in Tsimshian. I was so proud of him. Then in 1940 we lived in Sitka and I was confirmed by Bishop Rowe. He made us study, study, study! I will always remember his hands on my head and the wonderful blessing as I knelt at the altar that day.

~ Mildred Enloe
St. Peter's-by-the-Sea, Sitka

My memories of Alaska go back to the day Allen and I were married in St. Mark's Mission, Nenana in November 1938. Allen had made nuptial arrangements with Bishop Bentley for our marriage upon my arrival. It was a ten-day trip via Alaska Steamship from Seattle to Seward and a three-day train ride from Seward to Nenana. When the train approached the depot, I could see a good-sized crowd awaiting me — Bishop,

Mission children and townsfolk, all dressed in parkas and mukluks — and dogs and sled. Bishop Bentley invited me to ride to the Mission on the dog sled, and I did. Mrs. Bentley had prepared supper for us, but first I was treated to a nice warm tub bath. Those who have traveled the coal trains understand how much a bath was needed. Shortly after supper we four walked in the snow to the chapel. The Mission staff, Deaconess Thompson, Miss Blacknall, and Miss Bartberger, and the Mission children were present for the vow-taking. I remember the children's eyes were filled with awe. After the ceremony Allen and I trudged through the snow in minus 35 degree weather to our humble little log cabin. Bishop wrote my mother in Oregon about our wedding service and ended his letter by saying, "The moon was big and bright in the sky, but I'm sure they didn't even notice it." I appreciated so much the special attention Bishop and Mrs. Bentley gave me to make my stay in Alaska enjoyable.

Bishop conducted Sunday evening services in various homes. He had the great respect of the village people as well as the town folks. Social and community life revolved around the Mission.

While Allen was away, working aboard the steamer *Nenana*, the Bentleys would often invite me to their lovely lodge for meals, and during the summer on picnics aboard the boat *Godspeed*. They were so special to me. After their departure from Nenana, the village was never the same. It was a sad day for all when the Mission was closed and the staff departed.. The entire Mission staff were an exemplary group,

warm and friendly, tending painstakingly to the buildings and grounds, a show place, a place where one was proud to take out-of-town guests to visit.

Even more sad was the summer the Tanana River overflowed its banks and took buildings and land downstream. The M.V. *Tanana* was coming upstream at this time, and Allen, who was on watch, observed a huge object coming toward the vessel. Pilot house crew grabbed field glasses to watch and were shocked to see a large building approaching — the Mission dormitory! The Bishop's Lodge had been dismantled earlier, log for log, and sold. Even the land where the Mission stood was washed downstream. Now we have only memories!

~ Mrs. Allen E. (Alvina) Brown

After moving to Alaska I was involved in a stressful legal battle and had some bad weeks, then a letter from a friend urged me to "go to St. Christopher's." She herself had moved to Indiana but deeply missed her Anchorage church. My earlier experiences with organized churches had left me unsatisfied, but I followed my friend's advice. When I walked into St. Christopher's and participated in my first Episcopal service, I knew I had found a home. I have since become a member of Christ Church, Anchorage, and my feelings about the Episcopal Church remain the same. I think Bishop Charleston best summed it up at a Convention service when he said, "We don't care if you say the prayers the same way or sing the song to the same tune — we love you anyway. COME ON IN!" That, to me, is the strength of the Episcopal Church: we can allow individuality under a common whole and not demand that everyone follow the exact "cookie cutter" mentality to be a welcome member of the Church. And we say to all the world, "We love you — COME ON IN!"

~ Judy Blair

Now who on earth do you suppose could have been responsible for the appearance of a moose head in the bed of housemother Martha Webb at St. Mark's Mission, Nenana, in the early 1950s?

~ One Who Knows

Thank you, Diocese of Alaska, for gathering up my little family into the Family of God's People. On April 28, 1977 I flew from California to Chalkyitsik with my son, Benjamin, who was three and a half. And on April 29 I married Randall Jones, the high school teacher in the village. Our wedding was the last service in the "old" St. Timothy's — in fact, two days later, the windows were removed and hauled to the new church building.

I have thanked David Salmon before, and I thank him forever for "marrying" me into the Episcopal Church. That windy, slushy, holy April 29th was the pivotal day in my life, turning my path back to God. And St. Timothy's, filled with Chalkyitsik people, will always be in my heart wherever I am in the world, wherever my path goes.

Exactly two years later, April 29, 1979,

our daughter Claire was born. It seemed just right that she should appear on our own holy day. In Fairbanks that summer, we met David Salmon at St. Matthew's for Claire's private baptism, but the sacristy key was not to be found. With a smile, David scrambled down the river bank, returning with a container of Chena water and promising to make Claire into a "real little Alaskan." Sarah and Minnie stood as her godmothers.

After two years in Deering, we returned to Fairbanks and St. Matthew's. One Sunday after church, Father Don Hart asked if I could help him out in the office for a month or so until he hired a parish secretary, saying I could keep new baby Matthew with me there in a crib. I did. I stayed three happy years in the office, knowing that place was exactly where I was supposed to be.

From Fairbanks to Kotzebue to Austin, Texas, where I now live, my path went. When Randall died of a sudden heart attack November 19, 1991, at age 44, it was the train wreck of my life. I think I might have died too if I had not already been gathered up into the Church. I knew I needed to do something special to honor the sacredness we felt in our marriage and to honor Randall's deep love of Alaska. And so, part of his ashes are here, tucked into the rock garden at the side of St. George's, Austin; and part of his ashes were lovingly scat-

tered in the Chena by Father Scott Fisher, into the spring breakup, on our holy day, our wedding anniversary, April 29th.

Thank you, people of St. Timothy's and St. Matthew's, you have enriched my life forever. I am still with you.

~ Bonita (Bonnie) Snyder-Jones

I remember taking a group of students from UAF, following final exams in May/June 1970, to Minto. Sister Judy (Morin) and I had been asked by Bishop Gordon to help move the church from old

The last service held in the old St. Timothy's Mission at Chalkyitsik was the marriage ceremony of teacher Randall Jones and Bonita Snyder in April 1977. Left to right: Best man Karl Flaccus, groom Randy Jones, Bonita's son Benjamin, Bonita (Bonnie), Fr. David Salmon, and bridesmaid Lilly Herbert. (Photo courtesy of Bonita Snyder-Jones)

Minto to New Minto, and the Bishop helped fly us out.

There was a wedding and potlatch on the first night. I remember a debate taking place at the potlatch over whether a Native ought to be marrying a white soldier from "outside," and what this meant for the village and the Native culture. There was a cacophony of sound later as traditional drummers and dancers competed with electric guitars and rock and roll.

I remember a peat fire at the airport that we tried to contain through the night. We slept in the old mission house and I spent late nights learning from a deeply spiritual priest, Tom Kehayes.

I remember raking and cleaning up around the old village church, wanting to be helpful. And then Peter John, who had been watching me for several hours, called me over and asked, "Why are you doing this? The old village is going to be empty soon. Leave it alone and come sit with me. You work too much." It was true. I worked too much with things that weren't important. From that point on I spent most of my time sitting and listening to him and others, despite Bishop Gordon's original orders to "move that old church."

~ The Rev. Bob Nelson

The Bentleys were at our Outgoing Missionary Orientation conference in Greenwich, Connecticut in 1963, when Bishop Bentley was head of the Overseas Department of the National Church (Alaska was still classified as "overseas" at that time, four years after statehood). Knowing they had lived in Nenana, where we were headed, I was eager to talk with them. Mrs. Bentley was the epitome of gracious Southern womanhood, and it was hard to picture her in the rough-and-ready Alaska environment I imagined. Sitting beside her at dinner, I said, "You were in Nenana, Mrs. Bentley; did you like it?" She smiled kindly and said in her quiet voice, "If I had not, do you think I would have stayed for 17 years?"

~ Carol Phillips

It was a blown tire on the station wagon Bishop Gordon and Gordon Charlton had driven to Eagle that led to this saga. No such tire could be found in either the Village or the Town of Eagle. So, Bishop got on the radio and raised Norman Elliott in Fort Yukon. Would he look about? Sure enough, Norm found a tire and flew it down in the little yellow Piper Cub some of his friends had come to call affectionately "The Drunken Canary." He landed safely on the old parade grounds alongside the town church and mission house. The tire fit, and, in time, Norm prepared to take his leave. Up the gradual slope of the parade ground he maneuvered, the better to get a running start. He gunned the engine, but before he was halfway to the banks of the Yukon, he realized he didn't have quite enough speed to get airborne. He remembered an instructor's counsel that if, for example, a moose should cross the runway and he needed to avoid it, he might drop the flaps and at least jump the moose, even if he did not actually get airborne. Being already past "the point of no return," Norm figured, "Why not?" Sure enough, the plane lurched into the air, the dipping wing almost decapitating Bishop Gordon and Gordon Charlton, who were last seen diving into the high grass as the plane righted itself and dropped out of sight. At first no one knew whether it had plunged into the river or what. Then, as Bishop and Gordon scrambled to their feet, the "Drunken Canary" reappeared, wobbling along just above the water on its way back to Fort Yukon.

As it happened, Norman was scheduled to come to Eagle for an assignment soon

Father Norman Elliott and "The Drunken Canary," 1957

thereafter. Shortly upon his return to Fort Yukon (he did make it back!) he received a letter, penned as if from the good people of Eagle, saying they awaited his "soon return to Eagle with great anticipation, hoping that it would be accompanied by such miracles as had his recent departure, when:

- a mute villager shouted out loud,
- a lame man leapt into the air;
- and an avowed atheist cried out, 'My God!'"

~ Mark Boesser

In 1954, after Jan Waldron was born, her Dad, Roger Waldron, began going to church again after a period of 13 years. During that time church was all right for the rest of the family, but Roger was inclined to show up only on special occasions such as weddings and baptisms. Soon we were all going to church as a family every Sunday.

The following Lent I attended a communion service at All Saints' Church. During the prayers the priest, the Rev. Philip E. Jerauld, prayed for guidance in establishing a new mission and especially for acquiring some land. Call it a vision if you like, but suddenly I thought of our hillside on the homestead. On the way out of church I mentioned the fact that our hillside would be a beautiful spot for a church. Later I told Roger about mentioning my thoughts to Fr. Jerauld; lucky I did, as that very evening Fr. Jerauld called on us, and before the week was over Roger had donated six and a half acres, including the hill, to St. Mary's Mission.

John and Marcie Trent (Photo courtesy of Winnie Nowak)

One of the reasons the church is special to our family is that Roger and I homesteaded our first year in Alaska in a one-room log cabin in the very spot where the church was built. Also, all five of the Waldron children were confirmed by Bishop Gordon at St. Mary's Church. Also, John and Marcie Trent were married here in 1966, and three of the Trent children were confirmed.

~ Marcie Trent

Bishop Gordon came flying in to hold services. His sermon sent a clear message from God, saying we in the villages have to stand on our own two feet. Meaning — hold our own services, do our own paperwork. So that's what we are doing.... When one of our old-timers passes away and is put in our church, the whole church would light up, brighter than our electric lights.

I hope my great-great-grandchildren or even my grandchildren will take over where I leave off. I'm kind of worried about our church. In the future who will keep things running? Who will build the fire? Clean church? Who will keep books? Who will hold services every Sunday? I guess I just have to let God handle my worries.

~ Elsie Pitka
St. Matthew's, Beaver

The boarding home at St. Mark's Mission, Nenana, 1949. This building housed boys' and girls' dormitories, a storage room, and two staff bedrooms on the upper floor; dining/recreation room, kitchen, two staff bedrooms, infirmary and sick bay, a workroom, and porch with woodstove on ground floor; and bathtubs, washing machines, and drying lines in the basement. (Photo courtesy of Dorothy Vinson Hall)

Laundry day at St. Mark's Mission, 1949

A dance in the Big Room at St. Mark's, 1949 (Both photos by Dorothy Vinson Hall)

In the early days the mission schools operated by the Episcopal Church, the Roman Catholic Church, and others afforded many opportunities for village children to get a good Christian education and to develop a strong work ethic. One of the highlights of our family life while I was growing up in Nenana was the one and a half-mile walk to St. Mark's Mission for Sunday services and visiting with the dedicated mission people. At that time the Mission also served as residence for Bishop Bentley and his wife.

Over the years a strong kinship grew between the young folks of Nenana and the Mission children. It was decided that a social hour or two would be beneficial for all of us, and they instituted a Friday night dance which we all enjoyed thoroughly. Deaconess Thompson, a tiny, spirited Irish lady, had a hard and fast rule, however; the dance would start at 7:30 p.m. following a half-hour chapel service. Those who missed chapel also missed the privilege of dancing.

The maintenance man at the Mission, Fred Mueller, kept all the equipment in top condition. Ladders were hung neatly on the side of the carpentry shop. One day Fred noticed that the longest ladder had been sawed in half. Turned out that Bishop Bentley had done this to deter ardent local youth from climbing up to the Mission girls' second-floor quarters!

These are lighthearted remembrances of the Mission, but there were somber recollections as well, such as the martyrdom of Miss Farthing, the drowning of Father Reid and two of the Mission boys, and other tragic events. One cannot help but be inspired by the dedication displayed by the missionaries and their faith.

~ John B. (Jack) Coghill

✝

XII

𝄞 I sing a song

Counterclockwise from top middle: **John Starr**, *lay worker at Tanana;* **Walter Hannum**, **Mildred** *and* **Mark Boesser**, *and* **Louise Hannum** *at Meier Lake;* **Gary Herbst** *of Ketchikan;* **Bishop Gordon** *visits with* **Susie Boatman** *and* **Meda Lord** *on the lawn of St. Mark's Mission, Nenana;* **Judy Edwards Jones** *and son—she taught us what faith is all about;* **Charlotte Adams** *of Beaver;* **Mrs Bentley** *with Alaska-bound missionaries:* **Teresa Barling**, **Dick** *and* **Shirley Treadwell**, **Don** *and* **Betty Hart**, *1964*

of the saints of God...

Clockwise from top middle: **Joe** and **Alta Jerue** and the **Rev. Henry H. Chapman** at Anvik centennial, 1987; **David Salmon** and **Belle Herbert**, Chalkyitsik; **David Paul** of Tanacross; Church Army cadet **Tom Tull** at Fort Yukon; Escorted by **Walter Hannum**, **Mrs. Grafton Burke** "comes home" to Fort Yukon for 1961 centennial celebration; **Winnie Nowak**, St. Mary's, Anchorage; **Bishop Cochran**, **Bob Jones**, and **Hugh Hall** confer at the 1976 diocesan convention at Fort Yukon

They lived not only

*Counterclockwise from top middle: **Mary Nathaniel** and **Bruce Caldwell**, Fort Yukon; **Mary** and **Chuck Eddy**, St. Mary's, Anchorage; **Philip Peter** and **Titus Peter**, Fort Yukon; **Joyce Sarles** brings new daughter **Christine** home to Minto, 1966; **Bob Jones**, Kotzebue, Anchorage, and now Bishop of Wyoming; Father and son **Patrick** and **Elijah Attungana** at Elijah's ordination to the priesthood, July 1990, Point Hope; **Bessie Titus**, chair of the diocesan Standing Committee*

in ages post

Clockwise from top middle: **Wilfred Lane**, *Kotzebue;* **Donald Oktollik** *of Point Hope and* **Milton Swan** *of Kivalina;* **Norman and Stella Elliott**, *Anchorage;* **Joe Aprill**—*he developed the work on the Kenai Peninsula;* **Wilfred** *(Shorty) and* **Ann Files** *aboard the S.S.* Aleutian, *1938 (Photo courtesy of Will Files Jr.);* **Sam Rock**, *interpreter at Point Hope in the 1900s;* **James Hawley** *and* **Jerry Norton** *at Jerry's ordination at Kivalina*

there are hundreds

Counterclockwise from top middle: **Sarah Salmon** of Chalkyitsik; **Andy Fairfield**, now Bishop of North Dakota; **Bishop Gordon** and **George Edwin**, Tanana; **Malcolm Miner**, formerly of Anchorage, now of Hawaii; **Bob Nelson**, St. Mary's, Anchorage; **Shirley Gordon**, June 1994; she belongs to all of Alaska (Photo by Evolyn Melville); **Charlie Adams**, Juneau, 1985; **Margaret John**, Fort Yukon

# of thousands still,

*Clockwise from top middle: The **Curtis Edwards family,** Tanana, 1960; **David Keller** of Shageluk, Cordova, and Tanana; **Chief Bergman's family**, Allakaket; A community reception for **Margaret** and **Hugh Hall**, Kodiak; **Harry** and **Diane Brelsford**, Anchorage, May 1988; **Mary Parsons**, executive secretary, diocesan office (Photo by Luis Uzueta); **Bishop Peter Trimble Rowe**; Kids at Emmaus Center junior high camp: **Gypsy Walukones**, **Lael Harrison**, and **Kristin Hoefling***

DIOCESAN
HEADQUARTERS:

Bishop Rowe House
1205 Denali Way
Fairbanks, Alaska 99701

Phone: (907) 452-3040
Fax: (907) 456-6552

MAILING ADDRESS:

Episcopal Diocese of Alaska
1205 Denali Way
Fairbanks, Alaska 99701

*Above: Diocesan staff, 1995: left to right: Bishop
Charleston, the Rev. Canon Anna Frank, Mary Parsons,
Connie Moore, Lynn Slusher, the Rev. Canon Luis Uzueta;
Inset: Sarah Gonzales (Photo by Malcom Lockwood)*

Right: Bishop Rowe House

...that through the church the wisdom of God in its rich variety might now be known...

- Ephesians 3:10

XIII

THIS IS OUR DIOCESE

BISHOP
The Rt. Rev. Steven Charleston

DIOCESAN STAFF
The Rev. Canon Luis Uzueta
 Leadership Development
The Rev. Canon Anna Frank
 Missioner for Native Ministry
Lynn Slusher, Connie Moore
 Christian Learning
Edward J. Thielen
 Interim Administrator
Glenn Herring
 Accountant
Sarah Gonzales
 Administrative Assistant
Mary Parsons
 Executive Secretary, Editor

THE STANDING COMMITTEE
Bessie Titus, Chair
The Rev. Larry Spannagel
Nancy James
Andrew Tooyak Sr.
The Rev. James Hunter II
The Rev. Gary Herbst

THE COMMISSION ON MINISTRY
The Rev. Scott Fisher, Chair
Norman Omnik
Annie Demming
The Rev. Jan Hotze
Margaret Hulbert
LeRoy Funk
The Rev. Gregory Kimura

THE DIOCESAN COUNCIL
The Rt. Rev. Steven Charleston, Chair
Edward J. Thielen (Southcentral)
The Rev. Dale Sarles (Southeast)
Bertha Jennings (Arctic Coast)
John Starr (Interior)
(Also on the Diocesan Council are the members of the Standing Committee)

DIOCESAN OFFICERS
Chancellor: Eric Wohlforth
Treasurer: Paul Sherry
Vice Chancellor: Tim Middleton
Historiographer: Vacant

DIOCESAN PUBLICATIONS
Alaskan Epiphany, published quarterly, $10/year
Diocesan Dialogue, free monthly newsletter

SOUTHEAST DEANERY
Kathleen Wakefield, Dean

Haines
St. Michael & All Angels
Jan Hotze (V)

Juneau
Holy Trinity
Laura Lockey (*)

St. Brendan's
Wilson Valentine (R)
Ann Parsons (D)

Ketchikan
St. John's
Gary Herbst (R)
Earle Palmer (*)

Petersburg
St. Andrew's
Dale Sarles (I)
Bill Fulton (S)

Sitka
St. Peter's-by-the-Sea
David Elsensohn (R)

Wrangell
St. Philip's
Stephen Helgeson (L)

Retired and other clergy:
Charles Adams (r) Juneau
Mark Boesser (r) Juneau
Diane Tickell (r) Auke Bay

SOUTHCENTRAL DEANERY
Bob Orrin, Dean

Anchorage
All Saints
James Basinger (R)
Norman Nauska (*)

St. Christopher's
Scott Rathman (V)
Betty Lou Anthony (D*)

St. Mary's
Charles Eddy (R)
Robert Nelson (A)
Robert Thwing (*)
Michael Burke (S)

Christ Church
Larry Spannagel (V)
Raymond Dexter (*)
Allen P. Richmond (*)
Richard Stevens (S)

Cordova
St. George's
Spaulding Howe (V)

Eagle River
Holy Spirit
Gregory Kimura (V)

Homer
St. Augustine's
Paula Sampson (V)
Will Files (L)

Kenai
St. Francis-by-the-Sea

Kodiak
St. James-the-Fisherman
Paul R. Smith (R)
Steve Avery (D*)

Palmer
St. Bartholomew's
Ralph Wagner (V)

Seward
St. Peter's
Ronald Hiester (V)

Talkeetna
Denali Episcopal
Myron Ebling (L)

Valdez
Epiphany (Lutheran)
Mark Will

Wasilla
St. David's
Dyana Orrin (R)

Retired and other clergy:
Norman Elliott (r) Anchorage
Hugh Hall (r) Kodiak
Allen P. Richmond (r) Anchorage
George Beacom (r) Palmer
Keith Lawton (r) Palmer

ARCTIC COAST DEANERY
Oral Hawley, Dean

Kivalina
Epiphany
Raymond Hawley (V*)
Jerry Norton (A*)

Kotzebue
St. George's-in-the-Arctic
Wilfred Lane (V*)

Noatak
Episcopal Congregation
Evelyn Shy (L)

Point Hope
St. Thomas'
Seymour Tuzroykuke Sr. (V)
Elijah Attungana
Andrew Tooyak Sr. (L)

Point Lay
St. Alban's-in-the-Arctic
Willie Tukrook (L)

Retired and other clergy:
James Hawley (r) Kivalina
Clinton Swan (r)

INTERIOR DEANERY
Regional Deans:
Patti Salmon, Yukon Flats
Madeline Williams, Tanana Valley
Maudy Sommer, Yukon Koyukuk

Allakaket
St. John's-in-the-Wilderness
Johnson Moses (L)

Anvik
Christ Church
Julie Walker (L)

Arctic Village
Bishop Rowe Chapel
Trimble Gilbert (V*)

Beaver
St. Matthew's
Elsie Pitka (L)

Birch Creek
St. James'
Titus Peter (V*)
Randall Balaam (L)

Chalkyitsik
St. Timothy's
David Salmon (V*)
Mary Nathaniel (D*)

Circle
Holy Trinity
Alice Carroll (L)

Eagle
St. Paul's & St. John's
JoAnne Beck (L)

Fairbanks
St. Matthew's
Scott Fisher (R)
Helen Peters (D*)
Jim Eichner (S)

Fort Yukon
St. Stephen's
Teresa Thomas (D*)

Grayling
St. Paul's
Dolly & Henry Deacon (L)

Hughes
Hughes Mission
Susie Williams (L)

Huslia
Good Shepherd
Maudy Sommer (L)

Minto
St. Barnabas
Berkman Silas (V*)
Luke Titus (A*)

Nenana
St. Mark's
Stan Sullivan (V*)

North Pole
St. Jude's
James Hunter II (V)

Rampart
Episcopal Congregation
Paul & Linda Evans (L)

Shageluk
St. Luke's
Katherine Hamilton (L)
Stevens Village

St. Andrew's
Robert Joseph (L)

Tanacross
St. Timothy's
Irene Arnold (L)

Tanana
St. James;
John Starr (L)
Ginny Doctor (M)

Venetie
Good Shepherd
Margo Simple (L)

Other Congregations
Manley Hot Springs
Delta-Fort Greely

Retired and other clergy:
James Gilbert (r) Arctic Village
John Phillips (r) Vidzeek'oo
Everett Wenrick (*) Fairbanks
Glen Wilcox (r) Fairbanks
Paul Tritt (r) Venetie
Montie Slusher (D) Fairbanks
Richard Simmonds (*)

R =	rector
V =	vicar
A =	assistant or associate
X =	support priest
I =	interim
L =	lay worker
S =	seminarian
D =	deacon
r =	retired
M =	missioner
* =	self-supporting; not priest-in-charge unless otherwise noted

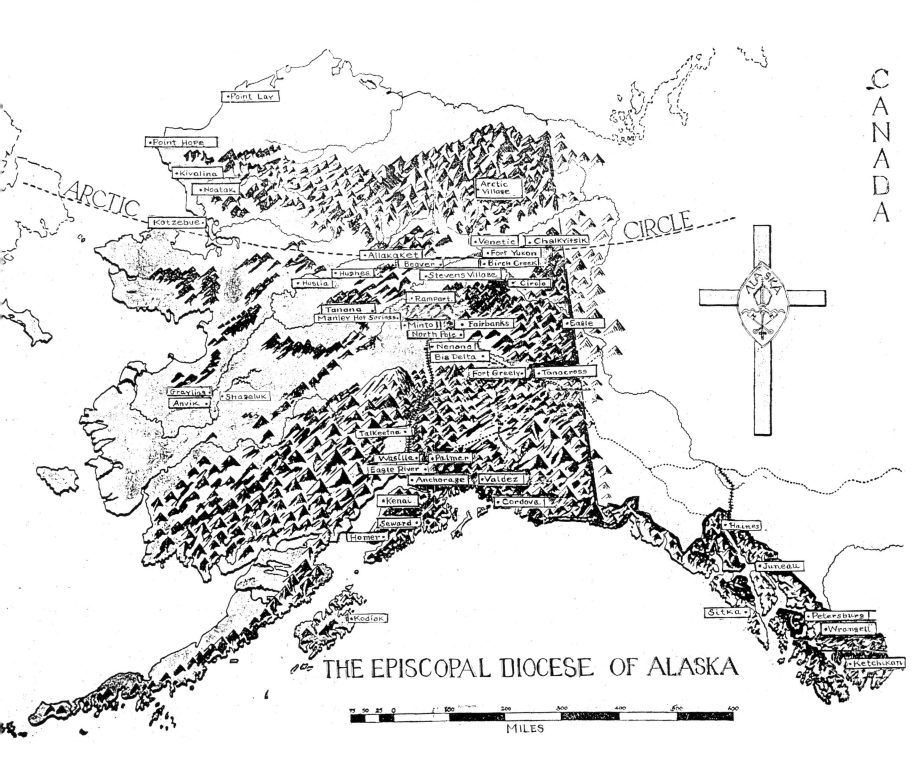

THE EPISCOPAL DIOCESE OF ALASKA

157

DIOCESAN ORGANIZATIONS, PROGRAMS & MINISTRIES

In addition to the many programs active within individual parishes and missions — altar guilds, acolytes' groups, young people's clubs, men's and women's organizations, outreach ministries of infinite variety — the Church sponsors several programs on a diocesan-wide basis.

The Presiding Bishop's Fund for World Relief is a national ministry of concerned Episcopalians who collect resources to aid in ministry development and, especially, for disaster relief.

The Episcopal Society for Ministry on Aging, Inc., also a national ministry, is dedicated to raising awareness of and support for seniors in the life of the church.

Faith Into Tomorrow is a capital funds campaign designed to raise money through pledges for an endowment fund that will provide ongoing income for support of the central areas of the diocesan ministry: Stewardship, Evangelism, Leadership Development, Christian Learning, and Communications. Initiated in 1993, the campaign has thus far been highly successful.

The Carpenters is a long-range planning committee for the Diocese, composed of representatives from each Deanery. The group sets goals for five-eight year periods; it reports to the Standing Committee and Diocesan Council, which in turn take recommendations to the annual Diocesan Convention.

The Daughters of the King has chapters in several parishes of the Diocese. It is a community open to women who seek to share in a life of prayer, faith, and spiritual service.

The Brotherhood of St. Andrew is a lay ministry of men focused on personal spiritual growth, mutual ministry, and Christian service; its sole object is "the spread of God's Kingdom among men."

Treasure Kids is a national ministry emphasizing the development of the Church's mission with children.

The Society of Mary is a national Church society for those who share special devotion to the Blessed Virgin Mary. The Bishop presents statues of Mary to parish chapters within the Diocese.

Meier Lake Camp in Wasilla is a diocesan ministry of hospitality, conferencing, and camping for youth of the Diocese and the larger Alaska community.

Emmaus Center in Petersburg is a ministry of the Southeast Deanery which has been focused on development of youth ministry.

The Society of St. Simeon and St. Anna is an honorary society for elders within the Diocese (see page 160).

Episcopal Church Women is a national organization of women in the Church which is active in ministries of support to both local and global mission (see page 161).

The United Thank Offering, a national ministry of the Episcopal Church, receives funds offered in thanksgiving for daily blessings and uses these funds to support the mission of the Church both here in Alaska and throughout the larger Church (see page 162).

Above left: A Cursillo group celebrates in worship and songs of praise.

Above right: Bishop Charleston presents a statue of the Virgin Mary to Fr. Scott Rathman at St. Francis-by-the-Sea, Kenai, in recognition of the parish chapter of the Society of Mary.

Left: A canoe trip at the junior high camp, Meier Lake, 1986

SOCIETY OF ST. SIMEON AND ST. ANNA

This is a unique honorary society for recognized elders within the Diocese. Members must be at least 60 years of age and active in ministry through the Church for a minimum of 15 years. They live a common Rule of Life in which they pray daily for the Church in Alaska. They alone are privileged to wear the golden cross of the Diocese.

These are the elders who have been inducted into the Society since its inception in 1991:

Adams, Caleb
Adams, Charlotte
Adams, Ruth
Alexander, Evelyn
Aprill, Elisabeth
Arndt, Hazel
Attungana, The Rev. Patrick
Bailey, Ann
Baldwin, Miriam
Barlow, Glenora
Bayer, Lorraine
Beacom, The Rev. George
Boesser, The Ven. Mark
Boesser, Mildred
Borden, M. Caroline
Charlie, Eli
Charlie, Mabel
Christian, Annie
Cruikshank, Moses
Davis, Dr. William E.
Demming, Annie
Dick, Mary
Elliott, The Ven. Norman H.V.
Elliott, Stella
George, Chief Paul
Gilbert, The Rev. James
Gordon, The Rt. Rev. Wm. J.
Hall, The Rev. Hugh
Hall, Margaret
Hamilton, Katherine
Hawley, The Rev. James
Hitt, Amy
Hoefler, Fred
Horn, Beverly
James, Annie
James, Elsie
Jerue, Alta
Johnson, Elliott Sr.
Kangas, Hana

Lane, Jacob Sr.
Leask, Karl
Lee, Mary Elizabeth
Linder, Carolyn
Littlefield, Martha
Luke, Solomon
Minano, Nina
Moses, Johnson
Neakok, Dorcas
Neakok, Warren
Nictune, Oscar
Nore, Betty
Nowak, Winifred
Paul, Julius
Pike, Mabel
Pitka, Dorothy
Richmond, The Rev. Allen P.
Richmond, Veva
Salmon, The Ven. David
Sandvik, Ruth
Sarvela, Mary
Shagloak, Virginia
Solomon, Hannah
Speck, May
Standerwick, Ruth
Swan, Charlotte
Swan, The Rev. Clinton
Swenson, Pauline
Taeschner, Elizabeth
Thomas, Tay
Tickell, The Rev. Diane
Towksjhea, Reuben Sr.
Trent, John
Trent, Marcie
Tritt, The Rev. Isaac
Volzke, Doris
Whitmore, Elsie
Williams, Susie

The Bishop invests honored elders of the Church into the Society of St. Simeon and St. Anna.

EPISCOPAL CHURCH WOMEN

S tarting in the early 1950s, the Episcopal Church Women throughout Alaska formed two Convocations: Denali, which comprised Southcentral and all churches north; and Southeastern, which covered from Juneau to Ketchikan. Each year the groups met separately, with a joint meeting every two years. Bishop Gordon attended these meetings and also flew in the village delegates in the "Blue Box." These events were a great inspiration as women joined in prayer and praise, shared and learned from each other. In the early 1970s the women's groups started to take different paths, and the Convocations were discontinued.

Women of the Missionary District gathered in Juneau in 1962 for the second Convocation of Episcopal Church Women (ECW). Left to right, front row: Doad Dorman, Ketchikan; Billie Williams, Anchorage, St. Mary's; Rene Bergreen, Ketchikan; Annie Demming, Palmer; Bertha Meier, Anchorage, All Saints; Dinah Frankson, Point Hope; Bee Courtenage, Ketchikan; Ena Jimmie, Minto. Second row: Mildred and Mark Boesser, Juneau; Grace Ramsey, Ketchikan; Bobbie Rice, Juneau; Dorothy Hall (District President), Fairbanks; Bishop and Mrs. Gordon; Winnie Nowak, Anchorage, St. Mary's; Hazel Pilkington, Anchorage, All Saints; Corinne Kenway, Juneau. Third row: Jeanie Elia, Tanana; Gwen Cobban, Seward; Alice Smoke, Stevens Village; Hilda Jones, Kotzebue; Winifred Coghill, Nenana; Anna May Orr, Fairbanks; Ulista Brooks, Salem, Oregon; Patty Dumville, Diocese of Michigan; Teddy Sorg, National Executive Board, Berkeley, California; Lucille Denning, (President of 8th Province Women), Bend, Oregon; Dorothy Olsen, Anchorage, All Saints; Mariette Trelease, Yukon Valley Missions; Marian Charlton, Wrangell; Marsha Jerue, Anvik; Louise Paul, Eagle; Annie Vent, Huslia. Fourth row: Martha Swan, Kivalina; Elsie Pitka, Beaver; Dorothy Webb, Wrangell; Jan Smalley, Juneau; Dee Reekie, Ketchikan; Mary Rowley, Sitka; Norma Banta, Cordova; Mary Smith, Petersburg; Katherine Hamilton, Shageluk; Dolly Deacon, Holikachuk; and Dorothy Clarke, Kodiak.

THE UNITED THANK OFFERING
WHAT IT IS — WHAT IT DOES

We in Alaska have been a part of the United Thank Offering from the time the very first grant was made in 1889. The first Alaska church building, at Anvik, was constructed with most of that first grant. In 1976 a two-year grant of $29,420 was made for NETWORK to help enlarge their program. More recently, a $75,000 grant was given to St. Francis-by-the-Sea in Kenai for their church and day care center. We have received 37 grants in Alaska for a total of $561,424. The grant monies have built churches and rectories, provided former Bishop Gordon's plane, the "Blue Box," and assisted in training priests and lay workers. The early grants helped build hospitals and schools and paid the salaries of missionaries and nurses.

The simple purpose of the United Thank Offering has remained the same during all these years: "Given in thankfulnesss... used to provide blessings for others." First known as the United Offering, the name was later changed to United Thank Offering, for through giving, women had come to know the joy of expressing thankfulness for everyday blessings.

Now, however, anyone may participate. It is something the whole family may join in by using the Blue Box frequently, depositing small coins of thankfulness.

United Thank Offering officers, 1980s: left to right: Helen Rogers, Veva Richmond, Mary Jane Harris, and Annie Demming

UNITED....... We
THANK...... God for His presence in our daily lives, for blessings great and small,
OFFERING..... our prayers and coins, which are
UNITED..... with those of thousands of other grateful people and sent to support the world-wide mission of the Church, giving still others cause to
THANK..... God and respond by
OFFERING..... their own prayers and coins in THANKSGIVING!

United Thank Offering Grants To Alaska 1889-1994

1889	Anvik	To build church	$	400
1931	Anchorage	To build basement for All Saints		
1949	Nenana	To build St. Mark's Rectory		2,000
1949	Fort Yukon	Addition to Hudson Stuck Memorial Hospital		10,000
1955	Shageluk	Repair and complete nurses' residence		3,000
1955	Circle	Church and quarters for priest		4,000
1955	Stevens Village	St. Andrew's Rectory		1,000
1955	Wrangell	St. Philip's Parish House		2,500
1958	Tanana	Enlarging St. James' Church		2,000
1958	Gift to	Miss Keefer and Mrs. Henry Chapman, on furlough from Alaska		100
1958	Fort Yukon	Furnishings for staff quarters		366.50
1958		Toward new plane (the "Blue Box") for Bp.Gordon		5,000
1958		St. Stephen's Rectory		10,000
1958	Palmer	St. Bartholomew's - toward new church		7,500
1958	Kotzebue	St. George's-in-the-Arctic-toward parish hall		10,000
1958	Fairbanks	Furnishings/repair residence of City Missioner		2,500
1961	Kodiak	St. James the Fisherman, new rectory		10,000
1961	Anvik	Christ Church - repairs		5,000
1961	Fairbanks	Two apartments, Bishop Rowe House, two cars		5,573
1961		For Bishop Gordon toward repairs to Blue Box II		5,000
1964-7	Ketchikan	St. John's Church - rectory		25,000
	Anchorage	St. Christopher's - land purchase		30,000
	Kotzebue	St. George's-in-the-Arctic - Church and foundation/rectory		15,000
		Training Program for Indian and Eskimo Lay People - Native Ministry		5,000
1970	Juneau	Alaska Homemaker Service, Inc.		20,000
		Training Program for Indigenous Ministry		14,000
1972		Diocesan Coordinator of Ministry - salary/housing for two years; self-supporting ministry		25,000
1976	Fairbanks	NETWORK coordinator to train lay and ordained indigenous leaders for two years		29,420
1977		Training of Church Growth Facilitator to assist parishes with outreach ministry and assist new congregations		1,300
1979	Kenai	St. Francis-by-the-Sea, Multi-purpose building		75,000
1984	Wasilla	St. David's - to help build church		35,000
1988	Juneau	St. Brendan's - to help build multi-purpose building		35,000
1989	Kodiak	St. James the Fisherman - new construction for programs		49,000
1991	Kotzebue	St. George's - Cudd Hall renovation		21,765
1992	Kenai	St. Francis Mission - to expand multi-purpose center		25,000
1993	Petersburg	St. Andrew's - to supplement donated labor & material for addition of a sanctuary and multi-purpose space		20,000
1994	Eagle River	Holy Spirit - to help complete sanctuary		50,000
		TOTAL:		$ 561,424.50

~ Compiled by Winifred T. Nowak,
Diocesan UTO Coordinator

THE ARMED FORCES MINISTRY

Many members of the Episcopal Church in Alaska serve in the National Guard and the Eskimo Scout Battalion as well as in the military throughout the world. Several have been appointed to the military academies by the state's senators and congressman. Recognizing the importance of their role and their dedication to their duties, the Diocese has always sought ways to minister to Episcopalians serving in Alaska. During the absence of an Episcopal chaplain at Fort Richardson in 1965, All Saints' Church entered into a contract with the Department of the Army to provide services for Churchmen and women stationed at that post. From that association St. Christopher's, Anchorage, was established.

Episcopal chaplains, although not members of the clergy of the Diocese, are active participants in the life and worship of congregations near their stations. In turn, chaplains have included local clergy in the services and activities at Base and Post chapels. Chaplain Charles L. Burgreen, having served at Fort Wainwright and Fort Richardson, became an assistant to the Bishop for the Armed Forces and in 1978 was consecrated as Bishop of that office.

Left: Governor William A. Egan reviews troops of the Eskimo Scouts of The Alaska National Guard at Point Hope, 1965.

Below: Capt. Michael Bailey, far right, was presented to Bishop Gordon for Confirmation in Nov. 1969 by Chaplain John A. Phillips of Nenana at the Ballistic Missile Early Warning System site at Clear Air Force Base. Left to right: Frs. Jack Randall and John Phillips, Bishop Gordon; Base Commander Col. John Barnard and Capt. Bailey.

Alaska clergy and four ordinands at All Saints, Anchorage, Feb. 17, 1952. Left to right, front row: Bishop Gordon, Albert J. Sayers, Robert Grumbine, Wilfred C. Files, Roy E. Sommers, Samuel A. McPhetres, and Canon Theodore Wedel of the College of Preachers in Washington, D.C. Back row: Henry H. Chapman, Kenneth Watkins, John S. Martin, J. Russell Clapp, Howard Laycock, Norman H.V. Elliott, Gordon T. Charlton Jr., and Hugh F. Hall. The ordinands were Frs. Grumbine, Martin, Laycock, and Elliott.

A Tour of the Diocese

In 1900 Fr. Jules Prevost's journey from Tanana to Nome required 43 days of arduous travel. Bishop Rowe spent 23 days on the 350-mile trail between Fairbanks and Valdez. The Rev. and Mrs. William Thomas made the trip from Point Hope to Nenana in 64 days. Archdeacon Stuck covered the hundreds of miles between the missions of the Interior in trips lasting for two or three months.

Now we invite you, for a relatively small investment of time, to join us for an armchair tour of the entire Diocese, from the panhandle of Southeast, through the state's most heavily populated areas in Southcentral, along the far north Arctic Coast, and ending in the Interior. Our tour, while lacking the depth, knowledge, and experience—to say nothing of the hardships—of our early leaders, will offer a brief but caring glimpse of the Diocese of Alaska.

We'll begin in SOUTHEAST, the gateway to Alaska, famed for its timber, mining, and fishing industries and its incomparable coastal scenery.

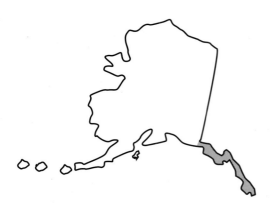

1. In the late 19th century, Ketchikan was a small Native community. Bishop Rowe wrote: "The only white man was a trader (who) offered me two acres of his squatter's claim if I would start a school for the Indian children.... I accepted, arranged for a school, and so the work began." A hospital and church soon followed. St. John's church building, constructed entirely by hand, without blueprints, by volunteer Native labor, was consecrated in 1904. During the years 1927 to 1961, the Native people had a separate church, St. Elizabeth's, and the Rev. Paul James Mather was the first Tsimshian priest, serving from 1926 until his death in 1942. The people united as one congregation (St. John's) and in 1955 became a self-supporting parish.

2. St. Philip's, Wrangell, was founded in 1903 by a group of Presbyterian worshippers who were received into the Episcopal Church in 1905. St. Philip's, consecrated in 1910, was built on land given by the Kik.setti Clan and is still in its original location. In addition to worship services and related activities, St. Philip's served the children of Wrangell Institute, a Bureau of Indian Affairs school.

3. St. Andrew's, Petersburg, was founded in 1950 and its building was dedicated in June 1954. Fr. Hugh Hall was instrumental in the establishment and construction of the parish hall, and Fr. Albert Sayers was the first resident priest. The parish operates the Emmaus camp and conference center.

4. Bishop Rowe moved his family to historic Sitka in 1896. The cornerstone of the church was laid on St. Peter's Day, June 29, 1899 and consecrated as the "Cathedral of Alaska" on Easter Sunday, April 15, 1900; the church building and See House are listed on the National Historic Register. Ministry is carried out from St. Peter's to students from around the state who attend nearby Mt. Edgecumbe school (see The Edgecumbe Experience, page 127)

5. Holy Trinity Church in Juneau was built in 1896 and served as the Pro-Cathedral of the Missionary District. The boom of mining activity also spurred establishment of St. Luke's on Douglas Island, and work continued among the mining camps and communities from 1910 until the industry diminished about 1917. The final service at Douglas was held in 1951. Holy Trinity has maintained its foundation of faith during Juneau's transitions from the years of heavy mining influence to its present position as the seat of state government and a leader in Alaska's rapidly growing tourism industry.

6. Mark Boesser's anecdote on page 52 describes the selection of the land for this thriving young mission in Juneau's Mendenhall Valley. Established in September 1985, St. Brendan's Church was consecrated in October 1989, with the parish hall added in 1991. (Photo by Fr. Wilson Valentine)

The Church's most recent work was established at Haines in 1991. On September 29th, the Feast of St. Michael and All Angels, this name was selected for the Haines church.

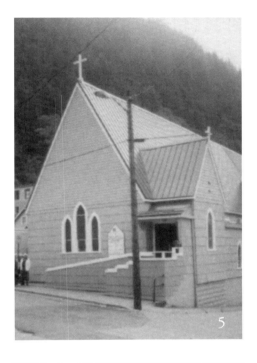

7. The oldest Episcopal Church in the Southcentral area is Epiphany, established in 1900 at Valdez by Fr. Jules Prevost. The work was carried on by lay leaders until 1906 when the first clergyman was assigned there. The townsite was moved following the heavy destruction of the 1964 Good Friday earthquake, and a new church, now headquarters of an ecumenical ministry, was built.

8. St. Peter's in Seward traces its roots to the early 1900s when the Rev. Frederick Taylor traveled from Valdez and held services in a tent on Resurrection Bay. The church has consistently provided a strong ministry in this town where fortunes have fluctuated with the tides of trade, railroad development, shipping, and other industrial factors.

9. Cordova, the copper mining and railroad boom town of the early part of the century, was fortunate to have the services of the Rev. E.P. Newton who came over from Valdez and established the Red Dragon

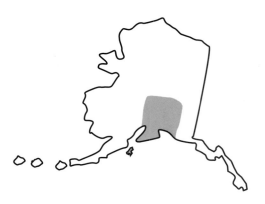

clubhouse, a place for Sunday worship and a refuge for working men who desired a more meaningful life than that offered by the local saloons. The town was also fortunate that in 1909 Fr. Newton's work was taken over by Eustace Ziegler, who founded St. George's Church, expanded the outreach work of the Red Dragon, and contributed significantly to the Church through his ministry and his art (See Frontispiece and page 21).

10. All Saints' Church, the first Episcopal church in Anchorage, is the strong root from which several other southcentral churches and missions have sprung. Established in 1916, its first building was situated at Third and K Streets in downtown Anchorage, then moved to the site of today's Town Square before the present building was constructed in 1951 at Eighth and F Streets.

11. The establishment and growth of St. Mary's, Anchorage, is documented in the article by Winnie Nowak (page 132) and the anecdote by Marcie Trent (page 146) The church recently completed an extensive building program, expanding the facility and, with construction of a new sanctuary, gracefully uniting all components of this large and extremely active parish. (Photo by Tay Thomas)

12. St. Christopher's, Anchorage, began with services for Episcopalians at the army base at Fort Richardson in the mid-1960s. Ground was broken for the church building in east Anchorage during the tenure of Fr. Bob Jones.

13. In the early 1980s the need for an Episcopal parish in south Anchorage became evident, and laymen from that area who attended All Saints' and St. Mary's volunteered to help develop this field of work. Today Christ Church shares worship and office space with Christ Our Savior Lutheran Church.

14. Clergy and layreaders from All Saints' initiated services in the pioneer farming community of the Matanuska Valley in 1957 (see Malcolm Miner's anecdote, page 139) In its early years the mission was served by the priest stationed in Valdez. Today St. Bartholomew's ministers in the scenic Palmer area. (Photo by Annie Demming)

15. St. David's was built in the 1980s to serve the fast-growing community of Wasilla and the Meier Lake Conference Center.

16. In the early 1980s interested lay people began investigating establishment of an Episcopal church in the Eagle River, Chugiak, and Peters Creek area north of Anchorage. Holy Spirit Church was chosen as its name, and the 1984 diocesan convention approved the formation of this mission. The congregation is active in support of deanery and diocesan activities as well as the Food Pantry that serves the community.

17. On a blustery spring day in 1987 this group of clergy and lay leaders met to consider the potential for the Church's work in the upper Matsu Valley. Shown left to right are Bishop Harris, Scott Fisher, Paula Ziegler (Sampson), Mary Louise Berndt,

ST. GEORGE'S CHURCH, CORDOVA, ALASKA

13

16

Andy Fairfield, Titus Peter, Elinore Ebling, Caroline Wohlforth, and Chuck Eddy. Denali Chapel in the unique community of Talkeetna began as outreach from St. David's, Wasilla, and is now served from Palmer, with the small congregation meeting in various homes in the area. (Photo by Myron Ebling)

18. Now turning south from Anchorage, we head down the Kenai Peninsula (bypassing the highway to Seward, visited earlier), and look west toward the town of Kenai. Here, through the missionary efforts of Fr. Joe Aprill (see Elisabeth Aprill's anecdote on page 138), the Episcopal Church of St. Francis-by-the-Sea, nicknamed the Wayfarer's Church, was established in the early 1970s. St. Francis is reputed to have been a friend to animals, and this photo suggests that the wildlife in Kenai return the affection. (Photo by Billy Wise)

19. At the far southwestern tip of the Kenai lies beautiful Homer, where Fr. Joe Aprill established St. Augustine's Church. At this time the Episcopalians share a building with the Seventh Day Adventist group, and newly ordained priest Paula Sampson has begun her ministry here. (Photo by Will Files Jr.)

20. From the Kenai we move over to Kodiak Island, where we find the Church of St. James-the-Fisherman. Founded in 1960, the church met first in the Navy chapel, then at the Russian Orthodox Church, then in rented space in the National Guard armory. The present building, completed in 1963, survived the 1964 earthquake and tidal wave, has shared its space with congregations of other denominations, and today is the attractive and active center shown here. (Photo by Ellen Lester)

From the communities of Southcentral Alaska we'll move north— far north and west—to our congregations of the Arctic Coast Deanery.

18

21. At Kotzebue the work of the Church began in the early 1950s with the establishment of St. George's-in-the-Arctic, "a small congregation in a 'big city,'" in the words of one parishioner. Here in this regional center and largest community of northwestern Alaska, a mixture of modern city and subsistence hunting and fishing lifestyles, the Church's ministry is in dedicated hands.

Thanks to the faithful ministry of lay leaders, the work of the Church is evident in the small village of Noatak on the river of the same name, northwest of Kotzebue.

22. North of Kotzebue Sound, on a gravel spit between the Arctic Ocean and a freshwater lagoon, the community of Kivalina is the home of Epiphany Church and a succession of strong Native clergy, beginning with Milton Swan, first Eskimo priest of the Episcopal Church. Epiphany was built in 1944 by Swan, Bishop Gordon, Daniel Norton, and Daniel Lisbourne, and Bishop Gordon spoke in his journal of his great joy when he nailed a cross he had made to the rooftop of the first church in Kivalina.

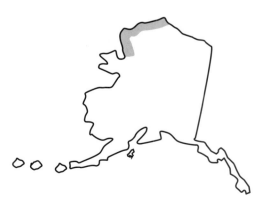

25

23. Few places can claim as rich a history in the Faith as Point Hope, where a medical missionary, Dr. John Driggs, first brought the Gospel and health care in the 1890s. The work of St. Thomas' Church has consistently attracted strong leaders. That tradition, established a century ago, prevails to this day, with leadership continuously emerging from within this far north Inupiaq community.

24. At Point Lay on the Arctic Ocean, St. Alban's-in-the-Arctic has a core of faithful people. And, since "the Church is people," we illustrate the work there with this photo of participants in the baptism of several youngsters by Bishop Harris in 1984.

25. Episcopalians in Barrow generally have moved to that farthest north community from other arctic locales for employment reasons. Services are held when and where possible (see Deacon Betty Lou Anthony's anecdote, page 136). Here are communicants at a service in Barrow conducted by Bishop Harris and the Rev. Montie Slusher.

23

21

24

22

26. From Barrow we look due south, across the rugged expanse of the Brooks Range and into the **Interior**, the vast heartland of Alaska. First stop, Allakaket, home of St. John's-in-the-Wilderness. One of the earliest of the missions, established in 1907 by Archdeacon Stuck, this church flourished through the ministry and ministrations of remarkable women nurses and teachers, clergy and lay leaders. Several articles about Allakaket are to be found in Chapter X, Stories from the Missions. (Photo by Fr. Luis Uzueta)

27. Downriver some 80-plus miles from Allakaket, a new church has been built in Hughes, where last summer's Koyukuk flood wrought widespread devastation. This is a great tribute to the strength and determination of this small community.

28. At Huslia, the work of Good Shepherd Church began in the 1950s, with clergy and lay leadership making this Koyukuk River mission a vital Christian center. Services were held in the community hall until 1960, when the church was built. Sidney Huntington designed the building and built the distinctive steeple.

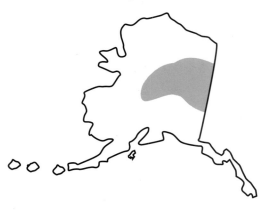

Coming down from the Koyukuk, we'll pay a visit to our three missions on the lower Yukon.

29. What can we add to all that has been said earlier about Christ Church Mission at Anvik? First Episcopal church built in Alaska...funded by contributions from the first United Thank Offering...ministered to for years by members of one selfless family and their equally dedicated assistants, teachers, nurses, layreaders, interpreters, and lay workers...home and haven to numerous children until funding cuts forced the painful closure of the Mission home during the latter years of Bishop Rowe's tenure (see page 28).

30. Work at Shageluk, on the Innoko River east of Anvik, began as outreach from Anvik, and St. Luke's Mission has been blessed through the years by strong leadership of both clergy and lay leaders. Here parishioners pose on the steps of their church.

31. The community of Grayling on the Yukon moved in 1960 from its earlier site at Holikachuk on the Innoko. St. Paul's Church moved with the people and continues to minister in this small village.

32. From the missions in the southwest region of the Interior, we move back to the mainstream of the Yukon, where, in almost the exact geographic center of Alaska we find the village of Tanana at the confluence of the Yukon and Tanana rivers. Site of early missionary activity, Tanana originally was manned by Anglican clergy from

Canada; the first priest of the American Episcopal Church arrived there in 1891. Strong ministry has been continuous since that time, with several of the Church's most effective leaders coming from within the community itself.

33. Barnabas traveled with St. Paul on his first missionary journey; when the village of Minto moved in the 1970s from its flood-prone location on the Tanana River, St. Barnabas Mission went along with it, into a new building in a safer location. Known for its nurturing of indigenous ministry, Minto is a strong link in the Church's life in the Interior.

34. The picturesque log church in Nenana is all that remains of the once extensive property of St. Mark's Mission. Time and the river have inflicted dramatic changes. Once nearly as remote as any bush village, Nenana now is an easy drive on one of Alaska's major highways. Once the home of bishops, archdeacons, nurses, teachers, and many children at the mission home and school, St. Mark's keeps quiet but faithful vigil in this rail-and-river community. (Photo by Marilyn Coghill Duggar)

35. The center of the Church's work in the Interior, and responsible for much early missionary outreach, is historic St. Matthew's, Fairbanks. Established in 1904 by Archdeacon Stuck and the Rev. John E. Huhn, this parish shares the colorful history of a place where events have reflected the boom-and-bust times of gold rush, military operations, exploration and development of huge petroleum resources, and the steady

26

28

31

27

29

30

32

civic growth and university development of the state's second largest city. (Photo by Ann Parsons)

36. North Pole has experienced rapid growth as a result of pipeline days and the military presence of nearby Fort Wainwright and Eielson Air Force Base. During the late 1970s St. Jude's Church was founded and is active and influential today in this community about 15 miles east of Fairbanks. (Photo by Evolyn Melville)

37. Work was begun at St. Timothy's Mission at Tanacross (Tanana Crossing) in 1912. The village moved across the river in the 1970s and is now accessible on the Alaska Highway. This new church building was dedicated in January 1981.

38. We'll turn back now to the Yukon area, starting at Rampart, 61 miles above Tanana. Rampart was the site of early missionary activity (1898) and the ministry of the Rev. John E. Huhn, who served there until his death in 1907. Last summer's Daily Vacation Bible School offered worship and fun to Paul Evans, Phoenix Moses, Marie Wiehl, Shane Wright, and Michael Burke, pictured here.

39. St. Andrew's Mission at Stevens Village has enjoyed many years of strong clergy and lay leadership from the time of its establishment in 1914.

40. About 50 miles farther along the Yukon, at Beaver, the work of St. Matthew's Mission began in the early years of the century. This new church building was erected in the 1970s.

41. Northeast of Beaver and just above the Arctic Circle lies Fort Yukon, the true historical beginning of the Anglican Church in Alaska. In 1861 the Rev. William Kirkby, a missionary from Canada, went to minister to Hudson's Bay Company traders and workers at Fort Yukon. On the strong foundation of the early missionary work, the Episcopal Church built and flourished through the efforts of leaders such as William Loola, Archdeacon Stuck, the Burkes, and a succession of deaconesses, teachers, nurses, and lay workers. The hospital established by the Church was a focal point of medical care that influenced the future health of the entire Yukon Valley. (Photo by Phyllis Fast)

42. Chalkyitsik, 45 miles northeast of Fort Yukon on the Black River, is sometimes known as "Fishhook," based on the meaning of its Gwich'in name. Of greater importance to us is its active mission, St. Timothy's, where Deacon Albert Tritt established the work of the Church. A new building replaced the old in 1977, and Fr. David Salmon has served a long and faithful ministry there.

43. Members of the Tritt family are shown at Good Shepherd, Venetie, a village on the Chandalar River in the Yukon Flats, where the Church's mission was started by the Rev. Albert Tritt in the 1930s, then further developed in the 1950s by clergy, deaconesses, lay workers, and volunteers.

44. The farthest northeast mission of the Church is at Arctic Village on the East Fork of the Chandalar, close to the controversial

Arctic National Wildlife Refuge (ANWR). The Rev. Albert Tritt founded Bishop Rowe Chapel in 1925 and carried out ministry for many years. His son, Isaac, continued the work, with other clergy and volunteers involved until another capable father and son team, Frs. James and Trimble Gilbert assumed the mission duties. Fr. Trimble Gilbert ministers at Bishop Rowe Chapel today.

45. Now moving upriver from Fort Yukon we find the town of Circle, where the Church founded a mission and hospital. Trinity Church at Circle was rebuilt in the 1980s by a youth group from California on land donated by the Roberts family.

46. The little village of Birch Creek is the home of St. James' Mission. On Easter Day, 1985, Bishop Harris confirmed this group presented by Fr. Titus Peter (at right), a well-known Native leader in the Interior.

47 & 48. Eagle is the site of historic Fort Egbert (where Roald Amundsen sent out word in 1906 that he had discovered the Northwest Passage) and once had two active missions, St. Paul's and St. John's, dating from the early years of the Missionary District. The community, on the Yukon near the Canadian border, was once the port of custom for travelers from the Klondike gold fields. Today the Church's work at Eagle rests in the care of lay workers, volunteers, and occasional visiting clergy.

These brief vignettes have covered thousands of miles and the events and people of many years past and present to offer a sense of the shape of the Diocese of Alaska today. Economic development, shifts in population, decreased funding, and lack of personnel have forced changes in the Church's ministry in the 49th State. The missions are steeped in colorful history and inspired by the accomplishments of leaders of past days. Today our people can reflect on this past with justified pride and nostalgia, but chiefly with determination to continue building on the rock-solid foundation of the Diocese as we move into our second Century of Faith.

✝

The clergy of the Missionary District met in Juneau in 1961 and gathered for this photo in front of Mendenhall Glacier. Left to right, kneeling in first row: Robert Kinney, Hugh Hall, Norman Elliott, Robert Shank, Keith Lawton, Walter Hannum, Bishop Gordon, Cameron Harriot, Dennis Walker, Sandy Zabriskie, and Pat Keller. Standing, second row: Henry Chapman, Isaac Tritt, Milton Swan, Page Kent (Church Army), Lee Stratman, Dick Simmonds, Mark Boesser, Randy Mendelsohn, Dick Clarke, Robert Grumbine, Malcolm Miner, David Salmon, David Paul, and Richard Walkley. Back row: Glen Wilcox, Tom Osgood, Murray Trelease, Tom Cleveland, William Warren, and Lew Hodgkins. Missing from the photo are Al Smith, Dick McGinnis, Dale Sarles, and Will Files Sr.

To everything there is a season, and a time
for every purpose under heaven...
~ Ecclesiastes 3:01

XIV

FOOTPRINTS IN TIME

1829 - Nov. Birth of Archdeacon Robert McDonald

1856 - Nov. Birth of Peter Trimble Rowe in Ontario, Canada

1858 - June Birth of John W. Chapman in Pikesville, Maryland

1861 - July Rev. William Kirkby, first Anglican missionary at Fort Yukon, holds first services there

1862 - Sept. Archdeacon Robert McDonald arrives in Fort Yukon

1863 - Nov. Birth of Hudson Stuck near London, England

1878 - Aug. Birth of Paul Mather in Metlakatla; he will become the first Alaska Native ordained to priesthood

1878 - Nov. Ordination of Peter Trimble Rowe to diaconate

1880 - Nov. Ordination of Peter Trimble Rowe to priesthood

St. Mary's Mission, Nome, founded in 1900 by Fr. Jules Prevost, closed after the population surge of the gold rush

1885 - May Death of Rev. Vincent C. Sim at Rampart House on the Porcupine River

1887 - July The Revs. John Chapman and Octavius Parker depart St. Michael for the lower Yukon village of Anvik where they establish a mission and Anvik's first school. Mr. Chapman remains in Anvik for 44 years at a salary of $600/year.

1888 - Thomas Canham sent by Bishop Bompas to Nuclacayette, site of Fort Adams and present-day Tanana

1888 - Oct. Special session of the House of Bishops establishes Alaska as a Missionary Jurisdiction

1890 - Dr. John Driggs arrives at Point Hope to begin a mission and a school. Driggs remains at Point Hope 18 years.

1891 - Rev. Jules Prevost is assigned to mission of Our Saviour at old Fort Adams near the present town site of Tanana, relieving Anglican priest Thomas H. Canham.

1892 - Jan. Birth of Walter Harper

1892/93 - Fr. Prevost travels up the Tanana and Goodpaster rivers to the head of Fortymile River, and on to the town of Fortymile; he is the first missionary to travel in this country.

1893 - May First logs laid for church building in Anvik

1894 - First church building in Alaska completed in Anvik

- Dr. Mary Glenton, first medical missionary on the Yukon River arrives at Anvik

1894 - Jan. First issue of *The Yukon Press* printed by Fr. Prevost in Tanana

1895 - Peter Trimble Rowe elected and consecrated first Bishop of Alaska

1896 - Birth of John Boyd Bentley in Hampton, Virginia

- Mar. Bishop Rowe celebrates his first Eucharist in Alaska in Juneau

- April Bishop Rowe departs Juneau for Chilkoot Pass and first trip into the Interior

- June Bishop Rowe reaches Circle and appoints William Loola as lay-catechist for Fort Yukon

- July Bishop Rowe's first confirmation in Alaska, 13-year-old Martha Mayo at Fort Adams below Tanana

- Bishop Rowe goes to Fort Yukon where he meets Bishop Bompas; then on to Fort Adams where he and Fr. Prevost move the mission site, establishing St. James' Mission

- Aug. Bishop Rowe confirms 16 in first confirmation service in Anvik

- Gold strike at Bonanza Creek

A brick from the church at Jamestown, Virginia, the first Episcopal church (1607) in colonial America, is embedded at the foot of the altar at Christ Church, Anvik, the first church built in Alaska (see page 32).

- Nov. Birth of George Edwin in Rampart

- Fr. Prevost moves from Tanana to Circle; establishes hospital

1897 - Bishop Rowe travels into the Interior again; also establishes a mission at Skagway, building a church and hospital

- July Stampede to the Klondike begins

- Aug. Isaac Fisher of Anvik is appointed lay assistant

1898 - Fr. Prevost establishes St. Mary's Mission at Nome; transfers from Circle to Rampart

- The Rev. Augustus R. Hoare first priest at Eagle

1899 - Fr. Prevost visits Valdez; builds Epiphany Church

- June Cornerstone laid for St. Peter's church in Sitka

- July Gold found on beach at Nome

- Bishop Rowe arrives in Nome to aid in construction of St. Mary's Mission

St. Savior's Hospital, Tanana, was a sister hospital to the Hudson Stuck Memorial Hospital at Fort Yukon. (Drane Collection, University of Alaska Fairbanks Archives, acc. #91-046-406- N)

- Sept. Rev. Leonides H. Wooden arrives in Fort Yukon from Skagway, the first resident priest from the American Church

- Nov. First service held at St. Peter's, Sitka

1900 - Apr. Bishop Rowe consecrates St. Peter's-by-the-Sea, Sitka

1901 - Aug. First resident priest arrives in Valdez

1903 - Church established at Seward

- Mar. Rev. Charles Rice and Esias depart Circle for the Fairbanks gold rush where

he holds his first service in the tent of a Fairbanks saloon

- June Bishop Rowe consecrates Holy Trinity, Juneau

- June Consecration of St. Savior's, Skagway

- July First confirmation class at St. Mary's, Nome, presents Bishop Rowe with gold nugget cross

- Dec. Ordination of first Athabascan Indian, William Loola of Fort Yukon, pupil of Archdeacon McDonald, to diaconate

1904 - St. Matthew's hospital formally opens and a mission is begun at Fairbanks under the direction of the Bishop and Rev. John Huhn. Hudson Stuck accepts position of Archdeacon.

- June Consecration of St. John's, Ketchikan

- June Ordination of Milton Swan in Kivalina as first Inupiaq ordained to the priesthood

- Aug. Hudson Stuck lands in Sitka and travels for the first time into the Interior

- Oct. First service held in St. Matthew's, Fairbanks

1905 - Aug. Rev. Charles Betticher arrives in Fairbanks as first rector of St. Matthew's. Betticher was influential in establishing a string of missions along the Tanana River. He also began *The Alaskan Churchman*, "the official publication of the missionary district of Alaska."

- Nov. Archdeacon Stuck leaves Fairbanks with six dogs on 2,000-mile trip to Fort Yukon, the Koyukuk, and the Arctic Coast

1906 -	Archdeacon Stuck establishes St. John's-in-the-Wilderness mission at Allakaket, the first mission on the Koyukuk River	

The congregation gathers outside All Saints' Church in Anchorage, May 7, 1922 to celebrate the fifth anniversary of the parish. At that time the church stood on the site of the present-day Town Square, 5th and F Streets. (Photo courtesy Anchorage Museum of History and Art)

1906 - Archdeacon Stuck establishes St. John's-in-the-Wilderness mission at Allakaket, the first mission on the Koyukuk River

- Rev. J. Edward Huhn dies of pneumonia two years after becoming rector of St. Matthew's and is buried in Rampart

- The people of Chena build their own chapel

- June Death of Bishop Bompas in Carcross; he is buried there by Bishop Stringer

- April Archdeacon Stuck returns to Fairbanks after completing the trip to the Arctic Coast and back by dog team

- July Consecration of St. Savior's Church in Tanana with Archdeacon Stuck and the Rev. Jules Prevost

- Nov. First issue of *The Alaskan Churchman* published in Fairbanks; subscription $1.00/year

1907 - A mission started at Nenana with Miss Annie Cragg Farthing in charge; St. Philip's Mission, Wrangell, established

- "The Red Dragon" (men's club) established by Rev. E.P. Newton in Cordova

- Apr. Work begins on church and mission house at Allakaket

- June Archdeacon Stuck dedicates first church in Allakaket

- Sept. Death of Archdeacon William Kirkby, first Anglican missionary to visit Fort Yukon (1861)

1908 - Dr. John Driggs retires from work at Point Hope and is replaced by the Rev. A.R. Hoare

- Tortella Hall, a 30-student boarding home dormitory, built at Nenana

- St. Luke's mission at Salchaket established

- April Bishop Rowe visits Seward for the first time

Chief Henry breaks ground for Huslia's new church in July 1960. Among the onlookers are Jimmy Huntington, George Attla Jr., Bergman Sam, John Sackett, and Edith Bifelt. (Photo by J. P. Davidson)

- June   Dr. Grafton Burke arrives in Fort Yukon as medical missionary

1910 - May   Consecration of St. Philip's, Wrangell

- Aug.   Dr. Grafton Burke of Fort Yukon marries Miss Clara Heintz in Allakaket

- Nov.   Death in Nenana of Annie Cragg Farthing who had served in Anvik, Circle, Fairbanks, and Nenana

1910-11 -   Mission and hospital established at Iditarod in response to the large influx of placer miners. This was a milestone in the history of the church. Because of the expense involved in establishing hospitals and missions to service transient populations such as Iditarod, Bishop Rowe decided to concentrate Church's efforts on the more stable Native population.

1912 -   Establishment of St. Timothy's Mission at Tanacross to serve the upper Tanana region

- Dec.   Fire in Fort Yukon destroys mission house, but no lives lost

1913 - Mar.   Archdeacon Hudson Stuck, Harry Karstens, Robert Tatum and Walter Harper begin ascent of Denali

- June   Hudson Stuck party conquers North America's highest mountain; Walter Harper is the first to set foot upon the summit of Denali

- Sept.   Death of Archdeacon Robert McDonald who worked along Upper Yukon and MacKenzie Rivers for 50 years; he translated Bible, Prayer Book and Hymnal into Takudh.

1914 - Jan.   Fire in Tanana destroys hospital, mission and dispensary

- Sept.   Death at Cape Lisburne of Dr. John Driggs, pioneer medical missionary

- Oct.   First service held in rebuilt church in Stevens Village

1915 -   Frederick B. Drane appointed Archdeacon, headquartered at Nenana

- Feb.   Bishop Rowe baptizes and confirms Chief John of Mentasta, the first confirmation on the upper Tanana River

- Apr.   Birth of David Rea Cochran in Buffalo, New York

Fr. Bob Jones officiates at the ground-breaking ceremony for St. Christopher's, Anchorage, 1968.

-     St. Matthew's hospital in Fairbanks closed

1916 -   Fort Yukon Hospital opened to fight tuberculosis

-     Mission boat *Pelican* arrives at Fort Yukon

-     All Saint's Church built in Anchorage

- Oct.   Deaconess Harriet Bedell arrives in Nenana; she serves for 15 years in Nenana, Stevens Village and Tanana.

1917 -   Chena Mission closes

- May   Rev. E.W. Hughes arrives in Anchorage to be the first resident Episcopal priest

1918 - Mar.   Death in Anvik of Simon's mother, the first communicant in Anvik

- May   Birth of William J. Gordon Jr. in Spray, North Carolina

- June   Death at Fort Yukon of William Loola, first Athabascan ordained to diaconate

- Oct.   The sinking of the *Princess Sophia* in Lynn Canal near Juneau in which all 353 persons aboard drown,

including Walter and Frances Harper

1919 - April   Bishop Rowe consecrates St. George's Church, Cordova

1920 - Jan.   St. Luke's in Salchaket closes

- April   Rev. A.R. Hoare who had served in Fort Yukon and Tanana is shot and killed in Point Hope by his young assistant from California

- Oct.   Death of Archdeacon Hudson Stuck in Fort Yukon

1922 - Jan.   First issue of *The Alaskan Churchman* with cover by Eustace Ziegler

- Apr.   The Rev. and Mrs. William Thomas arrive in Nenana after 64 days on the trail from Point Hope

- June   Ordination in Tanacross of Arthur Wright to diaconate

- July   Miss Amelia Hill arrives to serve in Allakaket

- July   Bishop Stringer of Yukon Territory dedicates Celtic cross, marking Archdeacon Stuck's grave in Fort Yukon

1924 - Sept. Fire in Fort Yukon completely destroys Mission and Stuck's library

1925 - Chandalar Village mission established; Bishop Rowe Chapel in Arctic Village consecrated by Dr. Burke

- July Albert Tritt of Arctic Village is ordained to diaconate at Fort Yukon

- Aug. The Rev. Frederick Goodman arrives in Point Hope where he stays for 18 years

- Dec. Birth of George Clinton Harris in Brooklyn, New York

1927 - Aug. Bishop Rowe flies from Nome to Point Hope in the first plane to land at Point Hope

1928 - Feb. Consecration of St. Elizabeth's, Ketchikan

- July Deaconess Bedell leaves Stevens Village after nine years of service and moves to Tanana

1929 - A mission is begun at Minto on the lower Tanana River

1930 - Rev. John Chapman retires from Anvik. A mission is begun at Kivalina

- Jan. Fire destroys Betticher Memorial Hall in Nenana

- Nov. Paul Mather becomes first Alaska Native ordained to priesthood in Ketchikan

1931 - Sept. Deaconess Bedell leaves Tanana after 15 years of service in Alaska

- Sept. John Boyd Bentley, second Bishop of Alaska, consecrated in Denver as Suffragan Bishop of Alaska

1934 - April Bishop Bentley consecrates All Saints, Anchorage

1935 - Mar. Budget cuts force closing of Anvik Boarding School

1936 - Feb. Death of the Rev. Harry Corser, serving St. Philip's in Wrangell 1903-1934; he started the first Boy Scout troops in Alaska

- Sept. First service held in new church in Allakaket

1937 - Sept. Death of Fr. Jules Prevost, first resident priest in Tanana; he translated Prayer Book and Hymnal, printed first newspaper in the Interior, and founded churches in Circle, Nome and Valdez.

1939 - Sept. Death of Dr. Grafton Burke who had worked in Fort Yukon since 1908

- Nov. Death of the Rev. John W. Chapman who served in Anvik for over 40 years

1942 - Jan. Death of Rev. Paul Mather, first Alaska Native ordained to the priesthood

- June Death of Bishop Peter Trimble Rowe in Victoria, British Columbia

- June Death of David Wallis, longtime lay reader and interpreter in Fort Yukon

- July Committal of Bishop Rowe's ashes in Sitka

1943 - Mar. William J. Gordon and Shirley Lewis arrive in Alaska

- July The Gordons are married in Seward by Bishop Bentley and leave on assignment to Point Hope

- Aug. The Venerable Frederick Goodman retires after 18 years in Point Hope

1944 - July Death of Peel Tooyak, longtime layreader and interpreter in Point Hope

- Nov. The Very Rev. Charles Rice of Holy Trinity, Juneau, retires

1945 - Jan. Rev. E. A. McIntosh retires after 12 years in Tanacross

- Aug. Death of John Fredson in Venetie

1947 - Feb. Fire nearly destroys St. Matthew's, Fairbanks

- May Death of the Venerable William Goodman, Archdeacon of the Arctic from 1925-1943

- May William J. Gordon Jr. elected third Bishop of Alaska at age 29

- May Bishop Gordon consecrated in North Carolina as third Bishop of Alaska

1949 - Feb. Birth of Steven Charleston in Duncan, Oklahoma

- April Bishop Gordon departs Fairbanks on first cross-country flight flying his own plane

- Sept. Fr. Robert Reid of Nenana, Enoch Tooyak of Point Hope, and Teddy Mueller of Nenana drown during a hunting trip on the Tanana River

1953 - July Miss Kay and Miss Hill leave Allakaket after combined 50 years of faithful service

1954 - Missions started at Kotzebue and Holikachuk

- June Philip Jerauld, organist for St. Andrew's in Petersburg, is ordained to diaconate by Bishop Gordon

1955 - Three more missions established: Beaver, Huslia and Shageluk

1957 - May The Rev. David Paul ordained to diaconate

1958 - The Rev. David Salmon ordained deacon

1960 - Jan. St. Bartholomew's dedicated in Palmer

- July Hudson Stuck Memorial Hospital at Fort Yukon closes after 52 years of operation

- Oct. Consecration of Church of the Good Shepherd, Huslia

1961 - Mar. First Yukon Valley Training School begins in Fort Yukon

- Mar. Fire destroys mission house in Tanana, killing Fr. D. Curtis Edwards and his three children

1962 - April First convention of Episcopal laity and clergy held in Anchorage with 66 present

- Oct. Ordination of David Salmon of Chalkyitsik, first Athabascan priest

- Nov. First service of St. James-the-Fisherman, Kodiak, in new unfinished building

1963 - Feb. The Rev. Henry Chapman retires after 40 years of service in Alaska

1964 - Jan. Bishop Gordon dedicates Bishop Rowe House in Fairbanks

- June Ordination in Fort Yukon of Titus Peter and Philip Peter to the diaconate, and Isaac Tritt to the priesthood

- June Ordination of Milton Swan, first Inupiaq priest of the Episcopal Church

1965 - June Presiding Bishop John E. Hines visits the newest mission: St. James-the-Fisherman, Kodiak

- July Seventy-fifth anniversary of the Point Hope mission

1966 - Jan. St. George's-in-the-Arctic consecrated in Kotzebue

- June — Bishop Gordon lands in Fairbanks in new Cessna 180 replacing "Blue Box II"

1967 - Aug. — Floods inundate Interior communities including Nenana and Fairbanks

1968 - Mar. — Ordination of the Rev. Donald Oktollik of Point Hope, the second Inupiaq ordained to the priesthood

- Spring — Ground broken for St. Christopher's, Anchorage

- Aug. — Group of Alaskans leaves for training at Cook Christian School in Arizona

- Nov. — Dedication of St. Paul's, Grayling

- Dec. — Dedication of St. Mary's, Anchorage

1971 - — Missionary District of Alaska becomes Diocese of Alaska

- Feb. — Ordination of George Edwin of Tanana to diaconate

- Mar. — First Arctic Coast Deanery Meeting - Point Hope

- June — First Interior Deanery Meeting - Tanana

- July — Dedication of Fort Yukon Community Center, financed in part by a $93,000 loan from the National Church

- Sept — Ordination of George Edwin of Tanana to priesthood

- Nov. — Dedication of St. Barnabas, New Minto

Bishop Gordon congratulates Bishop-elect David Cochran at the Diocesan Convention in Anchorage, April 1974.

1972 - Feb. — Ordination in Shageluk of Jean Dementi, first woman deacon in Alaska

- July — Burial service for the Rev. George Edwin in Tanana

1973 - Sept. — Bishop Gordon departs Fairbanks for Huslia and his last moose hunt up the Koyukuk

- Sept. — Funeral for Chief Jarvis of

Salchaket who drowned earlier in the summer

- Nov. — Dedication of new St. James' Church, Tanana

1974 - April — Bishop Gordon retires and leaves Alaska; David Cochran elected fourth Bishop of Alaska.

- Aug. — Consecration in Fairbanks of David Rea Cochran as fourth Bishop of Alaska

1976 - 1985 — Development and dedication of Meier Lake Conference Center, Wasilla

1977 - Jan. — Ordination of Jean Dementi to the priesthood, first woman ordained in Alaska

1980 - May — Beginning of first camp at Emmaus Center, Petersburg

1981 - June — George Clinton Harris is consecrated in Fairbanks as fifth Bishop of Alaska

1982 - Feb. — Death of Rev. Milton Swan in Kivalina

1984 - Oct. — Diocesan Convention approves Eagle River congregation as a mission

1985 - Sept. — St. Brendan's, Juneau, is established

1986 - Oct. — St. James, Birch Creek, is

established by 13th Convention as newest mission in the Diocese

1987 - Aug.   Bishops Gordon and Harris consecrate rebuilt St. Matthew's in Beaver

- Sept.   Bishop Harris consecrates new Good Shepherd church building in Venetie

- Nov.   Bishops Harris and Cochran consecrate new church in Circle

1988 - June   Death of the Rev. Jean Dementi in Fairbanks

1989 - June   Death of Bishop John B. Bentley in Hampton, Virginia

- Oct.   Steven Charleston elected sixth Bishop of Alaska

1991 - Feb.   Bishop Harris dedicates and consecrates new addition and renovation of St. James the Fisherman, Kodiak

- Mar.   Steven Charleston is consecrated in Anchorage as sixth Bishop of Alaska

- Aug.   First service in Haines of what is to become Church of St. Michael and All Angels

- Oct.   First installation of members of Society of St. Simeon and St. Anna

1994 - Jan.   Death of Bishop William J. Gordon Jr. in Midland, Michigan

- June   Interment of Bishop Gordon's ashes at Point Hope

✝

Church school members at Eagle, 1910

*...I have called you by name,
    you are mine.*
                            - Isaiah 43:1

XV
THESE ARE THE NAMES

The following names of communities and church workers bear witness to a powerful story of the Episcopal ministry in Alaska. The parish/mission roster in *The Alaskan Churchman* and *Alaskan Epiphany* served as the primary source for a record of service to the Diocese. Most names are listed as they first appeared in the roster. Regretfully this roll of service falls short of the full story of discipleship in the Episcopal Church in Alaska. This present effort is offered as an introduction to that story. Further information from readers of this book will be gratefully received.

SOUTHEAST

DOUGLAS

St. Luke's

1896	The Rev. Dr. Campbell
1906	The Rev. C.A. Roth
1918	The Rev. A.E. Butcher
1921	The Rev. Charles E. Rice
1944	The Rev. W. Robert Webb
1948	The Rev. Samuel A. McPhetres

HAINES

St. Michael and All Angels

1988	The Rev. Jan Hotze

JUNEAU

Holy Trinity

1896	The Rev. Henry Beers
1902	The Rev. C.A. Roth
1906	Miss Pritchard
1908	The Rev. Thomas Jenkins
	Miss Phoebe G.L. Girault
1910	The Rev. G.E. Renison
1916	The Rev. Guy D. Christian
1918	The Rev. A.E. Butcher
1921	The Rev. Charles E. Rice
1943	The Rev. William Forbes
1944	The Rev. W. Robert Webb
1948	The Rev. Samuel A. McPhetres
1959	The Rev. Mark Boesser
1964	The Rev. Walter W. Hannum
1966	The Rev. Charles H. Eddy
1969	The Rev. Richard K. Clarke
1970	The Rev. Dr. Robert Cavitt
	The Rev. Glen Wilcox
1970	The Rev. John E. Randall
1972	The Rev. Dale G. Sarles
1976	The Rev. Charles Adams
1977	The Rev. John Larson
1984	The Rev. Ann Parsons
1984	The Rev. George Masuda
1985	The Rev. Roger Wharton
1992	The Rev. Herb McMurtry
1994	The Rev. David Elsensohn
	Ms. Paula Sampson, seminarian
1994	The Rev. Laura Lockey

St. Andrew's by the Glacier

St. Brendan's

1972	Served from Holy Trinity
1992	The Rev. Wilson Valentine

KETCHIKAN

St. Elizabeth's/St. John's

1906	The Rev. Thomas Jenkins
1907	Dss. E.M. Deane
	Miss Edith Jones
	M.F. Loomis, layreader
	William Dickinson
1908	Miss Agnes M. Huntoon
1909	The Rev. Robert
1910	Dss. Louise Smart
	Miss Margaret M. Beebe
	Miss Ella Woods
	Miss Fullerton
	Miss Louise Mead
	Miss N.B. Harrett
1913	A.M. Sutphen
1914	Miss Margaret Wygant
	Miss Marlow
1915	Mrs. Ross
1916	The Rev. H.H. Kelly
	Mrs. Adella Cook
1917	Mrs. J.H. Molineaux
1918	Miss Edith Harper
1921	Miss Lillie J. Ames

Missionary District clergy met in Juneau in the mid-1960s. From left to right: first row: Hugh F. Hall, Norman H.V. Elliott, Lew Hodgkins, Milton Swan, Bishop Gordon, Glen Wilcox, Isaac Tritt, Walter Hannum, and Randy Mendelsohn. Second row: Lee Stratman, Mark Boesser, Don Hart, Jim Bills, Titus Peter, Dale Sarles, Dick Simmonds, Dick Clarke, Sandy Zabriskie, David Salmon, and Philip Peter. Back row: William Warren, Richard McGinnis, Don Bullock, Ned Caum, Murray Trelease, Jim Carrington, Richard Treadwell, Roger Lund, Bob Jones, John Phillips, David Paul, and David Keller.

1923	The Rev. Homer E. Bush
1924	Miss A. Wikon
1925	B. Ridley, layworker
1926	The Rev. Henry R. Sanborn
1928	The Rev. Paul Mather
	Casper Mather, layreader
1930	The Rev. Mark T. Carpenter
1936	The Rev. M.L. Wanner
1938	The Rev. Paul Maslin
1944	Gertrude Mather
1945	The Rev. Barclay Johnson
1947	The Rev. J. Kenneth Watkins
1954	The Rev. Lewis Hodgkins
1956	The Rev. Cameron Harriot
1958	The Rev. Norman H.V. Elliott
1962	The Rev. Hugh F. Hall
1969	The Rev. Donald M. Bullock
1976	The Rev. Earle C. Palmer
1985	The Rev. Morgan Sheldon
1985	The Rev. Gary Herbst

PETERSBURG

St. Andrew's

1954	Served from Wrangell
	(The Rev. Hugh F. Hall)
1956	The Rev. Albert J. Sayers
1959	The Rev. Henry H. Chapman
1963	Served from Wrangell
	(The Rev. Wilfred C. Files)
1964	The Rev. James H. Carrington
1967	Served from Wrangell
	(The Rev. Edward L. Caum)
1971	Served from Sitka (The Revs.
	Lee Stratman/George Beacom)
1975	Served from Ketchikan
	(The Rev. Donald M. Bullock)
1977	Martha Bateman
1979	The Rev. Stephen Kelsey
	The Rev. N. DeLiza Spangler
1982	The Rev. Susan Grove

1986	The Rev. Spaulding Howe
1987	The Rev. John Forney
1994	The Rev. Dale G. Sarles
1995	Bill Fulton, seminarian

SITKA

St. Peter's-by-the-Sea

1906	The Rt. Rev. Peter T. Rowe
1913	The Rev. George E. Howard
1926	Mrs. J.H. Molineaux
1938	Henrietta Barlow
1942	The Rev. William A. Thomas
1948	The Rev. Henry H. Chapman
1959	The Rev. Robert Grumbine
1962	The Rev. Lee Stratman
1963	Titus Peter
1964	Mrs. Elinor Stanland
1965	Miss Virginia Vere
1967	The Rev. Thomas E. Stevenson
1969	The Rev. George Beacom
1976	The Rev. Everitt Calhoun
1978	The Rev. Bruce Bayne
1981	The Rev. Robert Burton
1983	The Rev. Robert Clapp
1989	The Rev. Spaulding Howe
1991	The Rev. John David
1995	The Rev. David Elsensohn

SKAGWAY

St. Savior's Church and
Bishop Rowe Hospital

1897	The Rev. Dr. Campbell
	The Rev. Henry Beers
1899	The Rev. Cameron
1906	The Rev. C.A. Mullikin
	Mrs. C.A. Mullikin
1907	F.W. Lowle, layreader
1909	The Rev. Thomas Jenkins
1930	The Rev. Warren R. Fenn
1943	Emery W. Stanfield

1954	Served from Juneau
	(The Rev. Samuel A.
	McPhetres)

WRANGELL

St. Philip's Church and
Wrangell General Hospital

1903	The Rev. Henry P. Corser
1910	Dss Mabel Pick
	Miss Ella L. Woods
	Miss Blanche McCreery
1930	Miss Agnes Le Roi
	Miss Sarah Hart
1934	Arnold Krone
1942	The Rev. William Forbes
1946	The Rev. Thomas P. Maslin
1949	The Rev. Hugh F. Hall
1958	The Rev. John R. Lodge
1961	The Rev. Wilfred C. Files
1965	The Rev. Edward L. Caum
1975	Miss Alice Hunt, volunteer
1979	The Rev. Stephen Kelsey
	The Rev. N. DeLiza Spangler
1983	The Rev. Jan Hotze
1986	The Rev. Edward L. Caum

SOUTHCENTRAL

ANCHORAGE

All Saints'
1918	The Rev. Edwin W. Hughes
	The Rev. T.P. Howard
1922	The Rev. Burdette Landsdowne
1925	The Rev. W.A. Thomas
1930	The Rev. William MacPherson
1936	The Rev. Warren R. Fenn
1950	The Rev. Albert J. Sayers
1954	The Rev. Philip W. Jerauld
1956	The Rev. Malcolm H. Miner
	Miss Caroline Templeton, DCE
1958	The Rev. John M. Kinney
1959	The Rev. Lewis Hodgkins
1962	The Rev. Norman H.V. Elliott
1967	The Rev. John R. Herlocker
1972	The Rev. Malcoln H. Miner
1973	The Rev. Lee Stratman
1990	The Rev. James Basinger
1994	The Rev. Norman Nauska

St. Christopher's
1966	The Rev. Gary M. Noteboom
	The Rev. Bob G. Jones
1972	The Rev. Robert W. Bennett
1976	The Rev. Allen P. Richmond
1978	The Rev. David Schmidt
1979	The Rev. David Cates
	The Rev. Malcolm H. Miner
1983	The Rev. Allen Price
	The Rev. David Pettit
1984	The Rev. Bob Franken
	The Rev. Betty Lou Anthony
1985	The Rev. Jorgen Lilliebjerg
1986	The Rev. Mary Fisher
1987	Sister Mary Grace
1989	The Rev. Lee Stratman

1990	The Rev. Richard Staats
1991	The Rev. Betty Lou Anthony
1995	The Rev. Scott Rathman

St. Mary's
1966	The Rev. Alex. C.Zabriskie Jr.
	The Rev. Philip E. Jerauld
	Elaine Johnson, layreader
1969	The Rev. Charles H. Eddy
1972	The Rev. Everett Wenrick
1973	The Rev. Donald W. Spafford
1976	The Rev. Jorgen Lilliebjerg
	The Rev. Lawrence Spannagel
	The Rev. Robert C. Thwing
	The Rev. Diane Tickell
1977	The Rev. Raymond Dexter
1979	The Rev. Robert Nelson
1983	The Rev. Norman Nauska
	The Rev. Keith Lawton
1984	The Rev. Sue Hewitt
1985	The Rev. Veronica Knapick
1986	The Rev. Allen Price
1994	Michael Burke, seminarian

Christ Church
1981	The Rev. Raymond Dexter
1985	The Rev. Sue Hewitt
1991	The Rev. Allen P. Richmond
1994	Richard Stevens, seminarian
	Ms. Sue Smith, seminarian
1995	The Rev. Larry Spannagel

CORDOVA

St. George's
1908	(Served from Valdez)
	The Rev. E.P. Newton
1909	The Rev. Eustace P. Ziegler
1924	Miss Elsie Waitz
1925	The Rev. Leicester F. Kent
1928	The Rev. M.J. Kippenbrock

1939	The Rev. M.L. Wanner
1951	Served from Valdez
	(The Rev. Robert Grumbine)
1954	Page H. Kent
1956	The Rev. Lewis Hodgkins
1959	The Rev. Robert F. McClellan
1960	The Rev. John M. Kinney
1961	The Rev. Glen M. Wilcox
1967	Served from Seward
	(The Rev. Randall Mendelsohn)
1968	The Rev. David G.R. Keller
1969	Served from Valdez
	(The Rev. Dale G. Sarles)
1972	The Rev. Leslie L. Fairfield
1976	Served from St. Mary's,
	Anchorage (The Rev. Robert
	C. Thwing)
1979	The Rev. Diane Tickell
1991	The Rev. Ronald N. Hiester
1994	The Rev. Spaulding Howe

EAGLE RIVER

Holy Spirit
1984	The Rev. Norman Nauska
1986	The Rev. Bob Franken
1989	Dyana Orrin, seminarian
1994	The Rev. Greg Kimura

HOMER

St. Augustine's
1976	The Rev. Joe L. Aprill
1985	The Rev. Tom Taylor
1990	The Rev. Francoise Ray
	Nickie Stipe, seminarian
1995	Will Files, layworker
	The Rev. Paula Sampson

KENAI

St. Francis-by-the-Sea
1976	The Rev. Joe L. Aprill

Fr. Gregory Kimura

1978	The Rev. Allen Price
1981	The Rev. Noel Rich
1985	The Rev. Richard Simmonds
1989	The Rev. Scott Rathman
1991	The Rev. Dyana Orrin

KODIAK
St. James the Fisherman

1961	Served from Seward (The Rev. Hugh F. Hall)
1962	The Rev. Donald M. Bullock
1969	The Rev. Hugh F. Hall
1983	The Rev. Thomas White
1986	The Rev. Herb McMurtry
1992	The Rev. Francoise Ray
1994	The Rev. Steve Avery

PALMER
St. Bartholomew's

1958	Served from All Saints, Anchorage (The Rev. Malcolm H. Miner) The Rev. John M. Kinney
1960	The Rev. Thomas G. Cleveland
1961	Served from Valdez

	(The Rev. Dennis R. Walker)
1964	The Rev. Dennis R. Walker
1966	Served from Anchorage (The Rev. Lewis Hodgkins)
1967	The Rev. Bob G. Jones
1971	The Rev. James Carrington
1973	The Rev. Malcolm H. Miner
1976	The Rev. Larry Spannagel The Rev. George Beacom
1982	The Rev. Helen Peters
1987	The Rev. Ray Dexter
1991	The Rev. Ralph Wagner

SEWARD
St. Peter's

1907	The Rev. F.C. Taylor
1909	The Rev. Charles E. Rice
1917	The Rev. George J. Zinn
1929	The Rev. Wm. R. MacPherson
1940	The Rev. Warren R. Fenn
1943	The Rt. Rev. John C. Ward
1944	The Rev. Edward M. Turner
1949	The Rev. J. Russell Clapp
1956	The Rev. Carter van Waes
1958	The Rev. Hugh F. Hall
1962	The Rev. Randall Mendelsohn
1968	The Rev. Everett P. Wenrick
1971	The Rev. Donald Hart
1976	The Rev. Charles Lechner
1982	The Rev. Noel Rich
1987	The Rev. Mark Boesser
1988	The Rev. Myrle Diener
1993	The Rev. Ronald Hiester

TALKEETNA
Denali Chapel

| 1990 | The Rev. George Beacom |

VALDEZ
Epiphany and Good Samaritan Hospital

1906	The Rev. Frederick C. Taylor
	Mrs. Frederick C. Taylor
	Miss E.M. Deane
1907	Miss Phoebe L. Girault
	Miss Lottie Brown
1908	The Rev. Edward P. Newton
1909	Miss Henrietta Barlow
	Miss Margaret Wygant
1910	Miss Margaret M. Beebe
	Miss Anna Cora Eaton
1911	Miss Lucinda Fast
1912	The Rev. Winfred H. Zeigler
1913	Miss L.J. Holmes
1915	The Rev. E.H. Molony
1917	The Rev. George J. Zinn
1939	The Rev. M.L. Wanner
1951	The Rev. Robert Grumbine
1960	The Rev. Dennis R. Walker

*ecumenical ministry: Episcopal, Lutheran & Presbyterian churches

1964	Served from Cordova (The Rev. Glen M. Wilcox)
1967	The Rev. Dale G. Sarles
1973	The Rev. John H. Emmert
1975	The Rev. Kee Harrison
1977	The Rev. Allen Price
1978	The Rev. Eric Ottum, pastor
1981	The Rev. Tom Auer, pastor
1985	The Rev. Susan Frey, pastor
1990	The Rev. Katherine Radach
1990	The Rev. Mark Will, pastor

WASILLA
St. David's

1978	The Rev. Mark Boesser
1991	The Rev. Francoise Ray
1992	The Rev. Dyana Orrin

ARCTIC COAST

BARROW
1988   The Rev. Montie Slusher

KIVALINA

Epiphany
1930   Tony Joule
1938   Capt. Jack deForrest,
       Church Army (C.A.)
       Capt. Albert Sayers, C.A.
1946   The Rev. Milton Swan
1976   The Rev. Raymond Hawley
       The Rev. Jerry Norton
       The Rev. Clinton Swan
1982   The Rev. James Hawley

KOTZEBUE

St. George's-in-the-Arctic
1954   The Rev. Alwin Reiners Jr.
1955   Chester Seveck, layreader
1958   The Rev. Thomas M. Osgood
1962   The Rev. Bob G. Jones
       Paul Buckwalter, volunteer
       Reed Nelson, volunteer
1966   The Rev. Gary M. Noteboom
1971   The Ven. Walter W. Hannum
1972   Charlie Jensen, layreader
       Charles Huss Jr., layworker
1973   The Rev. Richard T. Draper
1976   The Rev. James Hawley
       The Rev. Wilfred Lane
1993   The Rev. Bob Swope

NOATAK
       (served from Kotzebue and
       Kivalina)
1995   Evelyn Shy, layworker

NOME

St. Mary's Mission
1899   The Rev. Jules L. Prevost
1907   J.A. St. Clair
1909   Guy D. Christian

POINT HOPE

St. Thomas's Mission and
Augustus Hoare Memorial Hospital
1890   Dr. John B. Driggs
       Sam Rock, interpreter
1908   The Rev. Augustus R. Hoare
       Harry Killbear, interpreter
1911   The Ven. F.W. Goodman
1918   The Rev. William A. Thomas
1919   Miss Virginia Thomas
1920   Miss Emilie Grunason, R.N.
       Miss Ruth Ward (Mrs. Wm. A.
       Thomas)
1936   Ebruluk Rock, interpreter
       Peel Tooyak, interpreter
       Mrs. E.E. Brown
       Jesse F. Brown
1938   Capt. Jack deForrest, C.A.
       Capt. Albert Sayers, C.A.
1943   The Rev. Wm. J. Gordon Jr.
       Andrew Frankson, interpreter
       David Frankson, interpreter
1948   Joel Bourne
1951   The Rev. Howard Laycock
       Daniel Lisbourne
       Roy Vincent
       Page H. Kent
1953   The Rev. Rowland J. Cox
1955   The Rev. Donald Oktollik
1959   Capt. Page Kent, C.A.
       The Rev. J. Keith Lawton
1966   The Ven. Walter W. Hannum
1975   Mr. & Mrs. Robert Waggner
1976   The Rev. Patrick Attungana

       The Rev. Herbert Kinneeveauk
       The Rev. Nelda Kinneeveauk
1984   The Rev. Seymour Tuzroyluke
       Sr.
1989   The Rev. Elijah Attungana
       Andrew Tooyak Sr., layreader

POINT LAY

St. Alban's-in-the-Arctic
1930   Tony Joule, layreader
1950   Samuel Agnassaga
1979   The Rev. Montie Slusher
1995   Willie Tukrook, layworker

The Rev. Donald Oktollik is accompanied by Vera Frankson as he sits beside the whalebone fencing of the Point Hope cemetery. Traditionally, two bones from each whale landed at Point Hope are added to the palings, now numbering more than 800, that surround the gravesites.

INTERIOR

ALLAKAKET
St. John's-in-the-Wilderness
1907	Dss. Clara M. Carter
	Miss Clara Heintz
1910	Miss Anna E. Cady
1912	Dss. Ada Knox
	Miss E.L. Jackson
1913	Dss. Bertha B. Mills
1916	Miss Eleanor Ridgway
1918	Miss Katherine Koster
1921	Dss. Muriel A. Thayer
	Miss Lossie deRosset Cotchett
1922	Miss Amelia Hill, R.N.
1924	Miss Florence Huband
1929	Miss Estella Wilcox
1930	Miss Mildred Boyes, R.N.
1932	Miss Bessie Kay
1953	The Rev. Richard S. Miller
1956	The Rev. Randall P. Mendelsohn
1962	The Rev. Robert S. Kinney
1966	The Rev. Jim V. Bills
1969	The Rev. Raymond Oppenheim
1971	Cadet Richard Stevens, C.A.
1973	The Rev. Joe Williams Jr.
1995	Johnson Moses, layworker

ANVIK
Christ Church Mission
1886	The Rev. Octavius Parker
1887	The Rev. John W. Chapman
1906	Mrs. John W. Chapman
	Dr. Mary Glenton
	Dss. Bertha Sabine
	Mrs. F.B. Evans
1907	Miss Alice A. Green
	Miss Phoebe L. Girault
	Isaac Fisher, layreader

Fr. John E. Huhn -- His grave is at Rampart.

1908	Charles Walter Williams
1910	Miss M.C. Graves
	Miss Celia Wright
	Miss E.L. Jackson
1913	Miss Ora Dee Clark
1914	Miss M.C. Matson
1916	David McConnell
1917	Dss. A.B. Sterne
1918	Mrs. David McConnell
1919	Mrs. F.H. Olsen
1920	Miss Marguerite Bartberger
	Miss Ada Chapman
1921	John Boyd Bentley
	Miss Susan E. Smith
1923	Miss Ella B. Lucas
1924	Miss Florence Keefe, R.N.

1929	Miss Hazel Chandler
	Miss Adelaide E. Smith
	Miss Jean Jones, R.N.
1930	Mr. Chase, volunteer
1937	The Rev. Wilfred C. Files
	Miss T. Gayle Wagner, R.N.
1940	The Rev. Henry H. Chapman
1941	Miss Julia Anderson
1942	Miss Bessie Blacknall
1943	Mrs. Harry H. Lawrence, R.N.
1946	The Rev. Robert P. Holdt
1948	The Rev. B.R. Peterson
	Miss Mary E. Rowley, R.N.
1949	The Rev. Albert J. Sayers
1951	Miss Almeria Gordon
	Miss Mary I. Gordon, R.N.
1952	Albert E. Rich, volunteer
1953	The Rev. Glen M. Wilcox
1954	Curtis Cowell, volunteer
	Miss Elsie Smithcors
1961	The Rev. Richard H. McGinnis
1967	Served from Grayling (The Rev. Richard K. Clarke)
1969	Served from Shageluk (The Rev. Jean Dementi)
1972	The Rev. Jean Dementi
1973	James Fulton
1995	Ms. Julie Walker, layworker

ARCTIC VILLAGE
Bishop Rowe Chapel
1925	The Rev. Albert E. Tritt
1956	Raymond Harrison
	Sandy Krumbhaar, volunteer
1959	The Rev. Isaac Tritt
	Gilbert Joseph
1964	The Rev. Titus Peter
1973	Tom Brawner, volunteer
1976	The Rev. James Gilbert
	The Rev. Trimble Gilbert

Clergy participated at ordination service at Tanacross, May 30, 1957, when David Paul became a Deacon. Left to right: Norman H.V. Elliott, Chaplain (Capt.) Robert Clark, perpetual deacon from Fort Greely, Malcolm Miner, Richard Simmonds, Chaplain William Doneghy of Fort Richardson, Bishop Gordon, the ordinand, David Paul, Robert Grumbine, Richard Lambert, Lee Stratman, Sandy Zabriskie, and Robert Greene. (Photo by Dick Kezlan)

BEAVER

St. Matthew's

1953	The Rev. Norman H.V. Elliott
1955	Capt. George S. Glander, C.A.
1960	The Rev. Alfred H. Smith Jr.
1962	The Rev. Richard Simmonds
1966	The Rev. Richard Treadwell
1970	David Sheldrake
1971	Scott Fisher, volunteer
	Charles Judd, volunteer
1973	Christopher McLendon
	Robert Davenport
1977	The Rev. Scott Fisher
1981	The Rev. David Salmon
1986	The Rev. Stan Sullivan
1995	Ms. Elsie Pitka, layworker

BETHEL

1986	The Rev. Tom Wilson

BIRCH CREEK

St. James'

1986	The Rev. Titus Peter
1995	Randall Balaam, layworker

CHANDALAR VILLAGE CHAPEL/ VENETIE

1925	Enoch John

CHALKYITSIK

St. Timothy's

1953	The Rev. Norman H.V. Elliott
1954	The Rev. Albert E. Tritt
1959	The Rev. David Salmon (Bishop Bentley Chapel/St. Timothy's)
1962	Reed Nelson
1964	The Rev. Isaac Tritt
1967	The Rev. Titus Peter

1970	Scott Fisher, volunteer
1990	The Rev. Mary Nathaniel

CIRCLE

Trinity

1906	The Rev. Charles E. Rice
	Mrs. Charles Rice
1907	Joseph Kluwell, layworker
1909	Dss. Bertha Sabine
	Joseph Minister, layworker
1953	The Rev. Norman H.V. Elliott
1956	Ned Sunderland, volunteer
1957	Bruce H. Kennedy, volunteer
1960	Sandy Roberts, layreader
1964	The Ven. Murray L. Trelease
1980	The Rev. John A. Phillips
1995	Ms. Alice Carroll, layworker

EAGLE

St. John's and St. Paul's

1906	George E. Boulter
1908	George B. Burgess
1919	The Rev. B.W. Gaither
1924	The Rev. Arthur G. Fullerton
	Walter Benjamin, layreader
	Mrs. Sarah Benjamin
1947	Miss Grace Crossen, R.N.
	L.A. Crossen
1953	The Rev. Norman H.V. Elliott
1957	The Ven. Norman H.V. Elliott
1964	The Ven. Murray L. Trelease
1965	The Rev. Richard A. Treadwell
1967	Served from Nenana (The Rev. John A. Phillips)
1976	John and Sandi Four Bear, volunteers
1981	The Rev. Donald P. Hart
1995	Ms. JoAnne Beck, layworker

FAIRBANKS

St. Matthew's Church and St. Matthew's Hospital

1904	The Rev. John E. Huhn
	The Ven. Hudson Stuck
1905	The Rev. Chas.E. Betticher Jr.
	Miss Isabel Emberley
1906	Miss Emma C. Johnson
	Miss Florence G. Langdon
1907	Miss Margaret R. Wightman
	B.F. Taylor, layreader
	Miss Jessie B. Alexander
	T. Pryor, layreader
1908	Dss. Ada Knox
	Miss Agnes Bolster
1909	H.W. Strangman, layreader
	Miss Margaret Graves
	C.W. Williams, layreader
1910	The Rev. Louis K. Buisch
	Miss Clara C. Johnston
	Miss Dorothy S. Tate
	Miss Alma Lewis
	Mrs. M.S. Love
	Miss M.V. Holgate
1913	Miss Barbara O'Conner
1914	The Rev. H.Hope Lumpkin
	Miss Beulah Frederick
	Miss Lillian Winter
1923	The Rev. Henry H. Chapman
1927	The Rev. Mervin L. Wanner
1931	The Rev. Warren R. Fenn
1933	The Rev. M.J. Kippenbrock
1936	The Rev. Claudius P. Shelton
1940	The Rev. Elsom Eldridge
1944	The Rev. Albert N. Jones
1951	The Rev. Roy E. Sommers
	The Rev. Gordon T.Charlton Jr.
	Miss Blanche Meyers
1953	Page Kent
1954	The Rev. Norman H.V. Elliott

1955	The Rev. Richard T. Lambert
1956	The Rev. A.C. Zabriskie Jr.
1957	Mrs. Glenn Ward
1959	The Rev. Wm. T. Warren Jr.
	The Rev. R.B. Greene
1961	The Rev. Richard F. Simmonds
1962	The Rev. Edward L. Caum
1965	The Rev. Roger M. Lund
1972	The Rev. Titus Peter
	Miss Elaine Johnson, lay-reader/youth worker
	The Rev. Glen Wilcox
1973	The Rev. Donald P. Hart
	The Rev. R. Stephen Sedgwick
1976	The Rev. Anna Frank
	The Rev. Raymond Dexter
1979	The Rev. Allen P. Richmond
1983	The Rev. Fredrick Smyithe
1984	The Rev. Ned Caum
	The Rev. Roger Williams
1985	The Rev. Helen Peters
	The Rev. Melissa Newlin
1989	The Rev. Lewis Hodgkins
1990	Wilson Valentine, seminarian
	The Rev. Montie Slusher
1991	The Rev. Mike Williams
	The Rev. Scott Fisher
1994	Jim Eichner, seminarian

FORT YUKON
St. Stephen's Church, Mission School & Hudson Stuck Hospital

1899	The Rev. Leonides H. Wooden
1906	Miss Lizzie J. Woods
	Miss Florence G. Langdon
1907	The Rev. William Loola
1908	The Ven. Hudson Stuck
	Miss Anne E. Cady
	Dr. Grafton Burke
1913	Walter Harper, layworker

1914	Dr. E.R. Murphy
	Miss Effie Jackson
	Miss Dorothy Tate
1915	Miss Agnes M. Huntoon
1918	Miss Frances Wells
	Moses Cruikshank
	Miss Numeviller
	Dss. Mabel Pick
1920	Dss. Smith
	Miss E.B. Gunz, R.N.
1921	Miss Nellie W. Landon
	Dss. Fannie E. Cleaver
1922	Dr. Ernest A. Cook
	Miss Lillie J. Ames, R.N.
	Miss Lucy Vigus, R.N.
	Miss Annie P. Cook
	Miss Sands
	Mrs. Beatrice Wood
1923	David Wallis, layreader/interpreter

Fr. Warren R. Fenn

1925	The Rev. G.H. Moody
	Miss Elizabeth Kellogg, R.N.
	Miss Agnes Bradley, R.N.
	John Fredson
1929	The Rev. M.F. Williams
	Miss Margaret Foster, R.N.
	John Helenius
	Miss Mildred Boyes, R.N.
1931	Miss Clara H. Dickinson
1936	Miss Alice L. Hanson
	Miss Irene Sargent
	Miss Lucy A. Test
	Dr. Robert C. Hume
1937	Miss Lillian Tifft, R.N.
	Miss Deborah Bacon, R.N.
	Miss Olive Forbes, R.N.
	Mrs. Katherine Loola
	Al T. Rowe
	T.F. Jones
	Miss Annie McDonald
	William Esau
	Rachel Titus
1938	Loretta J. Hamilton, R.N.
	N.J. Nicholson
1939	Mrs. Grafton Burke
	Mrs. Frances J. West
	Mrs. Elsie Redpath
	The Rev. C.P. Shelton
	Dr. H.J. Aldrich
	Miss Kitty Hope
1940	Mrs. Jack H. Neilson
	Vernon Smith
	Miss Helen Stewart
1941	The Rev. George H. Jones
	Dr. Lulu M. Disosway
	Miss Lois Peter
	Mrs. James Felix
	Miss Doris Alexander
	Alfred White
	Miss Mary I. Creese, R.N.

Miss Minnie Jonas
Miss Beatrice Steven
Miss Fannie William
Miss Elsie Peter
1942   Miss Laura E. Lenhart
Miss Victoria Fields
Miss Effie James
1943   Miss Helen Dutcher
Miss Mary K. MacLellan, R.N.
Miss Louie-Dean Virgin
Miss M. Louise Reiley, R.N.
Silas John
Miss Minnie Adams
Mrs. Edith P. George
1944   The Rev. John M. Balcom
Dr. Marion L. Bingham
Miss Grace Crosson, R.N.
1945   The Rev. Wilfred C. Files
Ned Thomas
Miss Fannie M. Parkin
1946   Miss Bertha Mason
Miss Margaret Eimon
Miss E. Anne Weitzel
Miss Nancy R. Wilson
Miss Gladys Rose
Miss Lois Wendt
1948   Dr. Edward H. Dunn
Mrs. Christie B. Newbert
1949   Luman Beckett
Grafton Bergman
Miss Marion Grout, R.N.
Miss Rebecca Drane
1950   Dr. Milton O. Kepler
Miss Addie Mae Page, R.N.
Miss Helen Kibbe
Miss Almeria Gordon
Miss Floride Hester
1951   Miss Barbara Clintsman, R.N.
1952   The Rev. Norman H.V. Elliott
Dr. Ben H. McConnell

Fr. Al Smith and some of his Stevens Village parishioners

Miss Mary O. Hayes, R.N.
Miss May Nelson
Ray T. Leight
R.J. Albert
1953   The Rev. Richard Lambert
Miss Carol Strathman
Gilbert Prince
Huntington Roberts
Harry E. Carter
Miss Harriet H. Keefer, P.H.N.
Miss Elizabeth Klem
1954   The Rev. Albert E. Tritt
Ned Thomas, layreader
Dr. S. Donald Palmer
Miss Irene Burnham, R.N.
Miss Arlene Chatterton, R.N.
Grafton Bergman
Capt. George S. Glander, C.A.

The Rev. Isaac Tritt
Miss Susan C. Lewis, R.N.
1955   The Rev. Walter W. Hannum
Mrs. Sophie Paul
Miss Betty Marvin
Miss Stella U. Burton
1956   The Rev. Norman H.V. Elliott
Dr. W. Burns Jones Jr.
Miss Bertha E. Mason, R.N.
Miss Susan E. Carter, N\R.N.
Miss Margaret E. Merrell
The Rev. David Salmon
1959   Capt. Page H. Kent, C.A.
The Rev. Murray Trelease
1961   Miss E. Louise Bottle
1964   The Rev. Richard A. Treadwell
The Rev. Philip Peter
Miss Teresa A.C. Barling

Rose Williams and Fr. Joe Williams Jr. with Bishop Gordon at Allakaket

HUGHES

1970	Albert Weeks, layworker
1972	Mike Kroenke
1974	Timothy Sam, volunteer
1995	Ms. Susie Williams, layworker

HUSLIA

Good Shepherd

1953	Don Gardner, seminarian
1955	Miss Arlene Chatterton, R.N.
1956	The Rev. Patterson Keller
1963	James Garrett
	Douglas Davidson
1964	The Rev. Donald P. Hart
1969	The Rev. Thomas E. Stevenson
1971	Robert Vent, layreader
1973	The Rev. Thomas C. Wand
1976	Miss Christine Twitty, volunteer
1995	Ms. Maudy Sommer

IDITAROD

Iditarod Hospital

1911	Mrs. N.S. Davis
	Miss Barbara O'Conner

MINTO

St. Barnabas

1929	The Rev. Arthur R. Wright
	Moses Cruikshank
1954	Served from Nenana (The Rev. Cameron Harriot)
	Miss Bertha E. Mason, R.N.
1956	The Rev. Richard F. Simmonds
1961	The Rev. Dale G. Sarles
1967	The Rev. Thomas C. Kehayes
1971	The Rev. Luke Titus
1974	The Rev. Anna M. Frank
1976	The Rev. Kenneth Charlie
	The Rev. Berkman Silas

	Miss Elaine Johnson, layreader
1966	Cadet Thomas Tull, C.A.
1970	The Rev. Titus Peter
1972	The Rev. Andrew H. Fairfield
1973	Bruce Landenberger
1975	Joe & Gail Cochran, volunteers
1976	The Rev. Scott Fisher
1977	The Rev. John A. Phillips
	Elliott Moses Sr., layreader
1986	Peter & Simcha Newton, layworkers
1987	The Rev. Spaulding Howe
1988	The Rev. Stan Sullivan
1989	The Rev. Bruce Caldwell
1990	The Rev. Teresa Thomas

HOLIKACHUK/GRAYLING

St. Paul's

1954	The Rev. Thomas G. Cleveland
1959	The Rev. John M. Kinney
1960	The Rev. Richard K. Clarke (change in village location and name to Grayling)
1963	The Rev. Richard K. Clarke
1969	Served from Shageluk (The Rev. A.H. Fairfield)
1971	The Rev. A.H. Fairfield (based in Grayling)
1972	Peter Hardy
1974	Dale Swartzentruber
1975	Served from Shageluk (The Rev. Jean A. Dementi)
1995	Dolly & Henry Deacon, layworkers

NENANA

St. Mark's Mission

1907	Miss Annie Cragg Farthing
	Blind Moses
1909	Miss Margaret Wightman
	Mrs. W.E. Chrysler
1910	Miss A. Agnes Greene
	Paul Williams
	W.E. Chrysler
	Miss M. Agnes Bolster
	Miss M.S. Grider
	Miss Laura M. Parmalee
	Guy H. Madara
	Miss Dorothy S. Tate
	Robert G. Tatum
1915	The Ven. Frederick B. Drane
	Mr. Arthur R. Wright
	Miss Alice Wright
1916	Miss A. Isabel Rountree
	Miss Bessie Blacknall
1917	The Rev. Wm. A. Thomas
	Miss Harriet M. Bedell
1918	Miss Irma Dayton
1919	Miss Myrtle Rose
	Miss Fern Rose
1921	The Rev. Robert G. Tatum
	Miss Evelyn Jardine, R.N.
	Miss Katherine N. Bridgeman
	Miss E.M. Nixon
1923	Miss Eola H. Clark
	Dss Agnes O. Willing
	Miss Lossie deR.Cotchett, R.N.
1928	Miss Elsie Waitz
	Dss. Kathleen Thompson
1929	The Rev. E.A. McIntosh
	Miss Marian E. Woods
	Miss Florence M. Hissey
1930	Jimmie Bruce
	Miss Ann Silberg, R.N.
	Miss Maude I. Pratt

1931	Fred Mueller
	Miss Bessie Cook Kay
1935	Miss Marguerite Bartberger
1938	Mrs. John H. Adams
1939	Fred Goodwin
	Miss Irene Westerlund
	Miss Rose Kennedy
1941	Miss A. Kathleen Eddy
	Miss Louie-Dean Virgin
	Miss Carrie Thomas
	Harold Mable
1942	The Rev. Arnbold Krone
	Miss Anna E. King
	Miss Ada Alexander
1945	The Rev. Robert P. Holt
	The Rev. John Balcom
	Miss Martha I. Webb
	Miss Olive Brower, R.N.
1946	Miss Madeline Tooyak
	Miss Mary Ellis Bunton
1947	Miss Pauline E. Watts
1948	The Rev. Robert Reid
	Miss Gladys E. Shreiner, R.N.
1949	Miss Dorothy Vinson, R.N.
1950	The Rev. Albert J. Sayers
	Miss Mary Ann Hakes
1951	The Rev. Norman H.V. Elliott
	Richard Miller
	Miss Jean Aubrey, R.N.
	Miss Clara Childs
	Miss Dorothea S. Jacobs
	Miss Ann Teague
1952	The Rev. Cameron Harriot
	Miss Edith L. Stricker
	Miss Mary Ann Arminstead
1953	Jan Wendland
	Miss Carol Strathman
1954	Miss Martha I. Webb
	Miss Bertha Mason

	Miss Rachel McDiarmid
	Fred Mueller
1956	The Rev. Lee W. Stratman
1962	Served from Minto
	(The Rev. Dale G. Sarles)
1963	The Rev. John A. Phillips
1969	The Rev. John E. Randall
1970	The Rev. R. Stephen Sedgwick
1973	Served from Fairbanks
	(The Rev. Donald P. Hart
	The Rev. Richard Simmonds
	The Rev. Glen Wilcox)

Fr. Richard K. Clarke

1975	The Rev. Luke Titus
1978	The Rev. Richard Simmonds
1983	The Rev. Melissa Newlin
1987	James Cavanaugh, seminarian
1990	The Rev. Stan Sullivan

NORTH POLE

St. Jude's

1977	The Rev. David Keller
	The Rev. Glen Wilcox
	The Rev. Mark Boesser
	The Rev. Everett Wenrick
	The Rev. Ray Dexter
	The Rev. Andrew Fairfield
1978	The Rev. Jean A. Dementi
1984	The Rev. James Hunter II
1986	The Rev. Veronica Knapick
1988	The Rev. James Hunter II

RAMPART

1995	Paul & Linda Evans, layworkers

SALCHAKET

1909	Miss Margaret R. Wightman
1915	Miss M.B. Stone Thompson
	Miss Beulah Frederick
1918	Miss Effie Jackson

SHAGELUK

St. Luke's

1953	The Rev. Glen Wilcox (based in Anvik)
1955	The Rev. Jean Dementi, R.N.
1961	The Rev. David G.R. Keller
1968	The Rev. Andrew H. Fairfield
1971	Served from Grayling (The Rev. Andrew H. Fairfield)
	Dale Swartzentruber, volunteer
1995	Ms. Katherine Hamilton, layworker

STEVENS VILLAGE

St. Andrew's

1914	Miss Effie Jackson
1918	Dss. Harriet M. Bedell

1924	Henry Moses, layreader
1953	The Rev. Norman H.V. Elliott
1955	Coleman Inge
1956	Miss Arlene Chatterton, R.N.
1959	The Rev. Alfred H. Smith Jr.
1962	Served from Beaver (The Rev. Richard Simmonds)
1966	Served from Beaver (The Rev. Richard Treadwell)
1995	Robert Joseph, layworker

TANACROSS

St. Timothy's Church and Mission School

1912	Miss M.C. Graves
	Celia Wright
	The Rev. Chas. E. Betticher Jr.
	Mr. Robert Tatum
1916	Mr. & Mrs. E.A. McIntosh
1919	Mr. & Mrs. David McConnell
1923	The Rev. Arthur B. Wright
1945	The Rev. John A. Balcom
1949	The Rev. Roy E. Sommers
1952	John Dixon
	The Rev. Robert B. Greene
1958	The Rev. David Paul
	Logan Luke, layreader
	John Paul, layreader
	Frank Luke, layreader
	Eldred Paul, layreader
1959	The Rev. Richard N. Walkley
1962	The Rev. Alfred H. Smith Jr.
1965	The Rev. Richard Simmonds
1968	The Rev. Douglass Ray
1970	David Sheldrake
	The Rev. Donald Hart
1971	William E. Simeone, layworker
1973	Served from Fairbanks
1995	Ms. Irene Arnold, layworker

TANANA

Church of our Savior/St. James' and Mission School

1892	The Rev. Jules L. Prevost
1906	The Rev. Augustus R. Hoare
1907	Miss Agnes Bolster
	Blind John
1908	The Rev. Winthrop Peabody
1909	H.W. Strangman
	Blind Paul
1910	Miss Florence Langdon
	Dr. Edgar Loomis
1913	Dss Mabel Pick
	Celia Wright
1914	The Rev. E.H. Molony
	Miss Dorothy S. Tate
	Miss Agnes M. Huntoon
1916	The Rev. Philip H. Williams
1918	Miss Bessie Blacknall
	Miss A. Isabel Rountree
1923	Dss. Gertrude M. Sterne
	Miss Nellie M. Landon, R.N.
1924	A.G. Fullerton, layreader
1929	Dss Harriet M. Bedell
1930	Henry Moses, layworker
1936	Wilfred C. Files
1939	The Rev. Wilfred C. Files
1945	The Rev. Jennings W. Hobson
1949	John S. Martin
1953	The Rev. Walter W. Hannum
1955	The Rev. Randall Mendelsohn
1956	The Rev. Coleman Inge
1959	The Rev. D. Curtis Edwards Jr.
1961	The Rev. Thomas G. Cleveland
1966	The Rev. Elwin R. Gallagher
1969	The Rev. David G.R. Keller
1971	The Rev. George Edwin
1972	The Rev. E. Timothy Sniffen
1974	The Rev. Helen Peters

1976	The Rev. Alfred Grant
1977	Thomas Brawner, volunteer
	Robert Davenport, volunteer
1995	John Starr, layworker
	Ms. Ginny Doctor, missioner

TANANA VALLEY MISSION

1908	The Rev. Chas. E.Betticher Jr.
	C. Walter Williams
1914	Guy H. Madara
1916	The Ven. Frederick B. Drane

TETLIN

St. Andrew's

1959	The Rev. Robert S. Shank Jr.
1962	Served from Tanacross
	(The Rev. Alfred H. Smith Jr.
	Served from Tanacross
	(The Rev. David Paul)
1965	Served from Tanacross
	(The Rev. Richard Simmonds)

VENETIE

Good Shepherd

1940	The Rev. Albert E. Tritt
1953	The Rev. Norman H.V. Elliott
1958	Miss Susan E. Carter, P.H.N.
1962	The Rev. David Salmon
1967	Dss. Marilyn Snodgrass
1968	Richard Heald, layworker
1969	Served from Arctic Village
	(The Rev. Isaac Tritt)
1970	Bradley Lennon, volunteer
1972	Joseph Wagner, volunteer
1974	Bruce Landenberger, volunteer
1975	John Williams, volunteer
1977	The Rev. Paul Tritt
1995	Ms. Margo Simple, layworker

In the course of Episcopal ministry in Alaska, Outstations often became opportunities for occasional services throughout the year. Some Outstations grew into organized missions or parishes. Over the years the following were listed as Outstations:

Annette Island	Eagle	Nome
Arctic Village	Eagle River	Palmer
Barrow	Glennallen	Point Lay
Beaver	Healy	Rampart
Bethel	Homer	Seldovia
Bettles	Hughes	Shageluk
Big Delta	Huslia	Skagway
Birch Creek	Kenai	Stevens Village
Canyon Village	King Salmon	Suntrana
Chalkyitsik	Kodiak	Tetlin
Chena	Manley Hot Springs	Tok Junction
Circle	McKinley Park	Venetie/Chandalar
Clear	Minto	Wrangell Institute
Coschacket	Mt. Edgecumbe	
Dot Lake	Noatak	

~ Compiled by Connie Moore

...there is a further vision for those days.
~ Daniel 10:14

XVI
A NOTE TO THE NEXT GENERATION

When I knew that I would be asked to write a part of our story of the church in Alaska, especially the part that would look ahead to the future, I did what I thought would be the best kind of careful research: I took a walk. I got away from the computer screen, the piles of paper on my desk, the sound of the telephone and fax machine, and stepped outside into God's beautiful Alaska world. I took my dog along as a research assistant, and together we walked through the snow to see the trees, the winter light, and the distant mountains. While we walked, I prayed, which is speaking to the Lord, and I prayed, which is listening to the Lord. Our quiet conversation brought me home to write this to the next generation of the Episcopal Church in Alaska.

My dear Brothers and Sisters in Christ, the first thing I want to say is that I hope you won't be too surprised by the mistakes we have made. Looking back over your shoulder at us, I am sure you can see how often we made the wrong choice, missed the best opportunity, or forgot the most simple lesson. For all of this, we have only one response: that we are as deserving of God's patience as has been every other generation of Christians before us, right back to Peter,

"The next generation" at Allakaket, 1960

James, and John.

We stand in history in a humble way. In this generation, I would hope that our testimony to you would not be the inflated claims of a church triumphant, but the humble offering of a church compassionate.

We longed most for community, which meant we strived most for justice. We tried to care for one another. We tried to love. In doing so we recognized just how very hard that can be. We were so different from

one another. And we honored that difference. Therefore, we cannot boast to you of our great successes. We can only hold up to you the mirror of our hope: that your community has been strengthened by the love we shared here during these one hundred years.

The second thing I would say is that I hope you have inherited some good measure of our joy. Like you, we were always guiding the frail ship of the church through a sea of troubles. We never seemed to reach that distant shore where there were more resources than needs, people than problems, or time than demands. We even spent some anxious moments bailing water, wondering if we would make it at all. But there is one thing I hope you remember about us: even when we were bailing water, we were singing.

While we never quite made it to the Promised Land flowing with milk and honey, we had a wonderful time together moving in that direction. We embraced the Good News. We praised God and preached about mercy, forgiveness, new beginnings, hope, healing, and salvation. We opened our doors to all people. We felt that no problem was too great for the grace of God. We rejoiced in the gospel.

If our legacy to you is that the Episcopal Church in Alaska is still a community centered in the ongoing joy of knowing Jesus Christ as Lord and Savior, then all our present-day struggles will have been worth it. We will have passed on the good humor and hope that were always the energy behind our ability to adapt, to change, to create, and to carry on.

Finally, I would share with you the wisdom that every older generation of Christians ought to bequeath to the next: whatever begins in Christ will end in Christ. He is the alpha and the omega.

Whatever plans we made, we always tried to measure them on the scales of our abiding faith in Christ Jesus. We felt that if what we said or did was somehow true to the Lord, spoken or done in the Spirit of God, then it would always come out all right. Therefore, we took the discernment of God in our lives very seriously. We prayed. We listened. We went back to the Book over and over. We wanted to keep our eyes fixed on the twin stars of His promise to us: the star of our tradition as Anglican Christians that told us where we came from, and the star of our vision in mission that told us where we were going.

Walking along this line between past and future, we kept our balance by keeping our faith. We proclaimed a simple message of belief in God, confidence in the Scriptures, prayer as constant, and hope as eternal. We tried to never let our theologies cloud the strength of our vision by obscuring those simple principles. Consequently, we walked by faith trusting God in all things.

Young people of the Diocese gather for a camp session at Meier Lake Center in Wasilla.

Now you are walking the same path. I pray, we all pray, that you have kept the wisdom we learned, and that you will pass it on for us. Remember, if you awaken with Christ and never lose sight of Him all the day long, then you will rest in Christ when your day is done.

Steven Charleston
Bishop of Alaska

Right top; Three appealing youngsters play outside their homes at Arctic Village, June 1989: left to right: Sheena Tritt, Yvonne Gilbert, and Amanda Tritt. Bottom right: Bishop Cochran and Fr. Andy Fairfield with confirmation class at Fort Yukon, 1970s Above left; Young people enjoy games at the Huslia mission house, 1950s. Above: Kivalina kids "havin' fun"

SUGGESTED READINGS

Episcopal Church History

Anderson, Owanah. *Jamestown Commitment: The Episcopal Church and the American Indian.* Cincinnati, Ohio: Forward Movement Publications, 1988.

At the time of writing, Owanah Anderson was the head of the Native American Ministry for the Episcopal Church of the United States. She is a Choctaw, raised in Oklahoma. Her book is a rare instance of church mission history written from the point of view of the Native American.

Donovan, Mary Sudman. *A Different Call: Women's Ministries in the Episcopal Church, 1850-1920.* Wilton, Connecticut: Morehouse-Barlow, 1986.

The author includes information about many of the pioneer women who served in the Alaska mission field.

Prichard, Robert. *A History of the Episcopal Church.* Harrisburg, Pennsylvania: Morehouse Publishing, 1991.

Stuck, Hudson. *The Alaska Missions of the Episcopal Church: A Brief Sketch, Historical and Descriptive.* Seattle, Shorey Book Co., 1968.

Originally published in 1920, this slim volume is written from a first-hand experience by the great Archdeacon of the Yukon. It has been, until the present volume, the only history of the Episcopal Church in Alaska and is still indispensable for its unique personal perspective and Stuck's acquaintance with all the key figures in the early years of the mission field.

Alaska - Original Sources

The principal location for pursuing the history of the Episcopal Church in Alaska is the Church Archives. The records of the Church, which include correspondence, administrative records, parish reports, parish registers, manuscripts, church histories, and photographs will be found principally in two locations: The Episcopal Church Collection at the Archives of the University of Alaska Fairbanks and the Alaska Collection within the Archives of the Foreign Missions Society papers at the Archives of the Episcopal Church of the USA in Austin, Texas. Generally speaking, papers belonging to the episcopacies of Bishops Rowe and Bentley are in Austin, while all succeeding papers, particularly those of Bishops Gordon, Cochran, and Harris, are at the Fairbanks facility.

Austin: The Austin collection covers the period 1884-1952. The collection has much correspondence and related papers of clergy and other church workers in Alaska. The arrangement is alphabetical by name. A major portion of the Alaska records has been microfilmed and is available in Fairbanks at the University Library. This includes a detailed finding aid. Also in Fairbanks is a calendar of correspondence of Hudson Stuck. See: Schmidt, Norma R. *The Episcopal Church in Alaska: The Venerable Hudson Stuck, Archdeacon of the Yukon, 1904-1920* (Alaska Historical Commission, 1983.

Also for the Austin archives, see: Simeone, William E. *The Episcopal Church in Alaska: A Catalog of Photographs from the Archives and Historical Collections of the Episcopal Church.* Anchorage: Alaska Historical Commission, 1981. This is primarily a catalog of the photographs in the Austin, Texas Archives.

Fairbanks: At the University of Alaska Fairbanks, the records cover the period from the 1880s to the 1980s with the largest group of documents being from the last half of the 20th century. Aside from some correspondence of the first two bishops and the official papers of the next three bishops of Alaska, there are personal papers of clergy and church workers. Included, for example, are papers of Frederick B. Drane, Frederick W. Goodman, Augustus R. Hoare, and Hudson Stuck. There also are additional papers of Drane in the Frederick B. Drane Collection, and of Stuck in the Hudson Stuck Collection. Included in the latter are the manuscripts of three books and his diaries for the years 1904, 1905, 1909-1912, 1914, 1916-1918. There also are papers of Albert E. Tritt in the collection entitled "Arctic Village Journals," and of John Fredson in the Fredson Collection. Photographs from the Fairbanks area, 1914-1920, will be found in the Lumpkin Collection (the Rev. H. Hope Lumpkin).

There also is microfilm of records from Sitka (1899-1945), Seward (1905-1981), Fort Yukon (1899-1971), and Point Hope (1908-1947).

Periodicals

Another primary source of great interest consists of two publications: *The Spirit of Missions* and *The Alaskan Churchman*. The former was the publication of the national Episcopal Church, beginning in 1836. It is available through the Austin Archives. *The Alaskan Churchman* began publication in 1906 and continued a monthly schedule (intermittently) until 1980, when it was succeeded by *Epiphany*, and then *Alaskan Epiphany*, the current periodical of the Alaska Diocese. The Fairbanks Archives has a good run until 1976 of *The Alaskan Churchman*, and there is an index for the first 50 volumes, to 1954.

Missionary Memoirs and Writings

Chapman, John W. *A Camp on the Yukon.* Idlewild Press, 1948.

Memoirs of the first Episcopal priest in Alaska, who was in Anvik from 1887 until 1930.

_____. *Alaska's Great Highway.* Church Missions Publishing Co., 1909.

Charleston, Bishop Steven. *Good News from Native America - The Words and Witness of Bishop Steven Charleston.* Fairbanks: Episcopal Diocese of Alaska, 1994.

A collection of sermons by the sixth Bishop of Alaska, who is the first Native American bishop (Choctaw) of the Episcopal Church in Alaska.

Cody, H.A. *An Apostle of the North: Memoirs of the Rt. Rev. William Carpenter* Bompas, D.D. Dutton, 1908.

This memoir, edited by H.A. Cody, is by the first Anglican bishop of the North. Bompas served first as Bishop of Athabasca (1874-1884), and then of the McKenzie River (1884-91), and finally in the Yukon (1891-1906).

Driggs, John B. *Mission Life at Point Hope.* Church Missions Publishing Co., 1906.

Missionary doctor who served at Point Hope from 1890 to 1908.

Sabine, Bertha. *The Junior Auxiliary in Anvik, Alaska and Other Sketches.* Church Missions Publishing Co., 1905.

_____. *A Summer Trip Among Alaska Missions.* Church Missions Publishing Co., 1908.
    The author was Deaconess at Anvik from 1893 to 1913.

Stuck, Hudson. *A Winter Circuit of Our Arctic Coast: A Narrative of a Journey with Dog-sleds Around the Entire Arctic Coast of Alaska.* Scribner, 1920.

_____. *Ten Thousand Miles with a Dog Sled: A Narrative of Winter Travel in Interior Alaska.* Scribner, 1915.

_____. *Voyages on the Yukon and Its Tributaries: A Narrative of Summer Travel in the Interior of Alaska.* T. Werner Laurie, 1917.

Biographies

Burke, Clara Heintz. *Doctor Hap.* New York: Coward-McCann, 1961.

A biography of doctor and priest Grafton Burke by his widow. Burke was the missionary doctor at Fort Yukon from 1908 until his death in 1938.

Dean, David M. *Breaking Trail: Hudson Stuck of Texas and Alaska.* Ohio University Press, 1988.

A well researched study by a professional historian of the Archdeacon of the Yukon, who served in Alaska from 1904 until his death in 1920.

Hartley, William and Ellen. *A Woman Set Apart.* Dodd Mead, 1963.

A biography of Deaconess Harriet M. Bedell who served between 1916 and 1931 at Nenana, Steven's Village, and Tanana.

Jenkins, Bishop Thomas. *The Man of Alaska: Peter Trimble Rowe.* Morehouse-Gorham Co., 1943.

A friendly, non-scholarly biography of the first Bishop of Alaska, written by a former priest in Alaska and later Bishop of Nevada.

Mackenzie, Clara C. *Wolf Smeller (Zhoh Gwatsan): A Biography of John Fredson, Native Alaskan.* Anchorage: Alaska Pacific University Press, 1985.

A carefully researched study of the first Athabascan to graduate from high school and college. Fredson was a layreader in the Episcopal church in Fort Yukon and the Chandalar-Venetie area as well as an effective community leader.

Sax, Lee, and Linklater, Effie. *Gikhyi: One Who Speaks the Word of God.* Whitehorse, Yukon: Diocese of Yukon, 1990.

A book about Archdeacon Robert McDonald of the Yukon written by his granddaughter and deacon (Effie Linklater) and a clergy wife, Lee Sax. It provides insight into the role of the Canadian Anglican Archdeacon (1862-1913) of the Yukon who preceded Stuck at Fort Yukon and who pioneered development of a Kutchin (Gwich'in) orthography, translating the Bible, the Book of Common Prayer, and much of the Hymnal into the local language.

Thomas, Tay. *An Angel on His Wing: The Story of Bill Gordon, Alaska's Flying Bishop.* Wilton, Connecticut: Morehead, 1989.

An appreciative biography of the third bishop of Alaska, who was the first to fly his own plane to visit his far-flung congregations.

Parish Histories

Campbell, Charles. "A History of the Episcopal Mission of Our Saviour in Tanana, Alaska" - 1985.

Griese, Arnold and Bigelow, Ed. *O Ye Frost and Cold: A History of St. Matthew's Episcopal Church, Fairbanks.* Fairbanks, circa 1979.

Horn, Beverly. St. James the Fisherman Episcopal Church: A Short History. (Kodiak). 1982.

McAlpine, Donna. "Christ Church and the Episcopal Mission at Anvik," in The Church in Alaska's Past: Proceedings. Anchorage, Alaska: Office of History and Archeology. Division of Parks, 1979.

Nielsen, Nicki J. *The Red Dragon and St. George's: Glimpses into Cordova's Past.* Cordova: Fathom Publishing Co., 1983.

In addition to the above published histories, which are available in the University of Alaska Fairbanks Library (some in a few other libraries), there are manuscript histories within the parish files of the Alaska Episcopal Church Collection at the University in Fairbanks. Among these are histories of the Allakaket-Bettles-Hughes area (by Fr. Richard Miller), of Fort Yukon (Fr. Walter Hannum), and Tanacross (Fr. E.A. McIntosh).

General Histories of Interest

Berkhofer, Robert F., Jr. *Salvation and the Savage: An Analysis of Protestant Missions and American Indian Response, 1787-1862.* Westport, CT: Greenwood Press, 1965.

Bowden, Henry W. *American Indians and Christian Missions: Studies in Cultural Conflict.* Chicago: University of Chicago, 1981.

Neither of these books mentions Alaska and there is little about the Episcopal (or Anglican) missions in either, but they are valuable for setting the Alaska experience in a broader context.

Thomas, Tay. *Cry in the Wilderness.* Anchorage: Alaska Council of Churches, 1967.

This book is a brief history of the Christian Church in Alaska, treated chronologically. The background for the division of the territory into religious "spheres of influence" is particularly useful.

~ Compiled by Barbara Sweetland Smith

INDEX

ACKNOWLEDGEMENTS

Many people have helped produce *A CENTURY OF FAITH*, from the writing of individual chapters to the sharing of the briefest anecdote. Every contribution has been vital in the preparation of this volume. Thanks and gratitude are offered:

To our writers: Janine Dorsey, Norman Elliott, Scott Fisher, Anna Frank, Connie Moore, Dale Sarles, Barbara Sweetland Smith, Tay Thomas, Anne Wenrick, Luis Uzueta, and Bishop Charleston, for their research and dedication to the project;

To the staff at the diocesan office for their helpfulness, hospitality, and random acts of kindness, with special recognition of one of our diocese's greatest assets, Mary Parsons;

To Ed Thielen for monitoring fiscal concerns;

To Heather Jones of the Yukon Archives, Whitehorse; Gretchen Lake of the University of Alaska Fairbanks Archives; Diane Brenner of the Anchorage Museum of History and Art; Mark J. Duffy and Stephanie Walker of the Archives of the Episcopal Church, Austin, Texas, for their research, advice and assistance with historical photographs and information;

To Madelyn Stella and Jim King for their faith and encouragement;

To Byron Birdsall for his unfailing artistry;

To Beth Fox and Craig Heisinger of After Hours Design for their creative translation of a vision;

To Evolyn Melville for assistance and good judgment with photo selection;

To Scott Fisher for permission to reprint ACS Hosannah cartoons and articles originally published in *Alaskan Epiphany*;

To Tay Thomas for sharing material from *Cry in the Wilderness*;

To David M. Dean for permission to quote from *Breaking Trail - Hudson Stuck of Texas and Alaska*;

To Connie Moore for her heroic work tracking down statistics and information on diocesan personnel;

To Mark Boesser and Scott Fisher for the centennial calendar that provided the basic framework for Footprints in Time;

To Corinne Whitesell for manuscript preparation, for recording and supervising book orders, and for assistance with indexing;

To Nancy and John Killoran for assistance with advertising copy;

To Billie Williams for sharing her memories and for Bishop Bentley's tapes which have enriched this volume beyond measure;

To Jo and Dick Keller at Keller's Custom Photolab, and to the helpful staffs at Time Frame and Northern Printing;

To Bonnie Elsensohn for design of the centennial logo;

To descendants of some of our early leaders, who have contributed unique material: Joan Prevost Fortune, granddaughter of the Rev. Jules Prevost; Frances Drane Inglis and Rebecca Drane Warren, to whom we are indebted for the preservation of the photographs and journals of their father, Archdeacon Frederick B. Drane; Laura Chapman Rico, daughter of Dr. and Mrs. Henry H. Chapman;

To the many individuals who contributed anecdotes, stories, photos, histories, especially Mark Boesser, Marilyn Coghill Duggar, Dorothy Vinson Hall, Winnie Nowak, Dorothy Mendelsohn, Richard S. Miller, Andrew Tooyak Sr., and numerous others;

To our people from many villages who shared their memories and experiences of past and present and their hopes for the future;

To Bishop Charleston for his initial vision for a centennial book and for his faithful support of the project;

And a special thanks to my pastor, mentor, and friend, Father Norman Elliott, for his endless store of memories, facts, anecdotes, wit, and wisdom. He is a fountainhead of information who gave tirelessly of his time and recollections, and this book could not have materialized without his guidance.

I am deeply indebted to all who helped create this tribute, this act of faith, this expression of devotion to Jesus Christ and His Church.

~ Carol A. Phillips
Editor
June 1995

EPILOGUE

Mobile music -- Becky Harris and Caroline Wohlforth sing praises as Fr. Bob Nelson plays the organ en route to a service in Kotzebue, early 1980s.

In the May 1911 issue of *The Alaskan Churchman*, an article by pioneer missionary John W. Chapman called "Twenty-Five Years of Alaskan Missions" began:

> *It is not altogether easy to compress within the limits of a few paragraphs an account of the work that has been done by the Church in Alaska during the past twenty-five years...(so) I shall probably be forgiven if I fail to bring forward many statistics, or to deal in elaborate descriptions of the work that has been done at particular stations.*

Similar words could well be written about this attempt to compress into a finite number of pages the events of the past hundred years of the Church in Alaska. The history and stories of the vast regions ministered to by the Church, and the personalities that enliven that history, could fill many more books and many years of research. The opportunities and resources for study by interested scholars are rich and accessible. But our centennial is here and now, and so we have tried to prepare a tribute worthy of the Church's past and present and hopeful for its future.

The goal of *A Century of Faith* is not to glorify the past but to renew and revitalize the dedication of present-day saints as they carry out their varied ministries in the Name of Christ, following in the footsteps of the spiritual giants who have led the way. Like John Chapman, we trust we shall be forgiven for the inevitable sins of omission within these pages. And we hope this book will be enjoyed for what it is: a Book of Remembrance and a labor of love.

Unto Him be glory in the Church by Christ Jesus
throughout all ages, world without end. Amen.

- Ephesians 3:21

A Century of Faith

Project Coordinators	The Ven. Norman H.V. Elliott Carol A. Phillips
Editor	Carol A. Phillips
Writers	The Rt. Rev. Steven Charleston; Janine D. Dorsey; The Ven. Norman H.V. Elliott; The Rev. Scott Fisher; The Rev. Canon Anna Frank; Connie Moore; Carol A. Phillips; The Rev. Dale G. Sarles; Barbara Sweetland Smith; Tay Thomas; The Rev. Canon Luis Uzueta; and Anne Wenrick
Desktop Publisher	After Hours Design
Cover design	Byron Birdsall
Photo Consultant	Evolyn Melville
Order Fulfillment	Corinne B. Whitesell
Map and Calligraphy	The Ven. Norman H.V. Elliott
Centennial Logo	Bonnie Elsensohn
Printed by	Northern Printing Anchorage, Alaska
Binding by	Lincoln & Allen
Published by	Centennial Press 1205 Denali Way Fairbanks, Alaska 99701

...The best commemoration of the past is a
living, dynamic and responsible **present.**
We cannot move into the future unless we
are faithful to the Lord today.

- Bishop George C. Harris
in *Alaskan Epiphany* 1987